PACIFIC BASIN BOOKS

Editor: Kaori O'Connor

大清國慈禧皇太后

PORTRAIT OF THE EMPRESS DOWAGER

This is the portrait which was exhibited at the St. Louis Exposition, is now owned by the United States Government, and is in the National Museum at Washington

WITH THE EMPRESS DOWAGER OF CHINA

BY KATHERINE AUGUSTA CARL

Introduction by Kaori O'Connor

KPI

LONDON AND NEW YORK

First published in 1906

This edition published in 1986 by KPI Limited
11 New Fetter Lane, London EC4P 4EE

Distributed by
Routledge & Kegan Paul, Associated Book Publishers (UK) Ltd.
11 New Fetter Lane, London EC4P 4EE

Methuen Inc., Routledge & Kegan Paul
29 West 35th Street
New York, NY 10001, USA

Printed in Great Britain by St Edmundsbury Press Ltd,
Bury St Edmunds, Suffolk

ISBN 0 7103 0218 5

TO SIR ROBERT HART

To whose helpful encouragement I owe so much, I affectionately dedicate this account of my experiences at the Court of the country he has so long and faithfully served.

KATHARINE A. CARL.

Contents

vii

Contents

viii

Contents

Contents

Contents

Bridges—Chinese Architecture—Utilitarian Spirit of the Chinese—Flowers and Fields in the Park of Summer Palace—Grand Peony Mountain—The Sacred Buddha-Temple of the Ten Thousand Buddhas—Ruins of Old Summer Palace—Views from the Summer Palace Belvederes—When Their Majesties Go Abroad.

The Chinese Love of Festivals—The Fruit of Immortality—The Little Handmaiden and her White Rabbit—The Play at the Palace Theater on the Mid-Autumn Festival—Dinner in the Imperial Loge—Procession to the Moonlit Terrace—Floral Pai-lou to the Moon—"Bowing" to the Moon—The Poem to the Moon—The Burnt-Offering—Return to the Palace on the Moonlit Lake—Continuation of the Portrait—Some Disadvantages of Too Much Pleasure—Hospitality of the Empress Dowager—Chinese Conventions and Traditions—Wonderful Opportunities for Picturesqueness in Painting the Empress Dowager—Restrictions Imposed by Chinese Tradition—First Exhibition of the "Sacred Picture"—Description of First Portrait of the Empress Dowager— How I Should Have Liked to Paint Her.

Reception to the Diplomatic Corps and Ladies of the Legation—The Ceremony of Reception of the Ladies—The Empress Dowager's Cordiality—Taking Tea in the Audience Hall—Luncheon in the Throne-room—Promenade on the Lake—Visit to the Palace and Temple on the Island—The Marble Boat—Lack of Harmony among the Guests at Garden Party—Chinese Comment on our Costumes and Appearance—Dislike of Blonde Hair.

Putting the Characters Representing Her Majesty's Titles and her Two Seals on the Portrait—Beginning the Small Portrait—Toilette d'Intimité—"Hailo" and "Shadza"—The Palace Painters—Their Manner of Working—New Variety of Chrysanthemum—The

Contents

" Peafowl Feather "—The Audience Hall Pianos—Her
Majesty's Ideas of Dancing.

The Posters—Sites for the Ring—The Turnip Field—
Their Majesties Go in State across the Lake—The
House-boats—The Young Empress's State Boat—The
Imperial Loges at the Circus—Invited Officials—
Bands of Music—A Glimpse of the Manchu Princes
and Some High Officials—The Son of the Imperial
Princess—The Opera Glasses of Their Majesties—
What Interested Them Most.

Early Rising—When the Empress Dowager Sleeps—
Her Bedroom—Irregular Hours except for the Au-
dience—Domestic Duties—Her Favorite Game—Her
Luck—Her Meals—Conventions Observed at the Em-
press Dowager's Table—Her Dishes—The Hour of the
Siesta—Her Promenades—The Days of the Theater—
When Their Majesties Dine Together—Rigorous Ob-
servance of Fasts at the Table of the Empress
Dowager—Court Etiquette—The Graceful Bow—Rigid
Observance of Court Customs—Her Majesty's Re-
proof of Too Indulgent Mother.

Her Anxiety—Exterior and Interior Troubles—Preparations for Her Majesty's Birthday—Her Desire to
Have Everything as Simple as Possible and to Spare
Expense—The Emperor's Wish to Celebrate with the
Usual Pomp, and Desire to Bestow a New Title upon
the Empress Dowager—Difference of Her Majesty's
Interest in her Own and the Emperor's Birthday—
When She Received the Congratulations—Early Hour
of Congratulation—The Interior of the Throne-room
and Decorations for the Birthday—Winter Court Dress
of the Ladies—The Empress Dowager's Fatigue.

The Empress Dowager's Love of the Summer Palace
—Return to Peking—Young Empress and Ladies Pre-

Contents

cede and Receive Her on the Threshold of her Own
Throne-room—City of Peking, the Palace within the
Forbidden City—Its many Walls within Walls—The
Guard Houses—The Ceremony of Reception—The
Throne-room of the Winter Palace—The Interior
Dome—Her Majesty's Sitting-room—Private Chapel
—Portraits of Queen Victoria—The Three Great Halls
—The Spirit-Stairway—The Central Hall—Presents
from European Royalties—Where I was to Paint—
The Emperor's Precincts—Tradition at the Winter
Palace.

Legation Quarter—Morning Ride to the Palace—Splen-
did Walls of the Palace and City—The Streets in the
Forbidden City—A Funeral—The Mongolians—Beg-
gars at the Gate—Unsatisfactoriness of Studio at
Winter Palace—Her Majesty Orders It Remodeled—
Beginning Portrait for St. Louis—Imperial Parapher-
nalia and Insignia of Royalty—Importance of Pro-
priety—The Throne—Her Majesty's Costume for the
Portrait—Pearl Mantle—First Sketch—Stretching the
Great Canvas.

Manchu Ladies of the Palace—Presentation, on Their
Marriage, of Manchu Noblewomen—Bridal Costume
—Sedan Chairs—By Whom Bride is Presented—The
Young Empress's Graciousness—A Daughter in a
Manchu Family—Comparison of Manchu and Amer-
ican Girl—The Unmarried Daughter of the Manchus
—Her Position in the Family—Social Qualities—The
Manchu Men—Sports—Costume—Young Dandies—
Concubinage—Early Marriages of Men—Secondary
Wives — The Family— Secondary Wives of an Em-
peror—Their Rank—Position in the Palace—Title.

The Palace as the Heart of Empire—Occasions on
which Presents are Given (Private, Official, and Festivals)—Style of Presents Given by the Empress
Dowager—Presents to the Ladies of Legation—Birthday Presents—Some Presents Received by Me from
Her Majesty,

Contents

Contents

Contents

List of Illustrations

xvii

List of Illustrations

INTRODUCTION

IT IS A commonplace that a picture can tell a story, but it is an uncommon tale indeed that hangs upon the portrait of Tzu Hsi, Empress Dowager of China. It was the first portrait to be painted of a ruler of the oldest Empire in the world. The artist, Katherine Augusta Carl, was the only Westerner ever to live as a member of the Chinese court. And *With The Empress Dowager Of China* – her fascinating account of the time she spent in the shadow of the Dragon Throne – is the only full and authentic record of life in the Forbidden City in the last days of Imperial China.[1]

China in 1900 was an Empire imperilled, a dragon at bay, threatened by enemies from within and without, encumbered by the forty centuries of tradition that had once been the source of its greatness. Within the Empire, the old rivalry between the Chinese and their Manchu rulers had been overshadowed by the bitter dissent between conservative elements who clung tenaciously to the customs of the past, and reformers who wanted to drag China and her four hundred million people into the modern age. The state examination system that for centuries had provided China with her officials was breaking down, and the administrative bureaucracy was grinding to a halt through lack of competent men. The public treasury was depleted, the army and navy ill-equipped and untrained in modern fighting methods. The lack of provisions for teaching modern scientific and agricultural methods left the country prone to waves of famine and disease, and conditions of near anarchy prevailed in many of the provinces. To many within

Introduction

the Empire, the Western 'foreign devils' seemed the very architects of the misfortunes raining down upon them, and anti-foreign sentiment was rife throughout the land.

With good reason, China had long tried to conceal her internal troubles behind a veil of obsessive secrecy and bureaucratic obfuscation. Before 1860, no foreign government had been allowed to maintain an embassy in Peking and it was not until 1894, when Japan successfully challenged China for control of Korea, that the weakness of the Celestial Empire became apparent. Following the lead of Japan, other powers moved in to take advantage of the situation. Unable to resist foreign pressure, China had been obliged to allow the establishment of eight[2] foreign legations in her capital, and had also been forced to ceed territories in addition to the original Treaty Ports. Germany now held Kuachou, which it planned to make into a German Hong Kong; Russia held Port Arthur, Japan had Taiwan, Great Britain held Weihaiwei, France had Kuangchousan and Italy was seeking to establish a foothold in Chekiang. Ever more aggressive in their demands for further territories and concessions, the foreign powers made no secret of the fact that they saw China as a huge prize ready to be divided between them.

It was a turbulent and testing time; conspiracies abounded, rumour and intrigue were the order of the day, and the eyes of the country and the world were turned towards Peking and the palace of Tzu Hsi, the enigmatic Empress Dowager who held the future of China in her hands.

Peking was an Oriental puzzle, a nest of cities within cities, all within their own walls some thirty to forty feet high. There was the Chinese City, adjoined to the north by the Tartar City; within the Tartar City was the Yellow or Imperial City and within the Yellow City lay the Purple or Forbidden City – the heart of the Celestial Empire, and home of the Empress Dowager. Here, behind great gates, lay a cloistered world of gilded palaces, pavilions, temples and towers whose very names might have drifted out of a pipe of dreams – Palace of

Introduction

Accumulated Elegance, Rain Flower Pavilion, Precious Moonlight Tower, Hall of Protecting Harmony, Studio of Eternal Spring. There were bright courtyards flanked by rows of vermilion columns, marble-staired porches sheltering under eaves carved in the shape of dragons, lacquer-screened verandahs overlooking lotus pools and flower gardens, airy galleries leading to shadowy chambers fragrant with incense. Within these precincts the Empress Dowager and her nephew the Emperor Kwang Hsu, his wife and his concubines lived in seclusion, attended by eunuchs who by law were Chinese and not Manchu, and by slave girls who by law were Manchu and not Chinese. Six thousand people comprised the Imperial household, but of its doings almost nothing was known. Mystery and majesty were never so closely allied as here, for to reveal the inner life of the court or to criticize the Imperial house in any way was, for subjects of the Dragon Throne, an offense punishable by death. Of all the secrets of the East, none had been so well kept as the secrets of the Forbidden City. And, to the foreigner, this very mystery only enhanced the irresistable fascination of the world and the woman behind the dragon-tiled walls.

Only the merest details of the Empress Dowager's life were known. Daughter of a Manchu noble, she had entered the palace at the age of seventeen as a concubine of the fifth rank to the Emperor Hsien-Feng. She bore the Emperor his only son when she was twenty, and when Hsien-Feng died in 1861 she had become regent during the minority of her son Tung-Chih, sharing the regency with her co-Empress Tzu-An, widow of Hsien Feng. This first regency lasted from 1861 to 1873, when Tung-Chih assumed the throne. When Tung-Chih died without an heir less than two years later, Tzu Hsi adopted her young nephew whom she proclaimed Emperor under the name Kwang Hsu, and resumed the regency. After the death of her co-regent Tzu-An in 1881, Tzu Hsi reigned alone until 1889, when Kwang Hsu assumed the throne at the age of nineteen. Ostensibly retired, Tzu Hsi had continued to direct

Introduction

affairs throughout the early years of the new reign. In 1898, events obliged her to return to the throne; by 1900 she had been the effective ruler of China for thirty nine years.

Beyond this, there was little but rumour and hearsay to give substance to the shadow. The Empress Dowager had never been photographed or painted, and she did not appear in public. She had been beautiful in her youth, when a court poet had celebrated her charms with these prophetic lines;

> O beauty Supreme! O brilliant Star
> Shining but for the Son of Heaven!
> From thy glowing soul radiate
> Love, daring, hope, intellect, ambition, power![3]

Although she was now over sixty, she was believed to be beautiful still. She had been called the shrewdest woman in Asia, and the only man in China. She was forceful and imperious, yet her strength of will was moderated by a legendary charm and manners of an exquisite perfection. She was implacable to her enemies, but loyal to those who served her faithfully. She could be unscrupulous – and by some reports, murderous – in her methods, but her patriotism and love for China were unquestioned. She was superstitious yet pragmatic; she could be selfish, but she never spared herself in the service of the state. In this country of contradictions and enigmas, hers was the very epitome of that Oriental character that foreigners found 'the more complex, intricate, baffling, inscrutable and exasperating each time and the longer one confronts it'.[4]

Foreigners were admitted to the Forbidden City by invitation only, and invitations were issued rarely, and with great reluctance. Before 1887, no foreign envoy had seen the Empress Dowager and it was not until 1889, when she first received the wives of foreign diplomats at court on the occasion of her sixty fourth birthday, that she was seen by Western women.

Introduction

A few months later, in the summer of 1900, the anti-foreign and anti-Christian feeling that had simmered throughout the land for so long finally erupted in the wave of violence that became known as the Boxer[5] Rebellion. Defying the attempts of government forces to control them, fanatical mobs swept through the countryside unleashing a human tide of destruction that left two hundred and forty-seven missionaries and some thirty thousand Chinese Christian converts dead in its wake. By early June, Peking itself had become a battleground, with the foreigners besieged in their legations while Boxers fired on them from the city walls to cries of 'Kill! Kill!'. The seige continued for two months; all but the American and British legations were destroyed and the final toll in the legation quarter amounted to sixty-six casualties, including Baron von Ketteler, the German Minister, and Mr Sugiyama, Chancellor of the Japanese legation. Allie dforces comprised of Japanese, Russian, French, British, American, Austrian and Italian troops arrived to relieve the legations on August 14, and before dawn on the next day the Empress Dowager and the court slipped out of the Forbidden City and fled to safety beyond the Great Wall. The troops then turned to pillaging; by all accounts, they '. . . made a hell of Peking. A rage for looting seized the officers and they left the men to do what they liked.'[6] Soldiers and foreign residents surged through the palaces, marvelling at the beauties before them and taking what they could for their own. Russians removed booty by the cartload, the wife of the British minister was seen scavenging along with the rest, and the French writer Pierre Loti who arrived some weeks after the vanguard was still able to secure what he believed to be a pair of the Empresses own silken shoes. But although they now enjoyed the long-desired acceess to the palace precincts, the foreigners found that theirs was a hollow victory for the queen had flown the hive, and they were little the wiser about life in the Forbidden City.

For some time, the future remained uncertain. Like a piece in a living game of chess, the Empress Dowager moved

Introduction

through the outlying provinces, awaiting the outcome of deliberations. Partition, the establishment of a new puppet dynasty, or restoration of the old regime with indemnities were the three choices that confronted the Allies. The size of the country and the general unrest that then prevailed made partition impracticable, so the Allies finally decided to restore the Empress Dowager, realizing that Tzu Hsi was 'the only leader of character who commanded enough obedience and respect to be restored to the Dragon Throne.'[7]

Abroad and in many foreign circles in Peking, sentiment against the Empress Dowager ran high. She was believed by many to have connived with the Boxers, and was pilloried in the world press as a Jezebel, a Messalina, an arch-fiend, a She-Dragon, an old Manchu odalisk, a female Nero. But the Empress Dowager was not without her foreign admirers, among the most fervent of whom was Susan Pike Conger, wife of the American Minister to Peking. A woman of strong character and independent mind, Susan Conger was a dedicated champion of women's rights and a firm believer in the importance of the role women could play in furthering international understanding. She was also remarkably free of the arrogance that was then so pervasive a feature of Western attitudes towards the peoples and cultures of the East. Writing to a nephew soon after her arrival in China in 1898 she observed;

> As I am here and watch, I do not wonder that the Chinese hate the foreigner. The foreigner is frequently severe and exacting in this Empire which is not his own. He often treats the Chinese as though they were dogs and had no rights whatever – no wonder that they growl and sometimes bite.[8]

Susan Conger had emerged from the ordeal of the seige of the legations with her regard for the Empress undiminished and, on the return of the court to the Forbidden City in January, 1902, took it upon herself to lead the way in establishing a new

Introduction

era of mutual trust and understanding. She opened the American legation to visits by Manchu and Chinese ladies of position, and was received by them in return. When, as doyenne of the ladies of Diplomatic Corps she found herself in the presence of the Empress Dowager at palace audiences, she took every opportunity to talk to her about Western ways. Mrs Conger's activities were far from popular with many of her peers, one such putting the case mildly when she wrote;

> The American Minister's wife speaks of "my friend the Empress Dowager" or "Her Majesty". But at each fresh foreign visit to the Old Buddha, as the Chinese call the Empress Dowager, Chinese Christian women weep and protest bitterly, thinking of their murdered relations, whom they esteem *martyrs*.[9]

Nor were her activities viewed without suspicion by the other side, for the sack of Peking and the crippling indemnities of £675,000,000 imposed by the Allies after the Boxer Rebellion had done nothing to diminish the court's dislike of foreigners. But Susan Conger persevered; alone among the Diplomatic ladies in Peking, she was always careful to show the Empress Dowager the respect and honour due to her position. It was this that finally led the Empress Dowager to conceive a warm regard for the Minister's wife, an affection which, in the words of a sympathetic contemporary, allowed Mrs Conger to do more 'than any other person ever did, or even can do, towards the opening of the Chinese court to the people of the West.'[10]

The restoration of the Empress Dowager had also entailed the restoration of court practices, and although foreigners were now received in audience more frequently, the Forbidden City was once again effectively closed to the world. Unfounded rumours and scurrilous speculations concerning the place and the august personage within therefore continued unabated, but by June of 1903 the resourceful Mrs Conger was writing to her daughter about an inspired new idea;

Introduction

For many months I had been indignant over the horrible, unjust cariacatures of Her Imperial Majesty in illustrated papers, and with a growing desire that the world might see her more as she really is, I had conceived the idea of asking her Majesty's permission to speak with her upon the subject of having her portrait painted.[11]

The artist Susan Conger had in mind was an American, Katherine Augusta Carl, sister of the Commissioner of Customs in Chefoo. Born in New Orleans, trained in Paris and now visiting in Shanghai, Katherine Carl had already agreed to undertake the commision, but the Imperial assent was not immediately forthcoming. In China, portraits were only painted after a person's death, the highly stylized representations then being placed in ancestor shrines as objects of veneration and respect; there was therefore concern at court that it might be unlucky for the Empress Dowager to be painted from life. Tzu Hsi was also reluctant to allow an unknown foreigner into the palace for the length of time it might take to complete a portrait, and in any case she was doubtful of the artistic merits of the Western style of painting. By chance, Katherine Carl had painted a portrait of the daughter of a former Chinese ambassador to Paris when both had been resident in that city, and the Empress Dowager asked for the portrait to be brought to her. A talented watercolourist herself, she was not favourably impressed with oil painting techniques, pronouncing the finish 'rough', and she also had reservations about the Western method of shading. But after much deliberation the Empress Dowager gave her consent, and an exultant Susan Conger wrote to her daughter;

. . . the Empress Dowager gave consent to allow her Imperial portrait to be painted by an American lady artist for the St Louis Exposition. The work is to begin in August. Only think of it! That this portrait may present to the outside world even a little of the true expression

Introduction

and character of this misrepresented woman, is my most
earnest wish. I do not, dear girl, forget the dark days of
the siege, the sufferings, the bloodshed, the sorrows; but
I would not have this darkness bury in oblivion all the
bright rays of sunshine. I have most earnestly wished that
our home people could see Her Majesty as I have many
times seen her. I well know that these departures are
testing, but I always feel that the Empress Dowager can
meet them successfully. Her intuitive ability to perceive
and conceive is not easy to surpass, nor even equal, by
man or woman.[12].

Katherine Carl came to Peking, but the Empress Dowager
would not allow work to begin until of the arrival of an
astrologically auspicious date that she had chosen with great
care. Mrs Conger and Miss Carl finally presented themselves
at the palace in a state of some uncertainty. Still somewhat
reluctant in the matter, the Empress Dowager had made it
known that she would only agree to two sitttings. For her
part, the artist was uncomfortably aware that the work '. . .
depended upon the fantasy and whims of a great Personage
from whom, according to current reports, I had but little to
expect.'[13]

In the event, the day chosen for the meeting proved to be a
fortunate one for all concerned. Katherine Carl spent nine
months with the Empress Dowager. During that time she
lived and worked in the Imperial precincts – the only Westerner ever to do so – and she painted four portraits. The first of
these, which was exhibited at the St Louis Exposition of 1904,
was the most famous portrait of its day, but the artist's true
masterwork is *With The Empress Dowager Of China*. Living as a
member of the court, hers was an unparalleled opportunity for
observation, to which she brought the trained eye of an artist,
and a hand that painted pictures as well with a pen as with a
brush.

Here, for the first time, the inner life of the Forbidden City

Introduction

was revealed to the world in a charming and fascinating account that, reflecting something of the Oriental complexities of its subject, is really several stories in one. There is, first of all, the story of the court in its seasons and celebrations. There are tales of the courtiers, concubines, eunuchs and the tragic young Emperor Kwang Hsu. We see the Empress Dowager at work and at rest; hear of her pet dogs, the flower teas she drank from a jade cup, her fondness for walking in the rain, her passion for theatricals. There is the story of the painting of the great portrait itself – of the difficulties the artist encountered in arranging sittings and lighting, of attempting to marry the artistic traditions of East and West, and above all of attempting to capture the Emrpess's character on canvas. And finally, there is the story of the changing relationship between the two women, as the artist fell more and more under the Empress's spell. It is an account that draws aside the veil of mystery that had for so long surrounded the Forbidden City, yet does nothing to diminish the magic of the place or the person.

When the St Louis portrait was finally unveiled at a palace audience in April, 1904, Susan Conger – who had played such an important part in the enterprise – was fulsome in her praise. As she wrote to a sister;

> Surely, Her Imperial Majesty was there upon her throne in all her Oriental splendor. Not a stroke of the brush but told its story. Everything in form, place and color had its significance . . . But that which was far more to me was the Imperial woman sitting there in her strength of character. As I gazed at the portrait I could recall a sweet tone of voice, a gentle clasp of hand, a cordial smile that bespoke a welcome not easy for any nationality to surpass. There is a chord in human nature when played upon by woman, that woman can hear and appreciate . . . I trust that the many thousands of people who look upon this portrait in america will study those eyes, – they are

Introduction

Her Majesty's; will study the pose and grace of manner, –
they are Her Majesty's . . .[14]

The portrait was not without its critics. As one such put it – 'In
it we fail to see the little old woman, five feet high and seventy
years old, who sat for so long upon an usurped throne. . .'.[15]
But, of course, *that* is not what the artist saw. As her account
makes clear, the work that began as a demanding but straight-
forward commission soon became a labour of love. Is the face
in the portrait really that of Tzu Hsi? To those close enough to
the Empress Dowager to have felt the force of her personality,
it *was*. Whatever the truth of the matter, it is entirely fitting
that even the portrait of Tzu Hsi is sublimely enigmatic.

When she left the palace in 1904, Katherine Carl was
handsomely rewarded by the Empress Dowager, and presented with the order of the Double Dragon and the Manchu
Flaming Pearl. She continued her painting career in Europe
and America, establishing a studio in New York, but later
returned to live in Peking, where the French diplomat Daniele
Varè recalled her, 'living again in memory the days she had
passed with the Empress'.[16] She died in 1938.

Tzu Hsi, the Empress Dowager, died in 1908 and the Ch'ing
dynasty did not long survive her, coming to an end in 1912.
Her mausoleum in the Eastern Tombs lies empty, pillaged by
robbers, and the calumnies raised against her in her lifetime are
long forgotten. The portrait, for which Susan Conger had
such high hopes, did not after all appease Tzu Hsi's critics. But
this account, written as the author explains to accomplish
what the portrait did not, is today the Empress Dowager's
finest memorial. Through its pages, we can in our turn savour
the vanished splendours of the Forbidden City, and fall under
the spell of the remarkable woman who ruled a third of the
world from the Dragon Throne.

Kaori O'Connor

NOTES

1 There exist a number of what the historian Hugh Trevor-Roper calls 'bogus Chinese memoirs' that purport to describe events at court in the latter days of the reign of Tzu Hsi. These include the so-called diary of Ching-shan which formed the basis of *China Under The Empress Dowager* by J. O. P Bland and Edmund Backhouse, the forged diary of Li Hung-chang, and the accounts by Derling Yu-Keng who wrote under the name of Princess Der Ling. These are not to be regarded as authentic, full and reliable sources. See Trevor-Roper, Hugh; *A Hidden Life, the Enigma of Sir Edmund Backhouse*. Macmillan, London, 1976; p 196.

2 In 1900, Russia, America, Great Britain, France, Japan, Germany, Austria and Italy maintained legations in Peking.

3 Sergeant, Philip W.'; *The Great Empress Dowager of China*. Hutchinson & Co, London, 1910; p 333.

4 Scidmore, Eliza Ruhamah; *China, the Long-Lived Empire*. Macmillan, London, 1900; p 6.

5 The term 'Boxer' is said to be taken from the Chinese name for the secret society – the *I Ho Kwan* or 'Patriotic Harmony Fists' – that led the anti-foreign movement. See Sergeant, ibid; 212.

6 Hardy, the Rev E. J.; *John Chinaman At Home*. T. Fisher Unwin, London, 1907: p 42.

7 Warner, Marina; *The Dragon Empress*. Weidenfeld & Nicholson, London, 1972: p 251.

8 Conger, Sarah Pike; *Letters From China*. Hodder and Stoughton, London, 1909: p 45.

9 Mrs Archibald Little in *Round My Peking Garden*. In Sergeant ibid; p 263.

10 Headland, Isaac Taylor; *Court Life in China*. Fleming H. Revell Company, London and New York, 1909; p 101–2.

11 Conger, ibid; p 247–8.

12 Conger, ibid; p 248.

13 Carl, Katherine Augusta; *With The Empress Dowager Of China*. KPI, London and New York, 1986; p xx.

14 Conger, ibid; p 292.

15 Sergeant, ibid; p 334.

16 Varè, Daniele; *The Last of the Empresses*. John Murray, London, 1936; p vi.

WITH THE EMPRESS
DOWAGER

WITH THE EMPRESS DOWAGER

CHAPTER I

MY PRESENTATION AND FIRST DAY AT THE CHINESE COURT

THE day of my first Audience at the Chinese Court, August 5th, we were up betimes at the American Legation, for it takes full three hours to drive out to the Summer Palace from Peking; and punctuality is the etiquette of Oriental as well as of Occidental potentates. Our audience was for half-past ten o'clock, and the portrait of the Empress Dowager was to be begun at eleven; that hour, as well as the day and the month, having been chosen, after much deliberation and many consultations of the almanac, as the most auspicious for beginning work on the first likeness ever made of Her Majesty.

We left the Legation at seven A.M. in the trap of the United States Legation Guard, that being the only vehicle available large enough to carry the party, Mrs. Conger and her interpreter and myself and my painting materials, which included a large canvas and

3

a folding easel.   After leaving the City, the drive out
to the Summer Palace is through fertile fields and
a fair, smiling landscape.   It had rained the night
before and everything was beautifully fresh.   The
wet, stone-paved road stretched ahead like a shining
stream; the wheat and corn fields along the road were
of a brilliant green, with here and there the somber
note of a clump of arbor-vitæ, out of which rose the
walls of a temple!   The distant hills, where lay the
Summer Palace, were delicately limned against a soft
blue-gray sky, and the whole made an entrancing
picture.

Soon after leaving Peking the mounted official
Legation servants that followed Mrs. Conger's carriage were joined by a Chinese Guard of Honor sent
by the Wai-Wu-Pu (Foreign Office) to escort us to the
Palace.   After an hour and a half's drive we rattled
through a busy village, past the yellow ruins of a
great lama temple, and along the park walls of the
summer homes of several Princes of the Imperial
Family, and soon came within sight of the beautiful
grounds of the Summer Palace with its hills, valleys,
canals, and lakes; the hills crowned with tea-houses
and temples, the waters of the canals lapping the
marble terraces of the Palaces.   The red walls and
glazed tiles of the yellow and green roofs, the brilliant
foliage, freshened by the rain, made a gay picture;
and the temples, arches, pagodas, and the many buildings that constitute a Chinese palace gave it the appearance of a whole town rather than of a single palace.

As in all Oriental palaces, upon the very threshold
of the outer courts sit the beggar, the lame, the halt,

and the blind, gathering rich harvests from the generosity of the high nobles and officials and their myriad retainers as they pass in and out of the Foreign Office and the outer courts of the Palace. The Foreign Office, during the residence of the Court at the Summer Palace, sixteen miles from the Capital, has offices on the left of the great Imperial entrance, in order that state business may be more easily transacted while Their Majesties are in villeggiatura.

We alighted at the Foreign Office and were met by a number of officials with their interpreters, coming out to receive us. After readjusting ourselves in the waiting-room, we were met, when we came out, by the Chief Eunuch of the Palace, who conducted us to the red-covered Palace chairs, each carried by six men. They bore us past the Imperial gateway (used only for Their Majesties), through a door of entrance at the left, when we were within the sacred precincts of one of the residences of the Sons of Heaven and within the walls of the favorite Palace of the Empress Dowager! Before we could take in our surroundings, we had been rapidly carried through various courts and gardens, and had come at last to a larger, quadrangular court, filled with pots of rare blooming plants and many beautiful growing shrubs. Here the bearers put down our chairs; we descended and walked through the court, preceded and followed by a number of eunuchs. The great plate-glass doors of the Palace in front of us, blazing with the huge red character "Sho" (longevity), were swung noiselessly back, and we were at last within the Throne-room of Her Imperial Majesty the Empress Dowager of China!

With the Empress Dowager

A group of Princesses and Ladies-in-waiting stood to receive us. The Ladies Yu-Keng, wife and daughter of a former Chinese Minister to France, stood near the Princesses; and their perfect knowledge of both Chinese and English rendered them delightful mediums of communication between the Princesses and ourselves. Having known these ladies in Paris, it was almost like seeing old friends. They seemed a link between the real, every-day world and this Arabian Nights Palace into which we had been wafted. As we arrived at a quarter-past ten, we were in the Throne-room a few moments before Their Majesties appeared! Their entrance was so simply made, so unobtrusive, that the first I knew of it, noticing a sudden lull, I looked around and saw a charming little lady, with a brilliant smile, greeting Mrs. Conger very cordially. One of the Ladies Yu-Keng whispered, "Her Majesty"; but even after this it seemed almost impossible for me to realize that this kindly looking lady, so remarkably young-looking, with so winning a smile, could be the so-called cruel, implacable tyrant, the redoubtable "old" Empress Dowager, whose name had been on the lips of the world since 1900! A young man, almost boyish in appearance, entered the Throne-room with her: this was the Son of Heaven, the Emperor of China!

After greeting Mrs. Conger, the Empress Dowager looked toward me, and I advanced with a reverence. She met me half-way and extended her hand with another brilliant smile which quite won me, and I spontaneously raised her dainty fingers to my lips. This was not in the protocol program. It was an involuntary and surprised tribute on my part to her unexpected charm. She then turned and with graceful gesture extended her hand toward the Emperor and murmured "The Emperor," and watched me closely while I made His Majesty the formal reverence. He acknowledged the salutation by a slight bow and a stereotyped smile, but I felt that he, too, was closely scrutinizing me as his shrewd glance swept my person.

After a few moments' conversation, interpreted by the Ladies Yu-Keng, Her Majesty ordered my painting things brought in, while she retired to be dressed in the gown she had decided upon as appropriate for the portrait.

After she had left the Throne-room, I tried to take in the conditions of the place for painting. The hall was large and spacious, but the light was false, the upper parts of the windows being covered with paper shades. The only place in the hall where there was any sort of light for painting was in front of the great plate-glass doors, and this was but a small space in which to begin so large a picture. To get a light upon the portrait, as well as upon the sitter, I should be forced to place my canvas very near the throne where she was to sit; and, with so large a portrait as I was to paint, this would be a great disadvantage. When I thought I must paint here, and begin at once upon the canvas which was to be the final picture, my heart fell! Her Majesty wished, above all, to have a large portrait, and I was told she would not understand my beginning on a small canvas or making any preliminary studies — that if I did not begin on the

7

big canvas at once she would probably not give me
any more sittings; in fact we had that morning been
told at the Foreign Office that Her Majesty was to
give me but two sittings, so there was no alternative!
There could be no preliminary poses, no choice from
several sketches, and only a few moments in which
to choose the pose, which must be final—and I totally
ignorant of the possibilities of my sitter or her characteristics.

Luckily, I had but a few moments to consider all
these adverse circumstances, for Her Majesty soon
returned! She had been clothed in a gown of Imperial yellow, brocaded in the wistaria vine in realistic
colors and richly embroidered in pearls. It was
made, in the graceful Manchu fashion, in one piece,
reaching from the neck to the floor; fastened from
the right shoulder to the hem with jade buttons. The
stuff of the gown was of a stiff, transparent silk, and
was worn over a softer under-gown of the same color
and length. At the top button, from the right shoulder, hung a string of eighteen enormous pearls separated by flat pieces of brilliant, transparent green
jade. From the same button was suspended a large,
carved pale ruby, which had yellow silk tassels ter-
minating in two immense pear-shaped pearls of rare
beauty! At each side, just under the arms, hung
a pale-blue, embroidered silk handkerchief and a
scent-bag with long, black silk tassels. Around her
throat was a pale-blue, two-inch-wide cravat, embroidered in gold with large pearls. This cravat had
one end tucked into the opening on the shoulder of
her gown, and the other hanging. Her jet-black hair

My First Day at the Chinese Court

was parted in the middle, carried smoothly over the temples, and brought to the top of the head in a large, flat coil.

Formerly all Manchu ladies who have marvelous hair carried the hair itself out from this coil over a golden, jade, or tortoise-shell sword-like pin, into a large-winged bow. The Empress Dowager and the Ladies of the Court have substituted satin instead of the hair, for this wing-like construction, as being more practicable and less liable to get out of order. So satin-like and glossy is their hair that it is difficult to tell where it ends and the satin begins. A band of pearls, with an immense "flaming pearl" in the center, encircled the coil. On either side of the winged bow were bunches of natural flowers and a profusion of jewels. From the right side of the head-dress hung a tassel of eight strings of beautiful pearls reaching to the shoulder.

She wore bracelets and rings, and on each hand had two nail-protectors, for she wore her nails so long the protectors were necessary adjuncts. These nail-protectors were worn on the third and fourth fingers of either hand; those on the left being of brilliant green jade, while those on the right hand were of gold, set with rubies and pearls.

Her Majesty advanced with animation and asked me where the Double Dragon Throne was to be placed. After the eunuchs had put it where I said, she took her seat. Although not more than five feet tall, as she wears the Manchu shoes with six-inch-high, stilt-like soles, to avoid throwing the knees up higher than the lap she must sit upon cushions, and when

9

she is seated she looks a much larger woman than when standing. She took a conventional pose and told me I might make any suggestion I wished; but I had made up my mind that the pose and surroundings must be as typical and characteristic as possible, and as I had had no time to study my August Sitter I thought she would know best as to her position and accessories.

It was nearing eleven!

Beginning anything is momentous. Every artist knows how the wonderful possibilities of the bare canvas in its virgin purity standing before him inspires him with almost a feeling of awe; how he hesitates about beginning, so great is the responsibility. This bare canvas may become a masterpiece, the full expression of his thought, or it may come forth a maimed and distorted effort. To-day in these strange surroundings, with these unusual and unfavorable conditions, my hesitancy was greater than usual; for upon this beginning depended my being able to go on with the portrait.

My hands trembled! The inscrutable eyes of the wonderful woman I was to paint, fixed piercingly upon me, were also disconcerting; but just then the eighty-five clocks in this particular Throne-room began to chime, play airs, and strike the hour in eighty-five different ways. The auspicious moment had come! I raised my charcoal and put the first stroke upon the canvas of the first portrait that had ever been painted of the Empress Dowager of Great China, the powerful "Tze-Shi." The Princesses, Ladies-in-waiting, the high eunuchs and attendants, stood in breathless silence around, intently watching my every movement, for everything touching Her Majesty is a solemnity.

For a few moments I heard the faintest ticking of the eighty-five clocks as if they were great Cathedral bells clanging in my ears, and my charcoal on the canvas sounded like some mighty saw drawn back and forth. Then, happily, I became interested, and absolutely unconscious of anything but my sitter and my work. I worked steadily on for what seemed to be a very short time, when Her Majesty turned to the interpreter and said "enough work had been done for that day"; the conditions had been fulfilled and the picture begun at the auspicious moment. She added that she knew I must be tired from our long drive out from Peking, as well as from my work. She said I must rest and we must partake of some refreshments. She then descended from the throne and came over to look at the sketch.

I had blocked in the whole figure and had drawn the head with some accuracy. So strong and impressive is her personality, I had been able to get enough of her character into this rough whole to make it a sort of likeness. After looking critically at it for a few moments, she expressed herself as well pleased with what had been done, and paid me some compliments on my talent as an artist! I felt instinctively, however, this was due more to her natural courtesy— her desire to put me at ease—than to an actual expression of her opinion. After she had looked at the portrait, she called Mrs. Conger and the Princesses to see what had been done, and it was discussed for a few moments. Then she turned to me and said the portrait interested her greatly, that she should like to see it go on. She asked me, looking straight into my eyes the while, if I would care to remain at the Palace for a few days, that she might give me sittings at her leisure.

This invitation filled me with joy. The reports I had heard of Her Majesty's hatred of the foreigner had been dispelled by this first Audience and what I had seen there. I felt that the most consummate actress could not so belie her personality, and I accepted, without a moment's hesitation, the invitation so graciously tendered. I thought thus I should be able to get a good beginning for a satisfactory likeness of this most remarkable and interesting woman. My sanguine heart even leaped forward to the possibility of probably finishing the portrait entirely at the Palace. Her Majesty seemed pleased at my acceptance and said she would try to make me happy. She then withdrew and we were served to luncheon.

The Empress Dowager always eats alone. When she has guests the Princess Imperial, as the first of the Ladies of the Palace, acts as hostess. The guests of honor are placed at her right and left. The Princesses, Ladies Yu-Keng, Mrs. Conger, and myself formed the guests on this occasion.

The table, decorated with flowers and fruit, groaned under the many Chinese dishes placed thereon. Foreign dishes were served à la Russe. The Chinese dishes, attractive to the eye as well as to the senses of smell and taste, appealed to me at once; though I had been told one must cultivate a taste for them. There were foreign table waters and wines as well as Chinese drinks. We did full justice to the viands, tasting everything and trying to use the chop-sticks, though knives and forks were also placed for each of the guests.

After the repast Her Majesty and the young Empress, the first wife of the Emperor Kwang-Hsu, came in. Her Majesty presented the young Empress with the same grace with which she had indicated the Emperor at the morning Audience, repeating her title, "The Empress," as she did so. Immediately behind the young Empress was the only secondary wife of the Emperor, who was also presented by the Empress Dowager.

Then Her Majesty told Mrs. Conger she had her Players at the Theater that day, and she invited us to come and hear them. The Empress Dowager and Mrs. Conger led the way and I followed with the young Empress and Princesses. We passed through several courts, all gay with flowers, and finally reached the largest of all, the Court of the Theater. The Theater projects into this rectangular court and consists of a covered rostrum, open on three sides with doors at the back for the entrance and exit of the actors. In front of the stage and across the open, flower-filled court, with splendid bronze ornaments here and there, is a building which might be called the Imperial loge. This is from sixty to eighty feet long with a pillared stone verandah and occupies one entire side of the court. Huge panes of plate glass, the full height of the building, enable Her Majesty and the Emperor to see, from within, all that passes on the stage, and they can, of course, hear everything perfectly. The buildings which form the other sides of this court, those which run at right angles to the Imperial loge, are divided into small stalls, each about the size of an ordinary opera box. There are no chairs in these boxes, the occupants sit Turkish fashion upon the floor, for no courtier can occupy a chair when in the presence of Their Majesties. These side rooms are for the use of the high officials and Princes who are sometimes invited by Their Majesties to be present at the Imperial Theatrical Representations.

On my first day at Court there were no other invited guests; the Players had been summoned in our honor. Her Majesty sat in a yellow-covered chair on the red-pillared verandah of the Imperial loge. The Emperor was seated on a yellow stool at her left, the place of honor in China. Mrs. Conger and I were on Her Majesty's right, the young Empresses, Princesses, and Ladies-in-waiting standing around. After seeing two or three acts of a play of which we understood little more than the pantomime, but which was interesting from its very novelty, Mrs. Conger arose to take leave of Their Majesties and the Princesses. After this was accomplished, I accompanied her to one of the outer courts and there told her good-by.

When she left, I was alone in the Palace, the first foreigner to be domiciled in any residence of a Son of Heaven since the time of Marco Polo, and the only foreigner who had ever been within the Ladies' Precincts. I had a curious feeling of having been transported into a strange world. A sense of loneliness crept over me, and I feared the strangeness of my position might affect my work, and that, after all, I should not accomplish what I had remained in the Palace to do. I stood for a few minutes pondering my position, but was soon joined by the Ladies Yu-Keng with a message from the Empress Dowager that I need not return to the Theater, as she had gone to rest. She sent word that she thought it would be well for me to go to my apartments and try to sleep a little. She hoped I would be happy in the Palace and find the pavilion she had set aside for me comfortable. She added that I must not hesitate to order anything I wished and must make myself perfectly at home.

The Summer Palace, like all Chinese palaces and temples, and even the dwelling-houses of the rich, consists of a series of verandahed buildings, built on stone foundations which rise about eight feet from the ground, generally of one story, around the four sides of rectangular or square courts, connected by open verandah-like corridors. The apartments set aside for my private use, while in the Precincts, were to the left of the Empress Dowager's Throne-room and quite near it—in order that I might go and come to my painting with ease. These apartments occupied an entire pavilion. It was charming. Its shining marble floors and beautifully carved partitions, its painted walls and charming outlook over flowery courts, made it a delightful spot. These pavilions at the Palace have movable partitions and the rooms may be made as small as closets or as large as the whole building.

My pavilion consisted of two sitting-rooms, a dining-room, and a charming bedroom, separated from each other by screen-like walls of beautifully carved open woodwork, with blue silk showing through the interstices. In the larger spaces were artistic panels of flowers painted on white silk, alternating with poems and quotations from the classics, in the picturesque, ideographic writing of the Chinese. On one of the solid walls was a large water-color painting on white silk, representing a realistically painted peafowl in a flowery field; an immense mirror formed the other solid wall. The plate-glass lower windows had blue silken curtains, the upper windows of white paper were rolled down, and the rich perfume of the flowers in the court came in. In my honor, several foreign "objets de virtu" adorned the tables and window-shelves. The bed, a couch built into an alcove, was covered with blue satin cushions; and the windows were shaded from the outside by blue silken awnings, which gave a soft subdued light to the room, that made it very cool and restful-looking. I found the couch so inviting I was soon really resting, and the events of the day passed before my mental vision in kaleidoscopic array. Although the cushions of the bed were harder than I had been accustomed to, and the dozen or more eunuchs, who had been set aside for my service, were whispering just outside my window to be ready for any call, I soon fell asleep from sheer exhaustion and reaction from the unusual events of the day.

At five o'clock one of the Ladies Yu-Keng knocked at my door to tell me the Empress Dowager was awake, and had asked that I come up to the Throne-room as soon as I was ready. When we went up she called me to her side and said she hoped I had rested well, that I found my apartments comfortable; she repeated again the wish that I would be happy with her. She said we would not paint any more for that day, but on the morrow we would have another and longer sitting for the portrait. She begged me to let her know if there was anything I cared for particularly, that she might order it for me.

The Empress Dowager then dined alone, after which the young Empress and the Princesses led me into the Throne-room, and we dined at Her Majesty's table, her seat being left vacant. The young Empress occupied the place at the left of this vacant seat, and had me on her left. When we had finished dinner, at which the young Empress and the Ladies were most considerate of me, seeming to try to make me feel at ease, we went up to take our leave of the Empress Dowager. After this was accomplished we left the Throne-room, and made our adieus to the young Empress and Princesses, and left the Imperial inclosure for the Palace of the Emperor's Father, which Her Majesty had set aside for the use of the Ladies Yu-Keng and myself while I was at work on the portrait.

CHAPTER II

I WAS eager to be off the next morning, to have the promised long sitting from Her Majesty. The sitting of the day before had but whetted my desire for further work on the portrait. When we arrived within the Precincts we met the Empress Dowager and the Emperor coming out of the Great Audience Hall from their joint Audience. When Her Majesty saw us she stopped, as did the whole train of her attendant Ladies and eunuchs. She called me up to her side, took my hand, and asked me how I had rested and "whether I felt ready for work." This question showed her penetration, for she had seen the day before, from my eagerness and the breathless haste with which I used every moment, that my work was my first object, and she smiled when she put the query. I walked along by her side from the Audience Hall to the Throne-room where I had begun the portrait of the day before. When we reached the Throne-room she was divested of her official vestments, took a cup of tea, and called one of her tiring-women to bring her the dress and ornaments worn the day before, and she prepared to sit for me the second time.

1 8

Personal Appearance of Her Majesty

At this second sitting I looked at the Empress Dowager critically. I feared that the agreeable impression I had formed, the day before, of herself and her personal appearance had probably been too hasty, the result of the unusual glamour in which I had begun the portrait; I thought perhaps the Oriental environment had dazzled me and prevented my seeing the Empress Dowager as she really was, and I looked forward to a disillusion. As she sat there, upon the throne, before she was quite ready for me to begin, before she had transfixed me with her penetrating glance, before she knew I was looking at her, I scanned her person and face with all the penetration I could bring to bear, and this is what I saw:

A perfectly proportioned figure, with head well set upon her shoulders and a fine presence; really beautiful hands, daintily small and high-bred in shape; a symmetrical, well-formed head, with a good development above the rather large ears; jet-black hair, smoothly parted over a fine, broad brow; delicate, well-arched eyebrows; brilliant, black eyes, set perfectly straight in the head; a high nose, of the type the Chinese call "noble," broad between the eyes and on a line with the forehead; an upper lip of great firmness, a rather large but beautiful mouth with mobile, red lips, which, when parted over her firm white teeth, gave her smile a rare charm; a strong chin, but not of exaggerated firmness and with no marks of obstinacy.[1] Had I not known she was nearing her sixty-ninth year, I should have thought her a well-preserved woman of forty. Being a widow, she used no cosmetics. Her face had the natural glow of

With the Empress Dowager

health, and one could see that exquisite care and attention were bestowed upon everything concerning her toilet. Personal neatness and an excellent taste in the choice of becoming colors and ornaments enhanced this wonderfully youthful appearance, and a look of keen interest in her surroundings and remarkable intelligence crowned all these physical qualities and made an unusually attractive personality.

When I was so far in my study of her appearance, the Empress Dowager had finished speaking to her attendants, had settled herself to her satisfaction on the throne, and she turned to me and asked "what part of the portrait I was to work on." I had been told she would be much pleased if I would paint in the face. Thinking it was important to please her at the outset, instead of perfecting and advancing the drawing of the whole figure, as I should have done, I began on the face; first correcting the drawing as far as possible and then putting in a thin wash of color. During the sitting the Ladies, attendants, and eunuchs were coming and going; she took tea and conversed, but she seemed to understand that she must keep her head in the same position, and she would look over apologetically at me when she moved it. I did not wish her to be stiff, and preferred her moving a little to sitting like a statue. Her Majesty, like all Oriental ladies, smokes, and during the sitting the eunuchs or some of the Princesses brought her either the graceful water-pipe, of which she would take a few whiffs, or she would indulge in European cigarettes. She never allowed the latter to touch her lips, but used a long cigarette-holder. She was extremely graceful in her use of both the cigarette and water-pipe.

After little more than an hour's work Her Majesty decided that enough had been done for the morning and that we both needed rest! She came over to look at the face, and it was easy to see that she liked it much better now that the color was being put in. She stood behind me, discussing it for some time, and said she wished it were possible for some one else to pose for the face, so that she might sit and watch it grow. She thought it very wonderful that on the flat canvas the relief of the face could be represented. She then turned to me and said she knew I must be tired both mentally and bodily, as I stand to my work, advised me to go to my pavilion, have lunch, and rest, and added that she would try to give me another sitting in the afternoon before we went out for some sort of promenade.

I returned to my pavilion with the Ladies Yu-Keng, whom Her Majesty had appointed to keep me company for the meals in my own quarters. There was a young Manchu girl at Court whose father had been an attaché at Berlin, who spoke German and English; she, also, had been ordered by Her Majesty to take her meals with us, so that I might have pleasant company and be able to converse in my own language and have proper relaxation during my meals. Besides, I did not know enough Chinese to direct the servants or make my wants known, and these Ladies were Her Majesty's interpreters.

The meals at the Palace were all of the most lavish description, twenty or thirty dishes being placed upon the table at the beginning of the meal, while macaroni, rice, and a few other things were served from a side table. The Chinese are passed masters in the culinary art, and the delicacies seen at good Chinese tables are fit for a repast of Lucullus. Sharks' fins, deers' sinews, birds' tongues, rare fish, bird's-nest soups, fish brains, shrimps' eggs, and many other extraordinary dishes make up the every-day menu. No one can cook goose, duck, and in fact all fowls and game, to such perfection as the Chinese. Their soups are of a delicacy and flavor quite unequaled. Their breads and cakes seem to the foreigner, at first, the least delectable of their viands; their bread particularly, which is steamed instead of baked, is not tempting; but when you get over or rather through the raw-looking outside, with its five cochineal spots surmounting its pyramidal form, it is very sweet and wholesome. It is made of gray flour, as the Chinese do not believe in whitening the flour as we do. They make delicious creams, as to consistency; and these and their sweets generally are much esteemed by the foreigners.

At the Palace the food is served in tall dishes of painted Chinese porcelain, and everything is placed upon the table at once—soups, roast, sweets, all except the rice and macaroni. These latter dishes the Chinese eat boiling hot, and they are kept on chafing-dishes until served. Each person has a bowl, a small saucer, and a pair of chop-sticks. A small square of very soft cloth is used as a napkin. There is never any salt upon the table. The small saucer at the side of each guest contains a very salty sauce; if extra salt is needed, this sauce is used. The Chinese consider powdered salt too coarse for seasoning food after it is cooked!

They rarely drink at meals, and when they do, only tiny cups, about the size of a liqueur-glass, of heated wine. This is poured out of silver teapots, and is kept hot by being placed in receptacles containing boiling water. Their wines are more like liqueurs than ours; they are generally distilled with flowers and herbs and have a delightful "bouquet." Some of these wines have most poetic names, such as "Dew from the Early Morning Rose," and "Drops from the Hands of Buddha." The Chinese never drink cold water, nor do they take tea at meals. For me, being a foreigner, champagne was always provided, as well as claret or Burgundy. The Chinese do not drink coffee. After leaving the table, they take tea without milk or sugar.

The middle of the day is set aside for the siesta, and during the heat of the summer, every one goes to her apartments for two hours after luncheon. As I found the Chinese bed-cushions too hard to rest well upon, I took to my pavilion a foreign, eiderdown cushion, which I used for several days, until one day, on going to my room, I found two lovely new cushions with pale-blue silk, removable slips. On touching them, I found them to be soft and deliciously cool and fragrant as well. They were made of tea-leaves and had been sent as a present from the Empress Dowager. I found them a great improvement over eiderdown or feather cushions, especially for summer use. Though I did not care for this long midday rest, I was forced to go to my room and remain there, as there was nothing else to do.

When Her Majesty awakes, the news flashes like an

electric spark through all the Precincts and over the whole inclosure, and every one is on the "qui vive" in a moment. The young Empress and the Princesses go up to Her Majesty's Throne-room to be present at her "lever." When her afternoon toilet is made, the Empress Dowager comes out of her private apartments into the Throne-room and generally partakes of some light refreshment, or drinks a cup of tea or some fruit-juice.

She gave me a short sitting after her nap this second day and then ordered the boats for a row on the lakes. Attended by the young Empress and Princesses, and with the usual train of attendants and eunuchs, we went out into the court of the Throne-room, passed through a small pavilion opening directly upon the beautiful white marble terrace, with its quaintly carved marble balustrade, which stretches all along the southern side of the lake. Her Majesty's own barge lay at the foot of the marble steps and numbers of other barges and boats lay around, forming quite a little fleet. She descended the steps and entered the barge. The young Empress, Princesses, and Ladies followed. Her Majesty sat in the yellow, throne-like chair in the middle of the raised platform of the barge. The young Empress, Princesses, and Ladies took their places as decreed by centuries-old tradition. They sat upon cushions placed upon the carpeted floor of the raised platform of the barge.

When I stepped on, Her Majesty motioned me to come near her and sit at her right. The young Empress was on her left. Several of the high eunuchs stood at the back of the Empress Dowager's chair with her

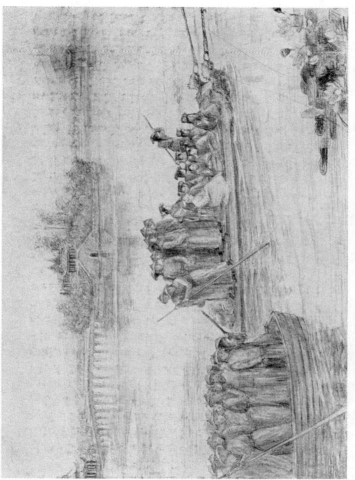

THE EMPRESS AND LADIES OF THE COURT IN THE IMPERIAL BARGE

On the Lake of the Summer Palace

extra wraps, bonbons, cigarettes, water-pipes, etc. There were two rowers on the barge who stood with their long oars to guide it, for it was attached by great yellow ropes to two boats, manned by twenty-four rowers each, and was towed along by them. Only the eunuchs of the highest rank, Her Majesty's personal attendants, went on the barge with her, and the two boatmen simply guided it. All the Palace boatmen stand to their oars, for they cannot sit in the presence of Her Majesty, even though not upon the Imperial barge. And it is only on the barge that the Empress and Ladies sit in the presence of the Empress Dowager without being invited by her to do so.

A number of flat boats followed the Imperial barge with the army of eunuchs that go to make up the train of Their Majesties when they move about the Palace or grounds. One boat carried portable stoves and all the necessary arrangements for making tea, as this is taken so frequently by Her Majesty and the Ladies, it may be called for at any time.

We were rowed across the lake to one of the islands; and when we looked back at the Palaces, the memorial arches, the temple-crowned hills, the curious camel-back bridges, and the beautiful white marble terraces jutting out into the lake with its islands, the scene was indeed fairy-like. We were then rowed into a field of beautiful lotus flowers, and Her Majesty ordered some pulled by the eunuchs to be given to the Ladies. She seemed delighted at my sincere admiration of this beautiful water-plant, so dear to the Chinese. After an hour on the lake, we were rowed back to our starting-point and disembarked. This time the Princesses and

With the Empress Dowager

Ladies left the barge first and stood to receive the Empress Dowager when she landed. When she had dined she asked us to dine with the young Empress and Ladies at her table in her Throne-room, after which we made our adieus and returned to our own Palace, without the Precincts.

[1] In the firmament of the Son of Heaven
A brilliant new star has risen!—
Supple as the neck of the swan
Is the charm of her graceful form.

From the firm contour of charming chin
Springs the faultless oval of her fair face,
Crowned by the harmonious arch
Of a broad and noble brow.

The stately profile, chiseled clear,
Is dominated by the pure line of noble nose
Straight and slender and singularly mobile,
Sensitive to all the impressions of the soul.

Dewy lips with gracious curves
Are the portals of a dainty mouth
Where often blooms the sweet flower
Of a most alluring smile.

Her face is lit by black and sparkling eyes,
Whose flames, in hours of ease,
With oblique caress, envelop and thrill
That happy mortal allowed to see.

When stern circumstance demands,
Her graceful form an attitude of firmness takes,
The soft glow of her brilliant eyes
Grows penetrating and holds one with proud authority.

O beauty Supreme! O brilliant Star
Shining but for the Son of Heaven!
From thy glowing soul radiate
Love, daring, hope, intellect, ambition, power!

From a Chinese poet—written when Her Majesty
was twenty-five years old.

CHAPTER III

THE Palace of the Emperor's Father, which the Empress Dowager had set aside for me to live in while I was at work on her portrait, was a splendid demesne, with a noble park and spacious buildings. It had been much injured by the foreign troops in 1900 and had been unoccupied since, until Her Majesty decided it would be a suitable dwelling-place for her "Portrait Painter." She had it hastily restored and refurnished for our occupation, but many of the pavilions and summer-houses in the grounds were in ruins, and the stables but partly rebuilt. Except the grounds immediately surrounding the buildings in which the Yu-Kengs and I lived, which were well kept and garnished, the greater part of the extensive park was in a fascinating state of natural wildness. The Palace, like all others in China, consisted of a network of verandahed pavilions built around spacious courts. There was a small Theater with the Prince's loge and stalls for his guests, and numerous tea and summer houses were scattered over different parts of the grounds.

I selected, as my abiding-place, a charming group

27

of buildings in a walled-in garden, fronting on a lotus-covered lake, with a winding stream at the back, spanned by a picturesque bridge. The principal pavilion of this group had a lofty central hall, out of which opened, on one side, bedrooms and dressing-rooms, and on the other dining-room and dependencies. Great doors in the center of the hall, which I had decided to use as my living-room, opened on a wide verandah which ran the whole length of the building. Marble steps led from this into a court filled with flowering shrubs. Two sides of the charming court had smaller pavilions similar to the central hall, and opposite this latter was a quaint stone wall, the upper part of tiled lattice-work, with curiously shaped openings at irregular intervals. In the center of this wall, massive wooden doors opened out on a beautiful terrace, shaded by fine old elms, over the lake. It was a charming dwelling-place, and this group of buildings soon came to be known as the "Ker-Gunia Fu," "Ker-Gunia" being "Miss Carl" rendered into Chinese, and "Fu" meaning "Palace," for the Chinese are very fond of nicknames. I learned later that these pavilions had been the dwelling-place of the Seventh Prince's son, the present Emperor Kwang-Hsu, after he had been chosen as Heir to the Throne and until he went to live regularly at the Imperial Palace.

As Her Majesty gave me my morning sittings after the Audience was finished (which lasted from eight A.M. to ten or eleven), I had plenty of time, after my cup of tea, to explore the grounds of our Palace, and I discovered new beauties each day. The Park was inclosed by high walls, for the Chinese are jealous of their privacy. Parts of the grounds were gently undulating, and all the eminences, where views could be had, were surmounted by charming summer-houses and belvederes. In one of these, where I loved to go in the early morning to refresh myself by the contemplation of the calm and peaceful lake beneath, and drink in the faint perfume of the stately lotus flowers, which grew in rich profusion on its bosom, I found an inscription on a large flat stone at the left of the entrance. I had seen enough of Chinese characters to know the inscription looked like a "poem." The Chinese poem is rarely more than a phrase: the expression, in elegant and concise form, of some dainty fancy, some bit of philosophy, and is more properly a "verse" than a poem.

I found, later, the inscription on the stone at the entrance of the summer-house was really a "poem," and had been written by no less a personage than the Seventh Prince himself! This had been his favorite place for rest and contemplation, and one day, as he reclined upon a cushion at the entrance, he had written this poem on the flat stone which lay conveniently near. The Chinese write with a brush well charged with liquid India ink, and their writing accommodates itself to almost any surface. Their characters, one for each word, take up less space than our combination of letters, and are infinitely more picturesque! Chinese gentlemen, or some attendant, generally carry about with them tablets of writing-ink and a brush, and they thus have the means at hand for jotting down a thought as it comes to them.

With the Empress Dowager

This little poem had been written with a brush, and some of the Prince's followers had afterward cut the characters in the stone, so that it became a permanent record of a fleeting thought. It had evidently been inspired by the lotus flowers growing beneath; so gloriously beautiful to-day, and to-morrow shorn of their splendor. It was a plaint on the transcience of worldly glory —

. . . .
. . . Which to-day, like the lotus fair,
   Lifts its head in pride;
But to-morrow lies low,
   Bathed in the stagnant waters of oblivion.

One day I came upon a number of small tomb-stones, in a beautiful shady corner, near the stables. I learned that these marked the last resting-places of the Prince's favorite dogs and horses. Each stone had an inscription with the name, and extolled the virtues of the favorite, whose bones lay beneath it. The Prince was a great lover of animals, and is said to have had the best kennels and stables of any of the Imperial Princes.

In my morning rambles, I also often came upon stones engraved with some character or a phrase from the classics. The ideographic Chinese characters, always picturesque, are doubly so when deeply engraved, or standing out in high relief on some rugged stone in a charming spot in the landscape. The picturesque form of the characters is sometimes heightened by being painted in vermilion or gilded; and the glowing color makes a delightful contrast with the cool gray of the

stone. Even though I could not decipher the characters, nor read the phrases, I loved to come upon them
in my morning walks. How much more interesting
they must have been to the scholarly Chinese who
understood them! How fine, when out for rest and
contemplation, to come upon some thought of their
great Sages cut in the living rock, or to see some
character meaning "Peace" or "Prosperity" standing out, in bold relief or glowing color, from some
shady nook, as if to bless him!

From another of the summer-houses in the Park I
could see the stone-paved highway leading from the
Capital to the Summer Palace. During Their Majesties'
residence at the Summer Palace, this is a busy thorough-
fare. When I did not care for peaceful contemplation
or quiet rambles over the grounds, I would go to this
summer-house, whence I could see the carts and
" chairs " of the officials, with their outriders, going to
and from the Palace; messengers galloping past, bearing despatches; all sorts of itinerant venders, with their
wares; heavily laden wagons, with small yellow banners flying, which showed they carried supplies to the
Palace. Sometimes a group of horsemen would dash
gaily past, the retainers of some splendidly attired
young Prince, who rode in their midst on a red-
saddled, handsomely caparisoned horse with silver
trappings. Anon, the cumbersome, red, fringe-be-
decked cart of some Princess, preceded and followed
by from fifteen to thirty outriders, according to her
rank in the Princely hierarchy, the black carts of her
women bringing up the rear.

One can tell the rank of the Chinese from the outsides of their chairs or carts. Only a reigning Emperor and Empress can go abroad in yellow chairs. The Emperor's secondary wives ride in orange-colored chairs. The relicts of an Emperor, first or secondary, go in yellow or orange-colored carts. Princesses go abroad in red carts. Mandarins of the first and second degrees ride in green chairs; those of the third and fourth in blue chairs; and there is still another shape and style of chair for the ordinary individual, who may prefer a chair to a cart. The rank and file go in carts. These carts, peculiar to Peking, curious two-wheeled vehicles with heavy, iron-studded wheels, are uniformly covered in blue cloth. The wealth and standing of their occupants are discernible from the quality of the cloth and its trimmings, and the richness of the harness and trappings of the mule which is always used in the Peking carts. The mule in North China is a magnificent animal, much finer than the Chinese horse, which is only a pony.

The Seventh Prince (Prince Ch'un) must have been a most interesting personality. He was brother to the Emperor Hsien-Feng, the husband of the present Empress Dowager; and his wife, the mother of the present Emperor, was Her Majesty's sister. This Prince was a valued friend of the two Empresses, the present Empress Dowager and She of the Eastern Palace, while they were Co-Regents during the minority of the late and a part of that of the present Emperor, and he remained, up to the time of his death, one of the most trusted advisers of the Regency. He was recognized by foreigners, as well as by the Chinese, to be an enlightened Prince as well as a man of fine character. The esteem in which he was held may have had something to do with the choice of his second son as the Successor of the late Emperor Tung-Chih, who died childless. The Chinese Emperors and their Council may choose the Successor to the Throne. If there be but one son, he is chosen as the next Heir; if there be a number, a selection may be made from them of the one seeming to be most suited for the exalted position. If there be no sons, the Successor is chosen from the nephews without reference to their age or to their being the sons of an elder or younger brother. The present Emperor's Father, Prince Ch'un, was the seventh brother of the Emperor Hsien-Feng, hence his Chinese name of "Seventh Prince."

CHAPTER IV

WE arrived at the Palace in good time the next
morning, as Her Majesty and suite were coming out of the Great Audience Hall. She greeted us
with a charming smile and made her usual inquiry for
my health. We joined her suite and went along to
the Throne-room where the portrait had been begun.
This Throne-room is a very spacious and lofty hall;
one side of the great room is almost entirely of glass,
with only the wooden columns that support the roof
between the windows—the lower half of plate-glass,
the upper of lattice-work with Corean paper as shades.
In the center of this side of windows is a huge plate-
glass door, reaching from ceiling to floor. The other
three sides of the hall, which separate it from the
apartments at the side and back, are of the same
beautiful, open woodwork carving I have mentioned as
serving as partitions in my pavilion. Those in Her
Majesty's Throne-room were, however, of greater
delicacy of workmanship and were more beautiful as
to the painted panels. The poems, written on white
silk, and alternating with the painted panels, were
from Her Majesty's favorite authors, original poems

34

Her Majesty's Throne-room

written by an Emperor or Empress, or laudatory verses dedicated to Her Majesty. There were satin portières at the doorways, and blue silk curtains over the plate-glass windows. Blue, being the Empress Dowager's favorite color, is used for all the hangings in the Palaces which are not intended for official purposes; where yellow is the color.

On the right of the Throne-room is a small chapel with an altar, over which presides a figure of the contemplative Buddha seated on the lotus. This altar was always sweet with offerings of fresh flowers and fruit. In front of the figure of Buddha stood the incense-burner, with perfumes constantly burning. On the left of the Throne-room are Her Majesty's sleeping apartments, and behind the openwork partition at the back of the hall is a large ante-chamber where the attendants and Ladies await their turn to make their entrance into the Throne-room. In the rear of the hall is a magnificent five-leaved screen of teakwood, inlaid with lapis lazuli, chalcedony, and many other semi-precious stones. In front of this screen, on a dais, stood an immense, couch-like throne, with a large footstool. These couch-like thrones, where Their Celestial Majesties may recline when holding Audiences, are not at all favored by the Empress Dowager, who always sits extremely erect, without leaning upon a cushion or the back of the throne. Except in the Great Audience Hall, where she uses the traditional throne of state of the Dynasty, she prefers a much lighter and quite modern one, which she has introduced into the Palaces. The thrones favored by Her Majesty are of open carved teakwood, circular in form, with cushions of Imperial yellow. One of these stood in the front part of this hall, on which she sat for the portrait.

The great throne, which I have described above, was hence relegated to the back of the Throne-room and kept for the sake of tradition, but never used by Her Majesty. On either side of it stood two immense, processional fans of peafowl feathers, with ebony handles placed in magnificent cloisonné supports. Superb cloisonné vases stood at either side of these ceremonial fans; and huge bowls of rare old porcelain held pyramids of fruits—apples, sweet-smelling quince, and the highly perfumed "Buddha's hand."

And there were flowers everywhere! It was the season of the year when bloomed a sort of orchid, of delicious fragrance, of which Her Majesty is very fond. These were growing in rare porcelain jardinières, placed at intervals around the hall. There were also vases of lotus flowers and bowls of lilies. The combined odors of all these fruits and flowers gave a subtle, composite perfume quite indescribable and delightful, but not at all overpowering, for the Empress Dowager is so fond of fresh air that there are always windows open in the Palace, even in the coldest weather.

Aside from the fruits and flowers, clocks were the dominant feature of this Throne-room, as well as of every other one I ever went into in any of the Chinese Palaces. The love of the Chinese for clocks and timepieces is well known, and there are thousands in each of the Palaces I visited. In this Throne-room there were, as I have said before, eighty-five:

magnificent jeweled and gold clocks, and specimens of all the varieties that were ever made; some with chimes; some with crowing cocks and singing-birds; some with running water; some with musical-box attachments, and others with processions of figures that came out at every hour and moved around the dial; some rare works of art and some commonplace examples of the clockmaker's trade. There are many foreign ornaments in the Palace, but, aside from the clocks and watches, Her Majesty the Empress Dowager does not seem to care much for European " objets de virtu." Unfortunately, what they have at the Palaces, aside from a few presents from European sovereigns, are generally very poor specimens of European art, and compare but lamentably with the beautiful Chinese curios. They are principally cheap modern stuff, bought by the Chinese nobles when abroad and sent as presents to Their Majesties. These presents, when they are accepted, are placed in apartments of the Palace not in general use.

When Her Majesty had her official garments removed (she always changed her dress after the morning Audience), and when the portrait had been placed upon the easel, she came over to look at it. After studying it for some time, she concluded that the nail-protectors on both hands were not artistic, and that she would have the gold ones (set with pearls and rubies) taken off, and show the uncovered nails on the right hand. I was delighted at this decision, for the nail-protectors destroyed the symmetry of the hand and hid the beautiful tips of her fingers. I had, of course, not presumed to make any suggestions as to her costume or ornaments. As the nail-shields are characteristic of the high-class Chinese ladies, it was well to have them on one hand.

After this change had been decided upon, she went over to a great vase, standing near, and took from it a lotus flower, held it up, in a charmingly graceful way, and asked me if that would not be pretty in the portrait, adding that the lotus was one of her attributes. As the color did not harmonize with the general scheme, I did not care for this suggestion, but temporized by saying "I was not ready to put it in then." After a little more than an hour's work, with the usual interruptions, she decided that enough had been done for that morning. When I suggested that I might work even after Her Majesty was tired, she said "No," that if she were tired sitting still, I could not fail to be more so doing the work and standing as I did. She said there was no hurry, that I had plenty of time to finish the picture, and must not run the risk of making myself ill.

After a short sitting in the afternoon Her Majesty ordered the boats, and we went out to the marble terrace, beneath which lay moored the Palace fleet, manned by blue-gowned oarsmen. We again took the Imperial barge, the Empress Dowager in the center, on her yellow chair, the young Empress and Princesses sitting around, Turkish fashion, on cushions. The barge, drawn along by the two great boats, glided as gently as a swan over the still waters of the lake. The air was soft and balmy. Two of the eunuchs were ordered to sing, and the minor chords of a curious air mingled their rhythm with the soft swish of the water.

Some Personal Characteristics

Beyond us lay the hills, the beautiful Western Hills, unchanging in form, but ever varying in color—sometimes blurred and gray, or a soft, warm violet; again a clear, deep blue, as if hewn out of lapis lazuli, and now and then, as a cloud passed over the sun, dark and threatening almost. I drank in deep breaths of delight!

The quaint picturesqueness of the marble-terraced banks, the summer-houses, the green and yellow tiled roofs, the vermilion walls and lacquered columns of the buildings, the curious fleet silently moving along, the eunuchs singing, the Empress Dowager sitting in state surrounded by her Ladies, the camel-back bridges—everything was strange, and, stranger still, I formed a part of this curious pageant! Only the beautiful hills beyond seemed familiar.

After drifting about for some time, we landed and went into the orchards and among the apple trees. The apple is a favorite fruit of the Chinese, and esteemed as much for its fragrance as its taste. It is emblematic of Peace and Prosperity, and is always placed among the offerings to Buddha, hence has also a sacred quality; but, though beautiful in form and color, the Chinese apple has very little taste, and the least savor of any of their fruits.

Her Majesty walked about among the trees and ordered several apples gathered, which she ate with greater relish than I could, for she graciously offered me one, and then told me to pull some for myself. A eunuch brought a basket and took them as I gathered them, and she told me to have them taken to my own apartments.

From the orchard she continued her walk to the

39

flower gardens, where she picked some small blooms and placed them behind her ears, Spanish fashion, telling the Ladies to do likewise, and herself choosing some for me and placing them over my ears. I knew these little marks of favor she showed me were not due so much to regard for me as to her desire to make the "stranger" feel at home. She hoped by showing me these special favors to insure a similar treatment of me by the Ladies and eunuchs. I have already alluded to Her Majesty's love of flowers. This was the one of her characteristics which seemed most incompatible with the idea I had formed of her from what I had heard, and her love of flowers and all nature caused me first to change that idea. It seemed to me no one could love flowers and nature as she did and be the woman she had been painted.

She had flowers always about her. Her private apartments, her Throne-rooms, her loge at the Theater, even the Great Audience Hall where she only went to transact affairs of state and hold official Audiences, all were decorated with a profusion of flowers, cut and growing—never, though, of but one kind at a time. She wears natural flowers in her coiffure always, winter and summer, and however careworn or harassed she might be, she seemed to find solace in flowers! She would hold a flower to her face, drink in its fragrance and caress it as if it were a sentient thing. She would go herself among the flowers that filled her rooms, and place, with lingering touch, some fair bloom in a better light or turn a jardinière so that the growing plant might have a more favorable position.

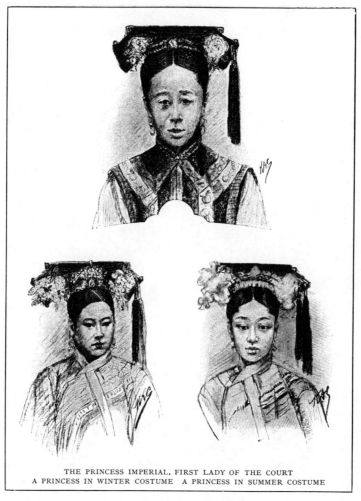

THE PRINCESS IMPERIAL, FIRST LADY OF THE COURT
A PRINCESS IN WINTER COSTUME   A PRINCESS IN SUMMER COSTUME

PRINCESSES OF THE COURT

Some Personal Characteristics

The Chinese do not place certain cut flowers in water, but keep them dry in bowls or vases, to get their full fragrance. The Empress Dowager had some quaint conceits about the arrangements of these. She would have the corollas of the lily bloom or the fragrant jasmine placed in shallow bowls in curious, star-like designs, beautiful to look at, as well as most fragrant.

Her passion for flowers being generally known among the courtiers, Princes, and high officials, they send daily offerings to the Palace of all that is rare and choice in the way of plants and flowers, for they know this is one present Her Majesty will always accept and appreciate.

There are some quaint customs in the Palace, as to flowers and fruits that grow within the Precincts. Though the Princesses and Ladies have the freedom of the gardens and may pull as many flowers and cull as many fruits as they wish, it is not etiquette for them to gather the smallest flower or to touch a fruit when in the presence of the Empress Dowager, unless they are especially told to do so. When Her Majesty tells them to pull a flower or fruit, the permission is gratefully accepted and that special flower or fruit religiously kept. The first fruits of every tree and vegetable, the first flowers of every plant and growing shrub in the Palace grounds, are considered sacred to Their Majesties, and no Princess, attendant, or eunuch would touch a flower or fruit until the Empress Dowager had been presented with the first of them. All these, apparently trivial, marks of respect to the Sacred Persons of Their Majesties were religiously observed!

CHAPTER V

THE YOUNG EMPRESS AND LADIES OF THE COURT

THE young Empress, the first Lady of the Court after Her Majesty the Empress Dowager, was, to me, a charming character. She is the daughter of the Duke Chow, General of one of the Manchu Banner Corps and a brother of the reigning Empress Dowager. She is thus a first cousin of the Emperor, and is his senior by three years. Her mother, a lady of high birth, ancient lineage, and great distinction, brought her up with much care. She also had the advantage of being a great deal at the Court with her august Aunt, and is highly accomplished, according to Chinese standards. She was affianced at an early age to the Emperor, but, as the custom is, their marriage did not take place for several years later. It was celebrated with great pomp at the Winter Palace in February, 1889, the week before the young Emperor himself took in hand the reins of Government, held, up to that time, by the Empress Dowager, and became Emperor in reality.

The young Empress has the erect carriage and light, swift walk of Her Majesty the Empress Dowager. She is small, not quite five feet tall, with exquisitely dainty hands and feet, of most patrician type. She

42

The Young Empress

has a narrow, high-bred face, with a thin, high nose. Her eyes are more of the Chinese type, as we conceive it, than either the Emperor's or Empress Dowager's. Her chin is long and of the type generally called strong. Her mouth is large and extremely sensitive. Her eyes have so kindly a look, her face shines with so sweet an expression, criticism is disarmed and she seems beautiful. She has a sweet dignity, charming manners, and a lovable nature, but there is sometimes a look in her eyes of patient resignation that is almost pathetic. I should not say she possessed any great executive ability, though full of tact, but while Her Majesty the Empress Dowager was in retirement and she was the first Lady at Court, she is said to have shown great capability in her conduct of affairs. Her dignity, perfect breeding, and natural kindness of heart would insure this.

The next Lady, after the young Empress, is the only secondary wife of the Emperor. She is said to have been extremely beautiful at the time she was chosen as his second wife by the Empress Dowager. She belongs to an excellent family, being the daughter of a Viceroy, but though only twenty-eight years old when I knew her, she was already very stout, and there were few remains visible of great beauty. She has very large, full-orbed, brown eyes, and still has a beautifully clear complexion, but her nose is flat, her mouth large and weak; the contour of her face is marred by layers of flesh, her forehead does not indicate much intelligence, and she has very little distinction in appearance. She seems good-natured, but is neither very clever nor tactful. She is not a favorite among the

43

With the Empress Dowager

Ladies generally, and is not nearly so interesting, in any way, as the young Empress. She is, however, treated with the most kindly consideration by the young Empress and has precedence over all the other Ladies, and her position at Court is second only to that of the young Empress. Whenever I mention the young Empress, it may be understood that the secondary wife followed immediately after her, coming before the Princesses or any other of the Ladies forming the Court of Her Majesty. I have often seen allusions made to the "Imperial Harem"; there is no such thing as an Imperial Harem at the Court of His Majesty the Emperor Kwang-Hsu. He has only these two wives.

Her Majesty's Ladies-in-waiting are principally Princesses of the Blood or the widows of Imperial Princes. Her first Lady, Sih-Gerga (Fourth Princess), daughter of Prince Ching, the Prime Minister, is a widow of twenty-four. She married, at the age of sixteen, a son of a high Manchu official, Viceroy of Tientsin, and was left a widow a few months later. She is a beautiful young woman, with face a perfect oval, large brown eyes, and a clear, magnolia-leaf complexion of exquisite texture. She would be called beautiful, judged by any standard. She has no children of her own, but, like most ladies of position who are widows or childless, has an adopted son. Adopted children in China are much closer relationships than is a child, by adoption, with us. In many instances their own parents are still living when they are adopted, and even these parents speak of their child as the son of the adopted mother or parents, and bow to her wishes in bringing up the child.

44

THE YOUNG EMPRESS YE-HO-NA-LAH
First Wife of the Emperor of China

The Young Empress

The next two Ladies of the Court are two Duchesses
—also widows. Widows in China never remarry, or if
they do, they lose caste and reputation. They are not
sacrificed on the funeral pyres of their departed hus-
bands, as in India; but a voluntary suicide on the
part of a widow in China is still looked upon as a
noble act. A widow who remains faithful to the
memory of her husband during a long life is rewarded
by the greatest respect and consideration during her
life, and honored after death.

If a girl prefers to remain unmarried, if a
widow remains faithful to the memory of her
husband, she is honored after her death with much
pomp and ceremony! And great memorial arches
are erected in her memory! All over China, one
is constantly coming upon these arches to widows
and virgins. If the family is not sufficiently wealthy
to raise these monuments themselves, public subscrip-
tions are taken, all the relatives contribute, and often
the inhabitants of the village or the country where the
heroine lived beg to be allowed to have their part in
raising a monument to her memory. These arches, of
stone or wood, are elaborately carved, sometimes with
remarkable sculptures of fabulous animals, flowers,
and thousands of birds of every kind (these latter
showing the immortality the soul has acquired).
Across the entablature of the arch, cut deep into
the stone or wood, and gilded or painted in glowing
vermilion, shines the name of the virgin or widow
to whom it is erected, and on the sides of the arch is
inscribed an account of her virtuous acts.

A girl is sometimes affianced at the early age of

45

from six to eight years, and the affianced is from that time spoken of as her husband. Should he die before they marry, which is never earlier than sixteen for the bride, she is considered a "widow," and must henceforth live the life of a recluse. She can never marry any one else. She may adopt a son, who will call her "mother"; but she may never hope for the joys of family life of her own, without calling down upon her head the obloquy of all whose respect she desires. She wears deep mourning the first three years after his death, and then second mourning; and she can never again put on the festive red, joyous green, or any other color except blue or violet—second mourning.

The Northern Chinese and the Manchu ladies use a great deal of paint and powder on their faces; but a widow can never add one artificial iota to the rose of her cheek, to the cherry of her lips, or the lily of her brow. She can nevermore use paint or powder. In most instances the Chinese ladies are but the prettier for this, for they have beautiful skins, and the use of powder and paint is carried to such an excess as to be quite unnatural.

There are only eight of Her Majesty's Ladies who live always in the Palace, but this number is increased about four times on festive occasions. The Princess Imperial, the Empress Dowager's adopted daughter, is the first of the Princesses at Court, and, when she comes to the Palace, ranks next to the Empress and the secondary wife of the Emperor.

One evening, at dinner, in the Throne-room, Sih-Gerga undertook to tell me the relationships of the different Princesses to each other and to the young Empress. Incidentally, this made them related to the Emperor and the Empress Dowager, but neither of Their Majesties' names was mentioned in this connection, for such would have been a great piece of presumption, amounting almost to sacrilege. They might be related, but no Princess would dare mention such a thing. It would be against all the laws of Chinese proprieties. I found, after this explanation of Sih-Gerga's, that the Ladies were all related by consanguinity or marriage to each other and to the young Empress.

There are a number of tiring-women and maids in the Palace who are called by outsiders "slaves"; but they are not slaves, or, if they are so, it is but for a time, a space of ten years. Every spring, the daughters of the lowest of the Manchu families, the Seventh and Eighth Banners, are brought into the Palace to be chosen from, by the Empress and Empress Dowager, for maids and tiring-women. One day, on going to the Palace, I saw a number of ordinary carts near one of the Postern Gates, and I learned they had brought crowds of these girls of the families of the Eighth Banner. They are first passed in review by the Head Eunuch, and he selects from them, those he thinks may please Her Majesty. These pass before her, and she tells the Head Eunuch which ones are to remain in the Palace. They are brought to the Palace from the ages of ten to sixteen years. They remain in service for ten years, after which time they are allowed to return to their families; and in case they have been satisfactory and pleased Their Majesties, they are given a comfortable dot and are provided with a handsome marriage outfit, which causes them to make much better marriages than they would otherwise do. During their so-called ten years' slavery in the Palace, they live upon the fat of the land, have beautiful clothes and many advantages. They wear, while in Her Majesty's service, blue gowns, with their hair plainly parted at the side and braided in a single long braid (tied with red silk cords), which hangs down the back. They wear bunches of flowers over each ear. The young Empress and secondary wife, as well as each of the Princesses, have their own maids and tiring-women, who remain in the private quarters of these Ladies.

Besides these young maids, there are in the Palace a number of old women, servants of Her Majesty, who have been married and have children; these overlook the younger women, direct the work of the lower eunuchs, and are in a position somewhat similar to housekeepers with us. Among these is a Chinese woman who nursed Her Majesty through a long illness, about twenty-five years since, and saved her life by giving her mother's milk to drink. Her Majesty, who never forgets a favor, has always kept this woman in the Palace. Being a Chinese, she had bound feet. Her Majesty, who cannot bear to see them even, had her feet unbound and carefully treated, until now she can walk comfortably. Her Majesty has educated the son, who was an infant at the time of her illness, and whose natural nourishment she partook of. This young man is already a Secretary in a good yamen (Government Office).

48

The Young Empress

No Chinese lady of position ever dresses herself or combs her own hair, and she generally has three or four personal maids. These are, in many instances, bought outright from their parents, and might be considered really slaves; but they are treated with great consideration and even friendliness by their mistresses, and have in most instances a happy lot. As these maids are bought when they and their mistresses are children, they grow up together, and though the maid never forgets the respect due her mistress, they are on a much more friendly footing than mistress and maid could ever be in Europe in such cases.

The first of a lady's maids stands behind her at table, no matter how many servitors there may be; goes out with her, sits with her, and sleeps either in her room or at her door, and is almost her constant companion. When the time comes for them to marry, they are given a comfortable outfit by their mistresses, and are cared for to the third and fourth generation; but the children of the so-called slaves are free, unless the mother or parents decide, of their own free will, to sell them, as they have been sold, to some good family.

CHAPTER VI

CONTINUATION OF THE PORTRAIT—HER MAJESTY'S DOGS

I HAD daily morning sittings from Her Majesty for the portrait, but always surrounded by the whole Court, with eunuchs coming and going. The sittings were long enough, for I had an hour in the morning and a half-hour in the afternoon with Her Majesty, but she did not expect me to work except when she posed, and this was not enough to make any headway on the picture, as there was a great deal I might have done at other times. Though there was so much going and coming in the Throne-room, it was a great advantage working in Her Majesty's own "milieu," surrounded by her favorite furniture, flowers, and fruits. This was some compensation; but I saw, if Her Majesty insisted upon my resting when she did—if I were allowed to work only in the Throne-room and only when she posed—the work could not go on as it should. Sitting for her portrait seemed to be looked on somewhat in the light of an amusement by the Empress Dowager, as a time for conversation and relaxation. She put me many questions while she sat, and I felt she was studying me as closely as I was studying her during that time.

Continuation of the Portrait

My interest in the personality of this wonderful woman increased each day. I loved to watch the extreme mobility of her countenance when she was at ease and was not invested in her official expression, nor her Buddha-like pose. Her voice was most musical, with no indication of age in it. Her enunciation was clear, and I loved to hear her talk. Though understanding but little of what she said, the music of her voice, the grace of her gesticulations, and the charm of her smile made her conversation most delightful to watch and listen to.

I was delighted that Her Majesty seemed to like me, and I appreciated her consideration in not wishing me to tire myself out with my work, and her kind hospitality which desired to make me acquainted with the charms of the Summer Palace and which allowed me to participate in her promenades and the simple amusements of her Ladies; but I felt it was important to advance the work on the portrait as quickly as possible. I knew that the "favor of kings" is uncertain, and I feared Her Majesty might soon tire of this new departure, of having her portrait painted! I feared the openly expressed opposition of the Chinese to a foreign lady being made a member of the Court circle, their superstition regarding the painting of a portrait of one of Their Majesties, which was against all Chinese tradition, might any day put a stop to the work; but, notwithstanding my fears and my desire to work, the days passed with little painting, and this was the only flaw in my perfect enjoyment of the fairy-like days and the unique experiences through which I was passing.

With the Empress Dowager

The walks with Her Majesty had all the pomp and ceremony of the boat-rides—Her Majesty's and the Empress's yellow-satin sedan-chairs, with their six bearers, leading off, followed by the red chairs of the Princesses and Ladies-in-waiting, according to their rank, with a rigorous adherence to precedence, and attended by an army of eunuchs and chair-bearers, etc. No one ever knew what our destination was to be when we started out on these walks, Her Majesty directing her chair-bearers as she was carried along, and the others following this lead; but we were always taken to some interesting spot, where there was something quite worth seeing. When Her Majesty's chair stopped, all the others were immediately put down by the bearers, and the Ladies got out and went up to where the Empress Dowager's yellow camp-stool was placed. She had excellent taste in the choice of stopping-places, and the views were always picturesque. She seemed to take great pleasure in showing off the charming points of view, as well as the flowers, grounds, and buildings.

On one of our walks, her dogs were brought out by their attendant eunuchs. Dogs are great favorites with all the Chinese, and especially with the Empress Dowager. She has some magnificent specimens of Pekingese pugs and of a sort of Skye terrier. The pugs are bred with great care and have reached a high state of perfection, their spots being perfectly symmetrical and their hair beautifully long and silky, and they are of wonderful intelligence. The King Charles spaniels are said to have been bred out of the first of these dogs ever carried to Europe. The Empress Dowager

Continuation of the Portrait

has dozens of these pets, but she has favorites among them, and two are privileged characters. One of these is of the Skye variety, and is most intelligent and clever at tricks. Among other tricks, he will lie as dead at Her Majesty's command, and never move until she tells him to, no matter how many others may speak to him. Her other favorite she loves for his beauty. He is a splendid, fawn-colored Pekingese pug, with large, pale-brown, liquid eyes. He is devoted to her, and she is very fond of him, but as he was not easily taught, even as a puppy, she called him "Shadza" (fool). Her dogs all have most appropriate names, given by herself. They know Her Majesty's voice and will obey her slightest word.

The Empress Dowager does not care for the small sleeve-dog; she hates the thought of their being stunted by being fed only on sweets and wines. She says she cannot understand animals being deformed, at man's pleasure. The day we first met the dogs in the garden was the first time I had seen them. They rushed up to Her Majesty, not paying the slightest attention to any one else. She patted their heads and caressed and spoke to her favorites. After a while they seemed to notice that a stranger was present, and they bounded over toward me. Some of them growled and showed other evidences of displeasure, some seemed surprised almost to fear; but as the instinct of a dog never deceives him as to who is his friend, this was all soon changed to friendly greetings. I bent down to caress them, and forgot my surroundings, in my pleasure at seeing and fondling these beautiful creatures. I glanced up, presently, never

53

dreaming Her Majesty had been paying any attention
to me, as I was standing at a little distance behind
her, and I saw on her face the first sign of displeasure
I had noticed there. It seems her dogs never noticed
any one but herself, and she appeared not to like her
pets being so friendly with a stranger at first sight.
Noticing this, I immediately ceased fondling them, and
they were presently sent away. It was but a momentary
shadow that passed over her face, and I quite understood the feeling. One does not like to see one's pets
too friendly with strangers, and I had been tactless in
trying to make friends with them at once.

A few days later, on another of our walks, some
young puppies were brought to be shown the Empress Dowager. She caressed the mother and examined
critically the points of the puppies. Then she called
me up to show them to me, asking me which I liked
best. I tried not to evince too much interest in them
this time, but she called my attention to their fine
points and insisted upon my taking each of them up.
She seemed to be ashamed of her slight displeasure
of the day before, and to wish to compensate for it.

The dogs at the Palace are kept in a beautiful
pavilion with marble floors. They have silken
cushions to sleep on, and special eunuchs to attend
them. They are taken for daily outdoor exercise and
given their baths with regularity. There are hundreds of dogs in the Palace, the young Empress, the
Princesses and Ladies, and even the eunuchs, having
their own. Some of the eunuchs are great fanciers
and breeders of them. One of them still breeds the
sleeve-dog. Her Majesty's known dislike to these

Continuation of the Portrait

latter is probably the cause of fewer being bred in the Palace now than formerly; and the race is slowly dying out. All the other dogs in the Palace, except Her Majesty's, are kept in the apartments and courts of their owners, and are not seen by her.

She dislikes cats very much, but some of the eunuchs have very fine specimens of the felines. They keep them, however, "sub rosa" and within rigid bounds, on no condition allowing them to come within Her Majesty's ken.

The pavilion at the Summer Palace where the Empress Dowager's dogs were kept was near her Throneroom, and also near the pavilion she had set aside for me. When the Court was taking its siesta, I used to go out where the dogs were basking in the sun in their court and look at and play with these interesting little animals. I was free to do as I pleased, and no one but the dogs' guardian eunuchs saw me there.

Among the younger set, of these pampered pets, was one that caught my fancy — one of those which had been brought for Her Majesty to look at in the garden. He was a beautiful white-and-amber-colored Pekingese pug. He soon learned to know me and would come running to me when I crossed the threshold of the court. Not long after I had discovered where the dogs were kept and had been paying them my daily visits, one night, when we had finished dinner at Her Majesty's table, one of her eunuchs brought in this very little dog and put it in my arms, saying Her Majesty had presented it to me from her own kennel! She had evidently learned of my visits to the dogs, though none of the eunuchs around her

person had seen me go there, at least so I thought!
I was delighted to own this beautiful animal, and
when the Empress Dowager came into the Throne-
room from her own apartments, I went up to her and
kissed her hand and thanked her for it. She seemed
much pleased that I liked it, and remarked that she
had heard it was my favorite of her dogs, that I was to
call him "Me-lah" (Golden Amber), from the color of
his spots. Her Majesty and the Princesses were all
much amused at the way he followed me around, not
leaving my side for an instant, nor paying any attention to their frequent efforts to attract his attention.
From that day, he became my constant companion
and faithful friend.

CHAPTER VII

PREPARATIONS were now beginning at the Palace for the celebration of His Majesty the Emperor's Birthday. This is not celebrated on the anniversary of the day he was born, but two days earlier. His Majesty must make the Autumnal Sacrifices to his Ancestors three days after the real date of his Birthday, and he must prepare himself for these sacrifices by a rigorous fast of three days. As it would be impossible to accomplish the ceremonial prescribed for the Imperial Birthday while fasting, the celebration of the Birthday was advanced, a special edict having been issued by the two Empresses, when Co-Regents for the young Emperor, ordering the Birthday celebrations to be advanced by two days, for the date of the sacrifices could not be changed—the sacrifice to one's Ancestors being the most sacred of obligations to the Chinese, and most rigidly and religiously observed. Even the Chinese Emperor's Birthday is not celebrated for two years after the death of his predecessor, so rigorous are the rules of respect to the dead and the rites accorded to one's Ancestors in China.

I knew no painting could be done during these

57

festivities, and I expected to go back to the United States Legation. I never dreamed I should be invited to participate in this celebration, hitherto unseen by any foreigner. A week before the Birthday itself, when out for one of our walks with Her Majesty, she called me up to her side and said the Emperor's Birthday was to be celebrated the next week, and invited me to remain in the Palace for these festivities. I was, of course, overjoyed at this gracious mark of her favor, and delighted to be able to see the Oriental pomp and pageantry that accompanied these ceremonial celebrations in China.

There were to be magnificent theatrical performances, splendid fireworks and decorations, and all sorts of pageants. The Imperial company of actors had already begun rehearsing special poems and plays, written to celebrate the occasion. Eunuchs were constantly bringing Her Majesty specimens of the work of the decorators and painters who were carrying out her designs as to special scenes and tableaux, or coming to ask for further instructions. The literati, who were preparing the original poems, sent in their manuscripts, that she might judge of their merits and make suggestions. She herself overlooked every detail, and seemed most interested and anxious to have everything successful.

The festivities began four days before the Birthday with gala performances at the Theater. Each day the decorations of the buildings, the courts, and gardens increased in beauty. In the principal courts, magnificent bronzes, all sorts of antique instruments of music, used only on these great occasions, were brought out as decorations; for music forms part of every ceremonial, official or religious, in China. Among the curious instruments were splendid bronze frames, with several superposed octaves of triangular musical-stones suspended therefrom; elaborately carved supports for different-toned bells; huge "triangles"; immense bronze "tam-tams," curiously and beautifully wrought; big drums on splendid bronze stands; wonderfully chased bells; and many other quaint instruments, used only for official and state processions in honor of Their Celestial Majesties.

The slanting and projecting, upturned roofs of the different buildings forming the Palaces were decorated with scarfs of vari-colored silk, knotted into a curious sort of fringe of rosettes, about two feet long; yellow, the Imperial color, and red, the festive color, predominating, but other colors were introduced into the color-scheme to accentuate these.

The large Square in front of the Imperial gateway, outside the Precincts, was filled with huge, tent-like, yellow satin umbrellas, with deep curtains around the edge. These umbrellas are used for all great festivities in China, and are generally of red. Those for the Emperor's Birthday were, of course, of the Imperial yellow, and were richly embroidered with emblematic designs. Presents for the Emperor were arriving daily from all parts of the Great Empire, and though everything was directed by splendid system the commotion was nevertheless great.

Finally, there was the first gala performance at the Theater. Her Majesty occupied her loge nearly all day, overlooking every detail, sending now and then to the stage one of her eunuchs to transmit her Imperial commands as to the speaking of certain lines or the using of certain postures. On the day of this gala performance she invited all the Ladies of the Palace to lunch, for the first time since I had been there, in the court of the Theater. Her Majesty lunched in the Imperial loge, and then ordered our repast to be served in the court, where tables were laid and served with all the pomp and ceremony that characterized the meals at the Palace. Even this "al-fresco" entertainment was ceremonious.

Most of the large courts of the Summer Palace have roofs of matting erected over them, to keep out the sun. These mat-roofs make, of the flower-filled courts, delightfully cool, outdoor parlors. The mat-sheds at the Palace are almost works of art. Tall poles, reaching from twenty to thirty feet above the roofs surrounding the courts to be protected from the sun, are painted in festive designs, and they support transversal beams, also gaily painted. Over these roof-beams are stretched strips of the beautiful matting which the Chinese excel in making. Matting-curtains drop from the roof of the sheds to a level with the Palace roofs. These side-curtains, as well as huge sections of the matting-roof, are movable, and may be opened and raised by means of cords and pulleys attached to the supporting pillars. The whole structure, supporting pillars and transversal beams, is tied together with ropes the same color of the beams, and not a nail is used. The mat-sheds are put up in June and taken down in September.

New ladies were arriving at the Palace every day

for a week before the Birthday—members of the Imperial Family from a distance, and the wives and daughters of Manchu nobles who were of sufficient rank to present their congratulations in person. The young Empress never failed to introduce me to these ladies. A foreigner in the Chinese Court is a much more extraordinary circumstance than a Chinese at a European Court would be, and this was, in most instances, the first meeting of these Princesses with any foreigner; but they were uniformly courteous and even cordial, never evincing the slightest curiosity as to my dress or my habits. I doubted whether a Chinese at a European Court, or at our White House, would have been treated with the same consideration by all, even to the servants. The children, of whom there were several at Court at this time, were as well-bred as their elders in their treatment of the "foreign lady."

After our first lunch in the court of the Theater, when the theatrical performance of the day was finished and the actors had left, I approached the stage of the Theater and began examining, with interest, its construction and appointments. The Palace Theater is raised about twelve feet from the ground, and its main floor is on a level with the Imperial loge. The building consists of three stories and a cellar. The latter is used for the few pieces of scenery of the scenic plays, and is where the simple devices used for moving it are manipulated. Like the Greek theater, the stage is open on three sides; and the actors come out and speak their parts, their entrance being to the left and the exit to the right of the stage.

With the Empress Dowager

Her Majesty was within her loge while I was examining the construction of the Theater; but she evidently noticed my movements, for the eunuchs soon threw open the great plate doors and she descended the steps of the Imperial loge and came across the court to where I was standing. She asked me if I would not like to go on the stage and look over the building and examine things thoroughly. She added, "You probably may never have such a chance to see a good Chinese theater again." She, herself, went up the steps leading from the court to the stage, and told me to follow her.

The stage is about twenty-five feet square, is roofed over, and projects into the court, its three sides being open. The fourth side has doors and curtains for the entrance and exit of the actors. There are no actresses in China. The men perform the parts of women, and represent them with such success that I was much surprised when I learned there were no actresses. At the back of the stage sit the musicians, who accompany all the theatrical performances in China.

Her Majesty, herself, led the way across the stage and we went behind the scenes. Here, I examined closely a number of "Floats" that were to be used, in the procession in honor of the Emperor, on the day of the Birthday. These floats had all been designed by the Empress Dowager. After we had looked at these, she suggested that I had better see the upper floors. These latter are not in general use in Chinese theaters. The theaters, even at the other Palaces, have but one stage. The steps which lead to the second stage, and thence to the third stage, are behind

62

the scenes. The two upper stages are used for spectacular plays and tableaux, when certain of the players group themselves in pyramidal form on these superposed stages and speak their lines therefrom. The upper stages have also trap-doors and pulleys for use in the spectacular plays. Her Majesty went up, herself, to show me these stages. She mounted the steep and difficult steps with as much ease and lightness as I did, and I had on comfortable European shoes, while she wears the six-inch-high Manchu sole in the middle of her foot, and must really walk as if on stilts.

Neither the Empress Dowager nor any of the Manchu ladies bind their feet; that custom prevailed in China before the Manchu conquest. The Manchus have adopted many of the manners and customs of the Chinese, but the Manchu women have retained their own individuality; and to-day, after more than two hundred and fifty years in China, they still wear their native costume, entirely different from the Chinese women. They still dress their hair in the picturesque Manchu fashion. They not only have never bound their feet, but they have as great a horror of it as Europeans have. Manchu ladies are not bound by the same rigid social conventions as are the Chinese women. They are less circumscribed and have more individual freedom than any other Oriental women. In fact, the Manchu woman seems to be, to other Oriental women, what the modern American woman is to her European sisters.

CHAPTER VIII

HIS MAJESTY THE EMPEROR KWANG-HSU

THE Emperor Kwang-Hsu was barely eighteen years old when Her Majesty the Empress Dowager, Regent of the Empire, handed over to him the reins of Government, admonishing him in a parting Imperial Decree to "discipline his body, develop his mind, love his People, and give unceasing attention to the administration of Government," which Decree His Majesty responded to in fitting terms, by another Decree, begging "Her Majesty the Empress Dowager to continue to advise him in important affairs," saying he "would not dare to be indolent," that only after prayer and sacrifice " to Heaven and Earth and his Ancestors would he Himself begin to administer affairs of State on the 15th day of the First moon of the 13th year of his Reign"! He began to reign by our count the 25th day of February, 1889, under the appellation of "Kwang-Hsu" (Glorious Succession). The name under which an Emperor of China reigns is not his own, but one chosen for him, and has generally some appropriate signification or some symbolic meaning.

His Majesty Kwang-Hsu is the twelfth Emperor, who has reigned over China, of the Dynasty of the

64

His Majesty the Emperor

"Great Purity," as the Manchu Dynasty is called.[1] His reign began at the age of five years, under the Co-Regency of the Empress of the Eastern and Empress of the Western Palaces. The former died in 1881, and from that time on Her Majesty, the present Empress Dowager, ruled alone as "Regent." His reign, counting the years of the Regency, has already lasted thirty years, the third in point of length of any of the Emperors of the Manchu Dynasty.

His Majesty the Emperor Kwang-Hsu was nearing the completion of his thirty-second year when I was first presented to him. I found him an interesting study, but not to the degree of Her Majesty the Empress Dowager, who has charm and is so fascinating. The Emperor is singularly devoid of this quality of "charm," and has but little personal magnetism. He interests one, nevertheless. Her Majesty is Universal, the Emperor is typically Oriental. In person he is of slight and elegant figure, not more than five feet four in height. He has a well-shaped head, with the intellectual qualities well developed, a high brow, with large brown eyes and rather drooping lids, not at all Chinese in form or setting. His nose is high and, like most members of the Imperial Family, is of the so-called "noble" type. A rather large mouth with thin lips, the upper short with a proud curve, the lower slightly protruding, a clear-cut, thin jaw, a strong chin a little beyond the line of the forehead, with not an ounce of superfluous flesh on the whole face, give him an ascetic air and, in spite of his rather delicate physique, an appearance of great reserve strength. His complexion is not so white and clear as that of the other members of the Imperial Family, for the Manchus have whiter skins than the Chinese; but this seems more the result of delicacy than natural with the Emperor. His luxuriant, very long hair, a characteristic of the Manchus, is beautifully silky and glossy and always arranged with the greatest care. It is said he much dislikes being shaved, but tradition, immutable in China, does not allow a man under forty, even if he be the "Son of Heaven," to wear a mustache or whiskers. Like all well-bred Chinese, he has small feet and hands, the latter long and thin and most expressive. The Emperor dresses with extreme neatness and great simplicity, wearing few ornaments and no jewels except on State occasions. His face is kindly in expression, but the glance from his rather heavy-lidded eyes is shrewd and intelligent. His manner is shy and retiring, but this does not seem to be so much from a lack of confidence in himself as from the absence of that magnetic quality, which gives one an appearance of assurance.

He seemed to me the ideal of what one would imagine an Oriental potentate to be, whose title is the "Son of Heaven." There is a Sphinx-like quality to his smile. In his eyes one sees the calm, half-contemptuous outlook upon the world, of the fatalist. There is an abstractness in the subtilty of his regard, an abstractness that embodies one's idea of the "Spirit of the Orient." At first it is difficult to tell whether this comes from a sense of power or from a knowledge of the lack of it, but that firm and fleshless jaw, that ascetic face and keen eye, show there must be reserve strength, that there can be no lack of power, should he wish to exert it. Over his whole face there is a look of self-repression, which has almost reached a state of passivity.

Does he dream of future greatness for the Empire? Does he feel that though his first efforts at governing have failed, he can bide his time—that all things will come to him who waits? Enigma, difficult to divine! But it almost seems so! He appears to fully realize, now, that he made a mistake in the choice of his instruments and time, in his efforts for Progress. But the look of eternal patience in the half-veiled regard of those large eyes seems to show that he will yet try to accomplish China's salvation—that he is but waiting his opportunity.

There is no evidence of the Emperor's feeling any animosity toward the Empress Dowager. Their relations, though rigidly formal, as is necessary from their exalted positions, seem to be most friendly. If there is any feeling on his part as to the check his Government received by the " coup d'état " of 1898, he does not seem to feel that Her Majesty is responsible for it. It was not she who put a momentary stop to his dreams of Progress. It was Chinese conservatism, a coalition of powerful ministers who put up the barriers of the "coup d'état" before him when His Majesty thought to drive on to Progress.

The Empress Dowager returned from her retirement and took up the reins of Government again, at the earnest prayers of the wisest Statesmen of China. She was persuaded by them, and she also believed, that the Emperor was driving the Chariot of State too fast over the difficult and ill-kept roads of traditional

Chinese routine. She felt that His Majesty, as well as the state, would soon be dashed to pieces if he continued as he was then going. It seems as if the Emperor realizes it all now. His unfathomable eye hides an infinity of possibilities, perchance a world of events. Is he quietly studying how to seize opportunity, when it next passes, and leap upon its back and lash it on to Progress or to—Ruin? He would meet either with that same stoical, Sphinx-like smile, I feel confident.

He seems, now, to give but little advice. He holds Audiences, however, and sees many of the officials alone. He issues edicts independent of Her Majesty; but on all grave affairs, and at the meeting of the Grand Council, Her Majesty is always present, and the decisions are the results of their two opinions. When despatches were brought into Her Majesty's Throne-room when the Emperor was present, they were first handed to her, and, after glancing them over, she would give them to him. He, after carefully reading them, handed them back to her with rarely a comment. One could see, though, that this was not from ignorance of the subject, but that he trusted, for the time being, to Her Majesty's greater experience.

Though the Emperor does not seem to feel that the time has come for him to act, he studies every event with the closest attention, and is well informed upon every subject connected with the welfare of the state. As long as the Empress Dowager sits upon the throne with him, I think he will not try to make any of his ideas paramount to hers. He knows that she also wishes Progress for China, and that her methods, more conservative and necessarily slower than his, may, in the end, accomplish just as good results. He seems to trust her thoroughly, and to be willing to have her take the lead. He knows, and the world will soon see, that Her Majesty the Empress Dowager is also vowed to Progress for China; that she is not anti-progressive, nor against reform, now that she feels the time has come for Progress and Reform. Her late edicts show this.

Whether the remodeling of China's laws, which will bring her into line with the Great Nations of to-day, will come during the Emperor's life; whether his power of waiting and his patience may enable him to reach the time when accomplishment shall crown his efforts, who can tell! In the meantime, he fulfils his duties as Official Head of the Empire, rigidly observing all public and private ceremonies incumbent upon him as Emperor.

The Emperor occupies a Palace fronting on the Great Lake as elegant and luxurious as Her Majesty's. He has his own eunuchs and attendants, and leads his own life, quite independent of Her Majesty and the Ladies. He pays his respects to his "august aunt and adopted mother" every morning before the Audience, and they go together to transact affairs of state, after which he returns to his own Palace and follows his own pursuits. On festivals, when the Theater is going, he comes into the Imperial loge during the representations, and, on these days, joins the Empress Dowager and the Ladies in their walks around the gardens or in boating on the lake. He also dines with Her Majesty on these occasions. He does not seem to care as much for the Theater as she does, nor to follow it with so much interest. He often leaves the Imperial loge in the middle of a play, and goes to his own Theater Throne-room, just behind the great Imperial loge, where he passes the time in reading or smoking, which he never does in the presence of Her Majesty.

He occupies himself daily with his studies, among which is English. He is a great reader. There is a special official, at the Palace, who buys His Majesty's books, and they say this is no sinecure, as he does not devote himself only to Chinese literature and the classics, but devours translations of foreign works and is constantly calling for new ones. They say he always reads a book a day, besides attending to his other duties.

He is passionately fond of music, plays on a number of Chinese instruments, and has even tried the piano. He has a good ear for music, and can pick out any air he has heard upon any instrument at his disposal. He is very clever, also, in a mechanical way, and can take to pieces and put together a clock, with fair success. He has been known, however, to fail in getting the very complicated mechanism of some of the Palace clocks properly together again. The Empress Dowager is constantly fearing that His Majesty will take some of her favorite clocks to pieces and not be able to put them into working order again; and he will not allow any one else to finish what he has begun.

He is a very early riser, often getting up as early

as two A. M. When there was some ceremony in Peking or some sacrifice to his Ancestors, he would go the sixteen miles, perform the ceremony or sacrifice and return in time for the Audience at eight o'clock, and it takes two hours and a half for the Emperor's swift runners to carry him the sixteen miles between the Summer Palace and Peking. He does not seem to care for young associates, either men or women, though he is very fond of children. He had but few favorites in the Palace, and quite ignored the pretty young girls and women of Her Majesty's " entourage." He seems to have great respect for cleverness.

There are certain distinctions made with reference to Her Majesty and the Emperor, which are rather curious. Her Majesty, being his Ancestress, is first in everything. She sits upon the Throne in the Great Audience Hall, while His Majesty sits on a stool at her left. He walks beside her chair when they go out, and stands in her presence, but when they dine together he sits in the place of honor at the end of the table. When Her Majesty dines alone, her chop-sticks and spoons, as well as the covers of her yellow porcelain dishes, are of silver. When Their Majesties dine together, the covers of the dishes are of gold, and His Majesty's chop-sticks and spoons are also of gold. I never knew what kind of covers or chop-sticks were used when the Emperor dined alone; for this was always in his own Palace, and I never saw his Palace except from the outside. It was not considered good taste, nor according to the " Proprieties," even to look that way when the Ladies happened to pass it in their promenades.

With the Empress Dowager

When His Majesty walked in the grounds with only his own attendants, without being in the train of the Empress Dowager, his walks were in parts of the grounds not frequented by the Ladies. On Festival days, when he went out in the Imperial barge, or walked with Her Majesty and the Ladies, as he sometimes did, he went through these promenades with his usual courteous demeanor, but he did not seem to enjoy them, and when they were finished he would return with his own attendants to his own Palace. He assisted Her Majesty when she was entertaining the Foreign Representatives, but one, who knew him, could plainly see that he was bored by these Audiences. He would slip away at the first opportunity, not because he objected to the foreigners, but that these state functions were not to his taste. Her Majesty would have preferred him to do his share in the entertainment of the Foreign Representatives and be more "en évidence." Though never out of temper or disagreeable on these occasions, and while he seemed to wish to do his duty, he seemed anxious to get them over. Whether from shyness or dislike at the functions, I could not tell.

1 Confucius says "Purity is the Essence of Heaven." Did the Manchus call theirs the "Dynasty of the Great Purity" with a knowledge of Confucian teaching, that the descendants of the Dynasty of the Great Purity (Essence of Heaven) might become literally the "Sons of Heaven," the appellation borne by the Emperors of China?

CHAPTER IX

THE EMPEROR'S BIRTHDAY

WE went to the Palace early the day of His Majesty's Birthday, and were in the Empress Dowager's Throne-room at six o'clock in the morning; but long before that time, the outer court was filled with the red and yellow chairs and carts of the visiting members of the Imperial Family, who had come in from Peking and from the neighboring Palaces for the day. The high eunuchs were in gala costume, wearing silken gowns of great beauty, embroidered in the Double Dragon. The eunuchs of lower rank were more simply gowned, as the representation of the Double Dragon on the Court gown is only allowed to those of a certain rank. Our chair-bearers were clad in the festive red, with brocaded figures, representing the characters for Longevity.

We passed through the beautifully decorated courts, past the gaily decked Palaces to the Throne-room of Her Majesty, where the Emperor had come to receive the private congratulations of the Princesses of the blood and the Ladies of the Court. It would have been against the laws of Chinese etiquette for these Ladies to go into the Emperor's Palace to congratulate him, even on such an occasion as his Birth-

73

day. When we entered the Throne-room, the Emperor was seated, or rather, reclining upon a lounge in the most informal manner. He was not averse, as was Her Majesty, to the reclining position when on the Throne. His greater Orientalism was evidenced here, for the Oriental proverb says, "'T is better to be sitting than standing, to be lying than sitting," etc. He sat up a little straighter on our entrance, and the Ladies made the formal Chinese bow, which he returned by a friendly nod and kindly smile. I made the European reverence as usual.

His Majesty was dressed a little more elaborately than usual, in a yellow gown, tightly belted in around his slender waist with a handsome belt-buckle of jade. At this morning salutation by the Ladies of his family, his hat lay beside him on the couch, which showed it was unceremonious, for ceremonies are carried on by the Emperor and all Chinese with their hats on. The great Imperial Pearl, one of the most precious of the Imperial jewels, formed the button of his hat on his Birthday. The seven official ranks of Mandarins are shown by the different colors of the buttons worn on their hats. The color of these buttons denotes the rank acquired by their wearers, those of the Manchu Princes, alone, being hereditary. The buttons of these latter are generally of jewels or semi-precious stones. The Emperor, the most simply dressed man I saw in China, wears, as a rule, a plain red silk button, but the Pearl, which can only be worn by a reigning Emperor, is used on state occasions.

After we had greeted His Majesty, we moved further into the Throne-room to await the "lever" of the Em-

The Emperor's Birthday

press Dowager. When she came out of her sleeping apartments, the Ladies fell upon their knees and simultaneously repeated the words of greeting used every morning to Her Majesty, "Lao-Tzu-Tzung Chee-Siang" (Great Ancestress, be happy). After acknowledging their salutations, she advanced and held out her hand to me, and I took it and, as was now my custom, raised the tips of her fingers to my lips. I, of course, never made any but a European salutation to either Her Majesty or the Emperor. She was very gracious and said I would be the first foreigner who had ever seen the birthday celebration of any of the Sons of Heaven, and she hoped I would enjoy it! She then commented on my dress and ornaments, examining the few jewels I wore. After this she turned to the Ladies and, with a quick glance, took in all the details of their Court costumes, calling their attention to the way their official beads hung and signaling any little deviation from traditional forms that she noticed in their attire. She was extremely rigid as to all the details of Court dress.

The Court costume of the Ladies is magnificent. That worn at the Emperor's Birthday (the summer costume) was of the stiff transparent silk I have described in the gown worn by Her Majesty for the portrait. The Court costume of the married ladies is of dark red, embroidered in golden dragons. The widows wear blue; the unmarried girls, bright red—all with the Double Dragon embroidered thereon. The married ladies and widows, when in Court attire, wear a magnificent court head-dress with jeweled crown. The young girls, even in Court dress, wear

With the Empress Dowager

the ordinary Manchu coiffure, with the long red silk tassels falling to their shoulders. The young Empress was charming on the Birthday. Her head-dress was of golden filigree, thickly set with jewels. Across the front, nine beautifully chased golden phenix, with jeweled tails outspread, held in their bills strings of pearls that fell to her shoulders and veiled her forehead. Square, conventionalized bunches of flowers projected from either side of this curiously and elaborately wrought head-dress. Her gown was of the Imperial yellow, embroidered with the golden Double Dragon. She had, around her neck, a solid piece of chased gold, like a huge open ring, with balls at the ends; and she wore the official beads that are always worn in Court dress by Princes and Officials and their wives. The Emperor and Empress Dowager are the only members of the Court who wear, neither the Double Dragon on their Court dress, nor the official beads. Suspended from the Empress's neck was a magnificently embroidered stole, about four inches wide, which reached to the hem of her gown. This stole is only worn by the wives of Emperors, during their husband's lifetime. The young Empress seemed unusually happy to-day, and this was the first time I had ever seen her and the Emperor in conversation. Next to the young Empress came the only secondary wife of the Emperor. She was dressed exactly as the young Empress was; the same gown, the same head-dress, the same embroidered stole, only her jewels were not so handsome, and her dress, instead of being of the Imperial yellow, was of orange. Yellow can only be worn by the first wife of an Emperor!

The Emperor's Birthday

After the salutations to the Emperor and Empress Dowager in Her Majesty's private Throne-room, Her Majesty went out into the court and took her place in her yellow chair of State, the Emperor following, on foot, as was his custom. The cymbals clashed. The flutes sounded and all the instruments of the Imperial Band played the curious minor air, with its tragic undertone of sound, its rhythm like a Gregorian chant, which is only played at the passing of Their Majesties for some great ceremony or official function, and which I soon called the "Imperial Hymn." This is the only approach to a National air that I ever heard in China.

Their Majesties went in ceremonious procession to the Great Audience Hall, where the Princes, Nobles, and high Officials privileged to enter Precincts, were to present their homage and congratulations to the Son of Heaven on the happy occasion of his Birthday. Besides these privileged visitors, there were a number of officials whose rank was not high enough to allow them to enter the Great Hall of Ceremonies. These kneel and make the prostrations in the outer courts.

The young Empress and Ladies of the Court did not follow Their Majesties to the Great Hall, but stopped at the Palace of the young Empress, to await there their turn for the official congratulations, which were not to be made until after those of the Princes and Nobles. The young Empress is a charming hostess, and her eunuchs and women handed us tea and cigarettes while we were waiting. She also had her dogs brought in for me to see. Her apartments opened on a sunny court, full of flowering shrubs and fruit trees. Around the other three sides of the court were built the pavilions for the use of her attendants and ladies. We spent half an hour in her pavilion, waiting for the congratulations of the Princes and Nobles to be finished.

The Emperor, for these official congratulations, was seated upon the Dynastic Throne, erect and stiff as an archaic figure; no longer the shy boy, but the Monarch clothed in all his power, and, for to-day, alone upon his great ancestral Throne. He was attended by his Master of Ceremonies, gorgeously attired, who stood in the rigid attitude prescribed for this ceremony.

Each splendidly garbed Prince and Noble knelt and made the prostration prescribed by the Book of Rites, and each presented His Majesty with a jade emblem, called by the Chinese "ruyie," [1] erroneously supposed to be a scepter by most foreigners; but the "ruyie" is simply an emblem of Good Luck, and may be presented on festive occasions to any one whom the givers wish to honor, and is not an emblem of Imperial authority. The Emperor held each of these "ruyie" in his hands for a few seconds after their presentation, bowed profoundly to the kneeling Prince, and then handed the emblem to an attendant eunuch, who placed it on a Dragon table at the left of the Emperor. When the Princes and Nobles had congratulated His Majesty and left the Throne-room, the young Empress and secondary wife, followed by the Princesses and Ladies, went in to make their official congratulations. The greeting in Her Majesty's

The Emperor's Birthday

Throne-room in the morning had been but a friendly salutation, without any official signification. The young Empress knelt and made her bow first and presented—as did each of the Ladies—a "ruyie." She made the same official salutation as did the others, but her "ruyie" was of a much richer style than those presented by the other Ladies.

After the ceremony of formal congratulations was over, Her Majesty, the Emperor, and Empress, followed by the Ladies and attendants, went in state to the Theater, with the same ceremonial and pomp with which they had gone into the Hall of Ceremonies. The Empress Dowager, who was always the most gorgeously attired person at Court, was, on His Majesty's Birthday, dressed with an extreme simplicity that amounted almost to plainness, and she wore no jewels. This plainness of attire was not an accident, but had been arranged with her usual forethought. She wished the Emperor and Empress to be the central figures of this day's festivities, and did not wish to vie with the Empress even in her attire.

The Princes and Nobles, who had come to the Palace for the official congratulations, were invited to the theatrical performance. They occupied the boxes that ran at right angles to the Imperial loge, which I have already described as forming the other two sides of the court of the Theater. A huge screen of painted silk, twelve feet high, was stretched from the last of the boxes occupied by the Princes to the stage— allowing the latter to be perfectly seen by the occupants of the boxes, but cutting off their view of the Imperial loge, whence Their Majesties, the Empress, and Ladies viewed the play. These invited guests are thus neither seen by the Imperial party, nor can they see the latter.

When Their Majesties and the Empress were seated in their loge, the principal actors came to the front of the stage, knelt, and "kow-towed" to the Imperial box. Then the play began. There was first a noisy burst of weird music, then the chief actor recited a laudatory, congratulatory poem in honor of the Birthday of the Emperor, wishing His Majesty "ten thousand years" of happiness and all the blessings possible. The poem was intoned like a chant by the actor, dressed in the gorgeous historic costume of an Imperial Herald of the time of Kublai Kahn. This poem was most impressive. One of the verses ran thus:

"The vast merits of His Imperial Majesty's August Ancestors have been handed down to Him from generation to generation.

"To the wisdom of His whole Dynasty we owe it, that we have lived in happiness,

"Ever ready to comply with the lofty teaching of our Rulers, leading us unto Good. . . ."

The poem went on to recite His Majesty's merits as a son, his respect for his August Mother, his filial piety, and ended with a wish that Great China might flourish and prosper—grow strong outwardly and inwardly, through the blessings of his reign and his desire for Progress.

After this poem had been intoned by the chief actor, with the whole company of players grouped around on the lower, as well as on the two superposed stages, all in splendid historic costumes, there was another noisy clash of weird music and the play itself began. The Chinese theater, which goes on from morning to night with a series of plays, generally begins with a short one, a curtain-raiser of a quarter to half an hour's length. To-day it began at once, after the poem was intoned, with a great historic drama. The exploits and high deeds of former Emperors were shown, and the actors were magnificently costumed in superb historic gowns which had been handed down from antiquity and were absolutely authentic.

At half-past eleven, with the Theater still in full swing, the eunuchs brought out tables of sweetmeats on the verandah of the Imperial loge, and set them before the young Empress and the Princesses and Ladies, and we were served to refreshments. Sweets and fruits in China are served between the regular meals. The sweetmeats to-day were "birthday food," and were all inscribed with some character meaning "Longevity," "Good Luck," "Happiness," "Peace," etc. There were pyramids of the delicious crystallized fruits which the Chinese excel in making; macédoines of queer fruits, nut pastes, almond creams, and all the fresh fruits in season. With this preliminary repast were served, also, some delicious Chinese wines.

Soon after the repast of sweetmeats was finished, we were served in the court of the Theater this time to the regular meal. It was an immense table to which we sat down on the Emperor's Birthday. There were so many Princesses, Duchesses, and Ladies of high degree from a distance, that our usual number

was more than quadrupled. The repast was a joyous
one. The Chinese are very witty and gay, and though
I could not understand all the scintillations of wit,
their gaiety was contagious! Each gave me special
delicacies that she liked, to try, and each seemed to vie
with the other in endeavoring to make the "stranger"
feel at ease. Some of the Ladies drank champagne
in my honor, and held up their glasses toward me as
they had seen the foreigners do. When the elders
had finished eating, the young people sat down.
These were the children of the Princesses and Nobles
who had been invited to join their parents for these
festivities at the Palace. No girl or boy under sixteen is allowed to sit down with their elders to a ceremonious dinner at the Palace.

Soon after we had finished our gay luncheon in the
court of the Theater the Ladies retired within their
loge, next to that of Their Majesties, and the screen
which hid the visiting Princes and Nobles from the
Imperial party was removed by the attendant eunuchs. When it was taken away, there sat, Turkish
fashion, the great Princes and high Nobles in their
splendid Court dress. Those of the highest ranks
occupied the boxes nearest the Imperial party. The
Princesses pointed out to me, from their box, their
brothers and kinsmen and others whom they recognized; but we saw without being seen, and were
only looking from behind the scenes.

The eunuchs then handed around refreshments to
the Princes and gentlemen, sweetmeats and fruits,
such as we had partaken of before our luncheon.
Then there were some huge steaming silver caldrons

brought into the court, and from these caldrons the eunuchs ladled into bowls some sort of white drink. As we had had nothing of this kind at our repast, I was curious to know what it might be. I knew it could not be wine, for that is served only in tiny cups, and this was served in the ordinary-sized eating-bowls. I was much surprised to learn that this drink was simply hot milk, flavored with almonds, and slightly sweetened, a drink of which the Manchus are very fond, and which is a special mark of Imperial favor, given only on great occasions. The gentlemen raised their bowls to their lips with both hands and drank it off with great ceremony, as if it were a sacred beverage, and seemed, in drinking it thus, to pledge the Emperor's Health and Happiness.

After the Princes had partaken of these refreshments, and while some eunuchs were removing the caldrons and dishes, another army of eunuchs came in, in pairs, each pair carrying between them trays of Imperial yellow, decorated with the red characters for Longevity. These trays contained presents from the Emperor to each of the invited guests, for His Majesty gives as well as receives presents on his Birthday! There was no difference made in the presents given, each tray being the exact counterpart of every other. Each contained a pair of porcelain vases from the Imperial Potteries, a bronze Incense-burner, a scroll with a quotation from the classics or an aphorism of Confucius written thereon. The scrolls were inclosed in silken covers, tied with the Imperial colors. There was also a jade "ruyie" in each tray, such as had been handed the Emperor at the morning ceremony, and an Archer's ring. After the contents of the trays had been delivered to each gentleman present, and the empty trays borne away by the Palace eunuchs, the dividing screen was again placed between the visiting Princes and Their Majesties, and the young Empress and Ladies went out of their loge to the verandah once more, and the theatrical performance again went on. In fact, it had been going on throughout our luncheon and the subsequent entertainment of the Princes, but we had paid no attention to it.

At four o'clock there was the grand "finale." The three superposed stages were occupied by all the gorgeously attired actors, and another Hymn of praise to the Emperor was intoned. He was extolled as the Son of Heaven and representative on earth of Buddha, and other extravagant wishes for "ten thousand years" of happiness were made. When this Hymn was finished, the floats, which we had seen the day before behind the scenes, came out in procession. These floats represented mythical animals, Buddhas, fairies, and personifications of the higher attributes. There were gigantic fruits which opened, disclosing figures representing eternal beauty, perfect happiness, and serene old age. Prominent among the gigantic fruits was the peach, the emblem of Longevity. Last of all, in this curious procession, came the Imperial Dragon, of huge proportions. Its contortions, as it struggled for the Flaming Pearl, emblematic of the unattainable, were most curious. All these figures made their obeisances to Their Majesties and the Empress. They were accompanied by splendidly clothed

The Emperor's Birthday

warriors, heralds, princes, and many gorgeously attired attendants, bearing banners and escutcheons. After the procession had made the tour several times, the dragon stopped with his huge head in the middle of the stage, made an obeisance to His Majesty, then raised it with a mighty roar and spouted forth—a copious shower of fresh spring water, which sprinkled the whole flower-filled court! The Empress and Princesses were all in the secret and knew what was coming, but they kept it from me, and much enjoyed my start of surprise as some of the spray fell upon me, as I had advanced to the very edge of the verandah in order to miss nothing.

When all was finished, the screen was again removed and the great glass doors of the Imperial loge were thrown open, so that Her Majesty and the Emperor could be seen. The visiting Princes and Nobles came forward from their places and knelt in a body, though still observing the laws of precedence as to their ranks. They knelt three times, and bowed their heads to the ground nine times to thank Their Majesties for the entertainment they had received. To receive these prostrations from the Princes, the Emperor and Empress Dowager assumed their Buddha-like poses and acknowledged the genuflexions by a formal inclination of their heads. When the Princes had retired, the actors, clothed in their usual garments, came to the front of the stage and knelt and "kow-towed," but Their Majesties did not return this salutation.

When the Princes and players had left and the Imperial party was alone, cushions were brought into the middle of the court, the Emperor and Empress and secondary wife knelt thereon, while their "Great Ancestress," the Empress Dowager, preceded by acolytes, swinging golden incense-burners which gave forth azure clouds of perfumed smoke, came down the steps to the weird accompaniment of the flutes and cymbals playing the "Imperial Hymn." The Emperor and Empress knelt to do Her Majesty homage, as the greatest living member of their Ancestors. When she reached them, they arose and followed her, and the three moved along in stately procession to the slow beating of the cymbals, followed by the Princesses and Ladies and all the attendant eunuchs. The subtle perfume of the incense, the stately rhythm, the splendid costumes, the flashing jewels and brilliant colors, made a magnificent picture never to be forgotten. The Imperial procession moved through several sunlit courts until it finally came to the entrance of the Sacred Hall, containing the Ancestral tablets; here the Empress Dowager stopped at the threshold until His Majesty and the young Empress had passed within, to complete the ceremonies of the day by worshiping and kneeling together before the tablets of their Ancestors. The music ceased. The ceremony was finished. His Majesty the Emperor Kwang-Hsu had accomplished another year.

1 Generally written "jui," but pronounced as I have written it.

CHAPTER X

THE Autumnal Sacrifices to his Ancestors and His Majesty's consequent three days' abstinence, to prepare for them, put a stop to further festivities after the Birthday, which would have otherwise continued for several days longer. The day after the Birthday was a quiet one at the Palace. Her Majesty was feeling tired and did not care to pose, after the Audience in the morning. The visiting Princesses and Ladies were preparing to leave the Palace; the eunuchs and Her Majesty's maids were bustling around, preparing for the moving of the Court to Peking, for Her Majesty and the Court, as well as the Emperor, were to go into one of the City Palaces the following day. Her Majesty ordered luncheon to be served in one of the beautiful summer-houses in the gardens, about a mile from the Palace, for she said a change would be good for all.

This summer-house, or rather Palace, situated on a hill overlooking the lake, was one of Her Majesty's favorite resorts. She often went to it, after a tiring Audience, and spent the rest of the day there, lunching and dining, and even taking her siesta there. Whenever she went to any of these Palaces inside the inclosure, she always invited all the Ladies of the Court to accompany her. It made a change in the monotony of their lives. This Palace was very luxuriously fitted up, and contained a splendid library, with thousands of volumes of the classics and Her Majesty's favorite authors. The view from its broad verandahs and fair marble terraces was one of the finest, even of the many beautiful ones, in the grounds. We lunched on the wide verandah and drank in the beauty of the scene. No wonder Her Majesty loved this spot! Beneath lay the beautiful grounds of the Summer Palace, with its calm lake and winding streams. On an eminence beyond, the graceful seven-storied pagoda that forms so characteristic a feature in all the views of the Summer Palace, proudly reared its stately height. On the right lay the temple-crowned hills, the upturned roofs of their buildings nestling on their slopes like a flight of gigantic gaily-hued birds, with wings outspread. In the distance, beyond a soft gray undulating landscape, with fields of brilliant green here and there, lay Peking, with its walls and towers, enveloped in a golden haze.

After luncheon and the siesta, Her Majesty called me up and said she was to go into Peking on the morrow, and asked whether I wished the portrait to be taken in for the three days the Court was to remain in the City. She said she would be much occupied with ceremonies and sacrifices, and there would be but little time for painting, but if I wished to work she might be able to give me a short sitting! I told her I did not care to have the portrait taken

AT THE AMERICAN LEGATION, PEKING

into the City, for I knew it would not be possible to get a room with the same light as that in which I had begun the picture. When she found I did not care to paint in Peking, she suggested that I go to the United States Legation and spend the time of the Court's sojourn at the Sea Palace. It had been more than two weeks since I had seen Mrs. Conger, or been in the Legation quarter, and I was delighted at Her Majesty's kind forethought in allowing me to spend these days at the Legation. She, however, suggested that, as I had not seen the Sea Palace, where the Court was to go, I might enjoy coming there for the day—and spending some of the time in seeing the Palace and grounds. She knew how I enjoyed seeing these beautiful Palaces, and this was another proof of her consideration. She said she would be much occupied with the ceremonies, but that she would map out a nice day for me, and would herself take me for a walk! She added, " This will give you a chance to study me, so your time will not be entirely spent in vain." She said we would resume the portrait on the Court's return to the Summer Palace.

After our return to her Throne-room, and when we had finished dinner, she told me I had better go into the room where the portrait and my materials were kept, when I was not working on it, and said I had better overlook its being put away myself. She followed me into the room, and herself aided and directed the arrangement of things. She ordered the "sacred picture" (for this is what the Chinese call a likeness of a reigning Emperor or Empress) to be attached to the wall with yellow cords and covered with a transparent yellow silk, box-like screen, which had been especially made to protect it from dust. The portrait was treated, from its very beginning, as an almost sacred object, with the respect a reverent officiant accords the Holy Vessels of the Church. Even my painting materials seemed to be invested with a sort of semi-sacred quality. When Her Majesty felt fatigued, and indicated that the sittings were finished, my brushes and palette were taken by the eunuch from my hands, the portrait removed from the easel and reverently consigned to the room that had been set aside for it.

The next morning early, I preceded the Court into Peking and went directly to the United States Legation, where I was warmly welcomed by my kind friends, Mr. and Mrs. Conger. The United States Legation occupied, at this time, a Chinese temple near the "Water Gate." This building had been given to the United States Government by the Chinese after the Boxer rebellion, and was occupied temporarily by the Minister of the United States during the construction of the new Legation on Legation Street. The temple had been transformed into a comfortable American dwelling-place—its Chinese individuality having been preserved wherever possible, consistent with comfort. The shaded court, filled with beautiful, growing flowers (many of them gifts from the Empress Dowager to Mrs. Conger), was a charming spot. While distinctly American as to its artistic comfort and furniture, the interior construction and decoration of the drawing-room were purely Chinese, which gave a touch of Oriental

" couleur locale " to this pleasant haven of American hospitality, where Mr. and Mrs. Conger dispensed their kindly favors.

Mrs. Conger, by her own individual initiative, has done much to bring about a friendly social feeling between the Chinese and foreign ladies. It was she who first thought of entertaining the Princesses and Ladies of the Court in her own home; and the United States Legation was the first of the Legations in Peking to issue an invitation to the Ladies of the Court, or to entertain them. It is the first Legation to entertain other Chinese ladies, wives of officials or of the gentry. Several other Legations have since entertained the Ladies of the Court, but in doing so they were only following Mrs. Conger's initiative. While doing so much to bring about friendly social relations with the Chinese, Mr. and Mrs. Conger receive all Americans, regardless of their importance or social position, with a kind cordiality. I was delighted to be in their charming family circle once more. I found my room at the Legation, with its sweet touches of homeliness, a delightful haven, and my visits to the Legation seemed always like going home.

The next morning at seven, a green official chair with its bearers came to take me to the Sea Palace. I was first carried to the Hsien-Liang-Hsu, the " Temple of the loyal and virtuous," where Li-Hung-Chang formerly had his home in Peking, and a part of which the Yu-Kengs had arranged for their home after their return from their mission at Paris, their own semi-foreign house having been destroyed by the Boxers.

With the Empress Dowager

At the Hsien-Liang-Hsu I was joined by the Ladies Yu-Keng, and we continued on to the Sea Palace. Our chairs, with their bearers, were preceded and followed by mounted attendants.

The Sea Palace is a comparatively new Palace, most of it having been built within the last fifty years. Our chairs were met at the northern entrance by the same eunuchs who had been set aside for our service at the Summer Palace. They led us to the boats in waiting to carry us across the lake, to the buildings occupied by Her Majesty and the Court. These boats were of the houseboat variety, with an inclosed cabin forming the center, and a platform running all around, on which the rowers walked up and down propelling it. The interior was carpeted, with a cushioned lounge, tea-tables, and chairs. The eunuchs and attendants sat outside on the prow. It takes twenty minutes to row across the lake in one of these boats, but the movement is delightful. When we reached the other side, we landed and went through several courts to that of one of Her Majesty's private chapels. She, herself, had just been making an offering here, and was coming out, preceded by acolytes swinging incense-burners, the musicians playing the "Imperial Hymn." When she saw us, Her Majesty called us to her side, asked if I had had a good trip into Peking, and how Mrs. Conger was. She then ordered the eunuchs to show us our apartments. We were led through corridors and courts to a charming pavilion which was to be our resting-place while at the Sea Palace. It had exquisitely and elaborately carved woodwork arches with heavy satin curtains, which divided it into five rooms. After we had rested a few moments here, we returned to the Throne-room. Her Majesty told me she had arranged for me to go out in one of the boats, and that I was to be shown all that I cared to see, or at least as much as I could see in that day. A eunuch standing near her held a number of strips of embroidery in his hand. They were embroidered head-dresses, which are placed upon the heads of the Buddhas during the great ceremonies in the Palace temples. She explained their use to me and then dismissed us, and we went out to the landing-place on the lake.

A number of boats lay at the foot of the steps— among them a charming open barge with blue silken awnings. As I had not been in a boat of this kind before, and as I was told to choose, I selected it for our row; and we started off, followed by several other boats carrying eunuchs and refreshments, with the necessary utensils for serving them. Our head eunuch, one of the six highest in the Palace, who had been appointed to look after me and the "sacred picture," was very intelligent, an enlightened lover of Chinese art, and a great collector of old Chinese paintings and curios. He had been, in his youth, one of Her Majesty's favorite players, was said to have great dramatic talent, and, when he was younger, had a fine voice for singing. Memory is among the most esteemed of the intellectual faculties by the Chinese, and reaches a high state of cultivation with them. Many of the eunuchs can repeat whole pages from the classics, and some are accomplished literati. This eunuch had a good speaking voice, and recited poems and told stories in a charming way. As we were rowed along, he stood at the prow and recited verse after verse of classic lore and told stories of the heroic times. He intoned them like a recitative—the rhythm so perfectly observed, the intoning so musical, it was a pleasure to listen to him, though I could not understand.

I lay back among the cushions, as we glided softly along, past beautiful pavilions, with splendid trees overhanging the lake and lovely flowers growing wherever there was a place to plant them. The tall figure of the splendidly attired eunuch, standing in the prow, repeating, with rhythmic cadence, poems and stories, gave one the illusion and charm of the "Arabian Nights," which I had fed upon in my childhood, and which I seemed to be living through to-day.

We soon came to a tiny islet in the lake, with a sort of open temple built over a black marble tablet which bore an incised inscription. I asked to land and examine it, and San-Gunia, the eldest of Lady Yu-Keng's daughters, a remarkably clever girl and well posted in Chinese literature, translated the characters. The inscription was a poem, a tribute to the Great Father who had graciously placed there this island, which "by night was bathed in the glory of the Moon and Sun-kissed by day, while the crystal waters of the lake formed a brilliant necklace on its breast."

Beyond the island I saw a temple. There was no landing-place, and the temple was under repair. The head eunuch, however, seeing how much I wished to go up, had the boat draw near and steps brought, up which we clambered, as best we could.

Peking – The Sea Palace

This was one of the temples so ruthlessly destroyed and unnecessarily desecrated by the Allies during their occupation of Peking. We passed through the vegetable garden of the monks—all shorn of its glory, but where a few vegetables and flowers still grew—and we went on through a beautiful grove of arbor-vitæ, with centuries-old trees, planted in the form of a cross, and came into the court of the temple. Even in its dilapidated state, with the workmen still in it, it was beautiful, and before it was so injured it must have been a splendid example of Chinese temple architecture. The cells of the lama monks were now unoccupied, and there were no officiating priests. Workmen were repairing and regilding the Great Buddha, and most of the effigies of the saints and images of the personified attributes were standing in dejected rows in the corridors awaiting the completion of their niches and chapels. The interior, of splendid proportions, glowed in beautiful somber colors. The carved-wood ceilings were in pendative designs, recalling those I had seen in the Alhambra; but the painting, in primary colors, of this elaborately carved ceiling gave it a greater richness of coloring and lent to the interior a warmer, deeper harmony than the white Moorish designs. The chapels behind the high altar were separated from the main temple and from each other by beautifully carved wooden screens, with rich brocaded silk of brilliant green (the color of Buddha), stretched behind the open work and showing through the interstices of the carving. These chapels are for the Sacred writings and for the vestments of the priests, and are also used for robing-

and retiring-rooms for the officiants. They correspond to the sacristies of the Catholic Churches in Europe.

The space behind the altar was of apse-like form, and opened upon a semi-circular marble terrace, thirty feet high, with a balustrade of the conventionalized lotus design so dear to the Chinese architects, From this terrace we had a beautiful view of the Coal Hill, surmounted by the curious Dagoba, so well known in all views of the Imperial City, as well as of the belvedere that marks the spot where the last Emperor of the Mings committed suicide when he was conquered. At the two extremities of the terrace were charming octagonal summer-houses, where the priests could go for rest and contemplation, and, while murmuring their prayers, could feast their eyes upon a charming view. After a few moments on the terrace, enjoying the beautiful view, we passed through the cells of the monks, which were large and comfortable, and, finally, out again into the sun-flecked shade of the marble-paved court, where we sat under low-hanging boughs of a splendid elm, and the eunuchs brought out tables and served us with tea and refreshments.

Then we took the boats and were rowed on further, till we came beneath a steep battlemented wall, surmounted by the rich green of arbor-vitæ trees. I was surprised to learn that this was another temple, for it looked more like an old feudal castle than a peaceful temple to the mild Buddha. We landed at the foot of the beautiful white Marble Bridge that spans the narrow northern portion of the lake, just under the stone wall on which the temple was built. We were carried up the steep, winding incline in our chairs. It was a most picturesque approach, and when we reached the top, with the beautiful temple lying peacefully on these martial heights, we found it well worth the climb.

There was a grove of arbor-vitæ trees leading to this temple. These trees seem to be sacred to the temples and burial-places in China, for all I ever visited in China were either built in a grove of arbor-vitæ, or had some of these evergreens growing near. Did the Greeks get their idea and name of the ever-living tree from the Chinese, who regard the arbor-vitæ as the tree of life and emblem of Immortality? This temple has a great Buddha of white jade, with jeweled stole and cuffs. Its expression of placid contemplation and kindly thought is typically Chinese. When Buddhism was first brought into China from India, the Buddhas had an Indian type; and not until the religion had taken firm hold of the people, was its divinity clothed in a Chinese personality, and a national individuality assumed. The day of our visit, the great jade Buddha was decked in a mantle of Imperial yellow satin, with a richly embroidered Manchu hood, such as I had seen that morning in Her Majesty's Throne-room, on its head. Tall, lighted candles, fresh offerings of fruit and flowers, and the smoking censer standing on the altar, showed there had been services that morning, and added to the religious atmosphere of the interior. The service had been a continuation of the commemorative celebrations in honor of the Emperor's Birthday and his sacrifice to his Ancestors.

With the Empress Dowager

The principal court of this temple is one of the most picturesque in the Sea Palace, shaded by magnificent cedars and stately elms. In the center, there was a magnificent cistern of verd-antique, splendidly carved in dragons. Over this cistern was a marble portico, its columns supporting a curious concave, copper roof. This roof had been a Palace "cooking utensil," that had been used in former times to prepare food for the poor; hence its extraordinary size. When it was worn out in this capacity it was used as the interior of the dome over the temple well, where the poor and weary could come to rest under its shadow and drink of the water of the well it protected. There were cells and outhouses for the monks in this temple also. But as we sat in the shady court, looking across the sunlit lake, the sky became suddenly overcast, and we took our chairs and hurried down the steep, paved road that led from the temple to the lake. We did not take the boats again on reaching the lake, but were carried, in our chairs, across the beautiful Marble Bridge. Just beyond us, we saw the towers of the first Catholic Cathedral ever built in Peking. It was built on land given to the Catholics by the Emperor; but, when finished, its towers were found to overlook the Palace grounds; so the Cathedral was bought by the Emperor, and land was given the Mission further on, and another Cathedral was built. The first Cathedral is now within the Walls of the Sea Palace, and is visible from every part of the grounds of the two Peking Palaces. It seems a strange anomaly to see this Christian Church within the Precincts of the Palace of an Oriental potentate, who is one of the representatives on earth of the "Great Buddha."

It began to rain, and the chair-bearers ran along to the Palace without stopping again, and we were soon called to dinner in the Throne-room, overlooking the small Theater, for there are two Theaters in the Sea Palace, one for winter use and one for summer. The latter is built on piles over the waters of a canal. Building the stage over water is supposed to give a peculiar musical resonance to the voices of the actors, softening the sounds and making them more pleasant to the ear.

After dinner in the beautiful summer Throne-room, with the rippling waters just beneath the windows, we made our adieus, first to Her Majesty and then to the young Empress and Ladies, and went out to be again rowed over the beautiful lake to the outside gates. The sun was setting! The arches of the Marble Bridge had become a beautiful, deep violet hue, and spanned the waters of the lake, now a gleaming mass of liquid gold. The sky beyond shone through the masses of foliage with a golden glow, and the towers of the old Cathedral were strongly silhouetted against this brilliant background. The scene was an ideal one. A beautiful silence pervaded everything, made the more rhythmic and intense by the regular movement of the oars in the water. When we reached the other side of the lake we were conducted to our green chairs, which were waiting without the gate, and were swiftly carried back to the Legation.

CHAPTER XI

SOME CHARACTERISTICS OF HER MAJESTY — SECOND VISIT TO THE SEA PALACE

I SPENT the next day at the Legation, and thoroughly enjoyed it, but I was glad to think that I was to spend the following day at the Palace again. The study of Her Majesty had now become to me like a thrilling novel. I could not bear to lay it down; and when I was forced to do so, I was longing to be able to resume it. She was such a delightful surprise to me. I had heard and read so much of her, before I went to the Palace, and nothing that I had heard or read had at all prepared me for the reality, so charming, so unusual was her personality. Not charming and interesting by fits and starts, but always so! She was so considerate and tactful, and seemed so really kind in her relations with those who surrounded her. I had been now nearly a month in daily contact with her. I saw her, not only when she sat for the portrait; I was with her the greater part of the day, and I began to let myself go in my admiration of her. The days seemed flat and stale when I could not see her—so full of interest and charm I found her. She was a woman of such infinite variety! There was always something new and fresh to study in her. She was the very embodiment of the Eternal Feminine. She was at once a child and a woman with strong, virile qualities. She would go into the Audience Hall, transact weighty affairs of State for three hours, and then go for her walks or excursions, and take a childish interest in the simplest pleasures. She would be seated in one of her Throne-rooms in trivial conversation with her Ladies, when an Official Despatch, in its yellow silk case, would be brought in, and presented by the eunuch on bended knees. Her face would immediately become full of serious interest; she would bend her brows and become the statesman; a few moments later, when she had duly considered, and given orders relative to the despatch, she became again the woman, full of interest in her flowers, dresses, and jewels.

A distinguished Frenchman once said of Her Majesty the Empress Dowager, " C'est le seul homme de la Chine," and she deserves the appellation of " man," if it goes to mean superior intelligence and executive ability; but it was not the " statesman" that I had the best opportunity of studying. It was the woman in her private life; and I had unusual advantages for this study, and the more I saw of her, the more remarkable I found her! Her favors to the Ladies of the Court were very impartially distributed. She had her favorites, but she did not allow them to gain any supremacy over her, nor to warp her judgment. Although her " entourage" never expressed an opinion contrary to hers, in her presence, and though she always accepted their *expressed* views in the most courteous manner, one could see she was not imposed upon, and that she knew, perfectly well, their real opinions, so great was her natural penetration.

I was astonished to find in what veneration the Empress Dowager was really held by the Ladies of the Court and her "entourage." Her favorite title, and that by which she has been longest known to the courtiers, is, "Lao-Fo-yeh," the "Old Buddha," which shows that they invest her with sacred qualities. After her return from Hsi-An Fu, where the Court went when the allied troops occupied Peking, and where the sacred Persons of Her Majesty and the Emperor suffered so many hardships and endured them so bravely, the courtiers gave her another, a closer and more affectionate appellation, "Lao-Tzu-Tzung" (The Old Ancestress). This was the title by which she was called in the Palace, by the Emperor, Empress, and Princesses, and by which she allowed me to address her.

On our arrival at the Sea Palace, the day of my second visit there, after making our bows to Her Majesty, we started, in our chairs, to the Hall of the Mongolian Princes. This is a magnificent hall in the northeastern part of the park, some distance away from Her Majesty's and the Emperor's Palaces. It is of one story, as usual, but this nearly forty feet high. The interior is spacious, with only a few dragon tables and chairs and no ornaments or other furniture. There is a raised dais at the back, with several steps leading up to it. Upon the dais stood a splendid Throne of archaic design, and over the Throne there are two huge tablets of black marble, with inscriptions in Chinese and Manchu characters. This

Second Visit to the Sea Palace

great hall is used only for receiving the Mongolian
Princes on their annual visit to Peking, when they
come in state, with hundreds of followers and retainers, to pay homage and tribute to the Emperor of
China. The rear of the hall opens on a court surrounded by smaller buildings, which are used as
waiting-rooms for the retainers and followers of the
Princes.

From this hall we were carried in our chairs along
the banks of the lake, beyond the Marble Bridge to a
distant part of the grounds, where stands the famous
Dragon Wall. Most of the Chinese houses have a
sort of stone screen opposite the principal gate of
entrance. This screen, called "A Wall of Respect,"
often has some sort of painted or carved representation of a dragon, which is supposed to chase away
evil spirits. This superstition does not seem to obtain
as regards the residences of the Son of Heaven, for I
never saw a dragon wall built in front of any of the
entrances to the buildings in the Palace inclosures.
Perhaps the Son of Heaven is immune from the visit
of demons, or is it that the rampant Double Dragon
on everything Imperial serves as sufficient protection
to the Palace? The Dragon Wall, in the Sea Palace,
must have formed a part of some of the outside palaces or temples which were brought into the sacred
inclosure when the Emperor Hsien-Feng decided to
make it a place of residence and enlarge its domain.
Many foreigners in Peking can remember when the
beautiful Marble Bridge, of such noble proportions,
of such exquisite design, now within the Precincts,
was used by the public. However it got there, the

With the Empress Dowager

Dragon Wall is at present within the Palace inclosure, though in an unused part of the grounds—not in front of any "residence," and hence not filling its mission as a "Wall of Respect," to keep the wicked spirits from crossing the threshold. This Dragon Wall of beautiful white marble is of great beauty, exquisitely carved in its minutest details, and fine in general conception and line.

Her Majesty had returned from the Audience when we got back to the Palace from our morning promenade. She was now attending to household affairs. The eunuchs were bringing up, for her inspection, the baskets of splendid fruits, which are daily sent into the Palace. Among others, there was a basket of magnificent grapes. She was delighted with their beauty, and held up one splendid bunch against the light, before she tasted them, remarking that "the beautiful color lent an added zest to the delicious fruit." Her Majesty then lunched, while we joined the Empress and Princesses on the verandah, after which we lunched again in this beautiful Throne-room. The meals taken with the young Empress and Ladies of the Court had now come to be gay reunions. Her Majesty would ask us every day to lunch or dine at her table, and I rarely took a meal in my own quarters. I had discarded the knife and fork and was learning to use the chop-sticks. I thought them such graceful implements when wielded by the beautiful hands of the Chinese Ladies, that I determined to learn their use. Though I never became an adept with them, I found these dainty implements perfectly adapted for eating the Chinese food. They are used

CHINESE ARCHITECTURE

Second Visit to the Sea Palace

both in the same hand like twin fairy wands, and seemed to me much more delicate and graceful than a knife and fork. My efforts at using them, and my desire to try all the new dishes, amused and pleased the Ladies. Each would give me special tidbits from her favorite dishes; they tried to teach me the Chinese names of the viands. My efforts at pronouncing these names, or my giving them to the wrong dishes, sometimes raised peals of laughter from the whole table. Her Majesty often heard the merriment, and would ask us, when we went into her private apartments after the meal, what had been the cause; and sometimes she would say, "What has 'Kergunia'[1] said?"

We had scarcely finished luncheon, on this my second day at the Sea Palace, before the chairs were ordered for a promenade. It had begun to rain, and the air was chilly; but Her Majesty had made up her mind to have a walk at that hour, and nothing ever interfered with her plans, in so far as she was able to carry them out. No weather, however disagreeable or severe, ever kept her from an outdoor promenade that she had planned. The open chairs were brought, as if the day were fine. Her Majesty and the Empress took their seats in their yellow chairs. Their attendant eunuchs unfurled the huge yellow umbrellas, used only for Their Imperial Majesties and the young Empress; the second Empress took her orange-colored chair; the Princesses and the rest of us seated ourselves in our red chairs, and our eunuchs raised the red umbrellas over us. Her Majesty the Empress and Princesses, clothed in the brilliant colors daily worn, the eunuchs still wearing their richly embroidered gala costumes, the chair-bearers still clad in the festive red, the yellow and red chairs with the big yellow, orange, and red umbrellas made a quaint procession, bright with color, that started off through the courts into the gardens.

Her Majesty loves every phase of nature and every kind of weather; but it seemed to me as if she particularly loved rain. She once said it lent such a poetic charm to the landscape, bathing it in a soft mystery and washing away all defects. Peking is a dry place, and rain is a rarity, which probably accounts for this predilection. Her Majesty was in great good humor, but her partiality for rain was not shared by the other Ladies of the Palace, and these rainy promenades were never indulged in by them with any great show of delight. Her Majesty likes moving swiftly, and the chair-bearers always run when she leads the procession. We sped along for about fifteen minutes, when the chairs suddenly stopped. I looked to see for what reason, as we were in the open, with no shelter anywhere near, and the rain still falling. I was surprised to see Her Majesty was already out of her chair and walking off toward a "gourd-arbor" at the side of the paved walk.

The gourd is much esteemed by the Chinese. It is emblematic of Fruitfulness and Prosperity, and is a special favorite of Her Majesty's. Those cultivated at the Palace, and known all over China as the "Imperial Gourd," have long been famous; but have reached a greater state of perfection than ever before, under the special care and training given them during

Second Visit to the Sea Palace

Her Majesty the Empress Dowager's reign. They are of one shape only, with a contracted neck and two equal parts above and below; but they are of all sizes, from one to twelve inches, the one-inch size being as perfect as the larger ones. They are grown on trellises, about seven feet high, and the vines are very carefully trained, so that each of the much-prized fruit may attain its best development and have its proper quota of light and sun.

Her Majesty walked through the mud to the arbor. The white kid six-inch-high soles of her shoes sank deep into the soft, rain-soaked soil. The eunuchs made vain attempts to protect her from the rain, but she went imperturbably on and was soon under the gourd-arbor. Here she leisurely tried several of the gourds, to see if they were properly ripe; for they must be pulled at a certain time or they do not dry well. After looking at and trying a number, she had several gathered and went back to her chair. The young Empress and the other Ladies had, of course, got out of the chairs when Her Majesty stopped. Luckily, she did not ask us to go into the arbor with her; but etiquette obliged us to stand on the marble walk, which though not muddy and not so disagreeable as the walk to the gourd-arbor, was, however, running with water. When Her Majesty took her chair again, we resumed ours, with a sigh of relief; for, though we were unprotected even in the chairs, we felt the truth of the Oriental saying, "It is better to be sitting than standing," etc.

After another quarter of an hour, the chair-bearers stopped again. We had come to another gourd-arbor! Her Majesty got out of her chair and examined the gourds in this arbor with the same deliberation and interest as she had looked at those where we first stopped. The rain was now falling in torrents, but Her Majesty's spirits seemed to go up in proportion to its coming down. The Ladies were again obliged to get out of their chairs! They stood in two dejected lines, with the eunuchs holding, as best they might, the red umbrellas over each, and they vainly tried to keep up an appearance of interest and enjoyment. The brave finery of the eunuchs, who may not carry umbrellas when on service, was now hanging in limp folds about them, and their fine feathers were much bedraggled. The Chinese Ladies had their two-inch-high, kid-covered cork-soles to protect their feet from the water; but mine, in thin kid slippers, were soaking. The picture of the dejected Ladies, the rain-soaked eunuchs, was, however, so amusing, that I quite forgot my own discomfort and thoroughly enjoyed the situation. After another twenty minutes' run, with the rain still falling, Her Majesty gave the word and the procession turned toward the Hall of the Mongolian Princes. The great doors were thrown open, and we were, at last, under shelter.

A yellow chair was placed for Her Majesty in front of the dais, and she had some of the gourds she had gathered brought to her. She selected one for herself, gave one to her principal Lady-in-waiting, Sih-Gerga, and handed one to the Chief Eunuch Li—the Princess and the Chief Eunuch both being proficient in the art of scraping them. A sharpened piece of

Second Visit to the Sea Palace

bamboo was brought to Her Majesty and she began to work on the gourd she had taken, scraping off the outer skin. She told me to stand near and watch her scrape it, as it was a very difficult thing to do well! She certainly did it well, and it was most interesting to watch her beautiful little hands, as they gracefully moved the piece of bamboo back and forth, quickly removing the outer skin, in the most approved way. Though apparently thoroughly interested in scraping her gourd, she asked me how I had enjoyed my promenade of the day before, and what I thought of the Sea Palace. She called my attention to the inscriptions on the tablets behind the Throne, saying they were in Manchu and Chinese characters, pointing out their difference of form and also speaking of the differences in the two languages. She said she thought Manchu would be easier for a foreigner to learn than Chinese, as Manchu has an alphabet and is constructed more on the lines of a European language. Presently Her Majesty turned to speak to some one else, and I immediately withdrew, as is the custom at the Palace. We went out and joined the Empress and Princesses, who had already retired from the Throne-room and were having tea and cigarettes reclining on the couches in one of the rooms in the rear. After an hour's rest in the Mongolian Hall, the rain having ceased, we continued our promenade through the grounds much more pleasantly than we had begun it, and Her Majesty took me for a walk in the Gardens of the Sea Palace, as she had promised.

After dinner, we were rowed over the lake to the Gates.

With the Empress Dowager

Just beyond them a company of archers was practising with their bows and arrows; for archery is still in vogue in China, and fine marksmanship among the archers is rewarded by substantial advancement in the army. Archery is also practised as a sport by the young Manchu nobles. It is said to educate the eye and materially develop the chest and arms. The Chinese pay great attention to position in archery. They stand stiffly erect, the chest thrown well forward, the head held high, the bow and arrow at rigidly prescribed angles; and if this position be not observed, however true the flight of the arrow, it goes for naught. From the shelter of my chair, I watched the company's practice until I heard the "Sunset call" resounding through the Palace grounds; echoed and reëchoed until it reached the outer gates, which began to move upon their huge hinges until they clanged together for the night.

[1] My Chinese name.

CHAPTER XII

RETURN TO THE SUMMER PALACE

THE next day the Court returned to the Summer
Palace. The festivities and sacrifices in connection with the Emperor's Birthday being now over and
the Court settled down to its usual routine, I hoped
I might be allowed to go regularly to work on the portrait, and that Her Majesty would allow me to paint
when she was not posing. There was much I could do
between times, and she could pose but for a short time
each day. Up to that time, Her Majesty had treated
me as a guest at Court, whose amusement was the most
important thing to be looked after. She seemed
much interested in the work, but my painting was an
incident and even the "Sacred Picture" a secondary
consideration. All these walks, these delightful excursions, were perfectly charming, and, had I gone to the
Palace to enjoy myself, or to study Her Majesty and
Chinese manners and customs, I would have been perfectly satisfied. I had, in the Empress Dowager, a
psychological study full of ever-varying and constant
interest. I was living through a unique experience,
seeing what I could never hope to see again, but I
was not allowed to paint on the portrait as much as
I should have liked. Could I but have had permis-

sion to work more, I should have been very happy. Had I been able to speak Chinese well enough, I felt I would obtain what I desired; she had shown herself so uniformly kind. She probably felt I was enjoying myself more in this way than working at my painting.

While I thoroughly enjoyed the promenades with Her Majesty, I loved the daily sittings. Every portrait-painter knows the sort of intimacy that establishes itself between him and his sitter, however unsympathetic the latter may be at first sight, which was certainly not the case in this instance. The effort of the painter to get under the exterior and discover the real person of his sitter; the desire to see the best side and make the most of it, meets generally with a sympathetic response. If the "rapport" is properly established, they get to know each other better by the time the portrait is finished than they could otherwise have done, perhaps in years. Though I saw Her Majesty so intimately at other times, I felt I was not seeing her "face to face" (figuratively speaking), except at the sittings.

The morning after our return to the Summer Palace, my easel was again placed in the Throne-room. The portrait was taken down from its resting-place and work resumed. Her Majesty gave me a long sitting, and the portrait made a step ahead. If I had only had a place to work alone, where I might study the picture, when she was not posing, I could have made so many improvements! But I was obliged to possess my soul in patience, and work along for the short space of an hour or so a day and stop the mo-

ON THE ROAD FROM PEKING TO THE SUMMER PALACE

ment Her Majesty felt fatigued, when my brushes
and palette were whisked away, as if by magic. There
was no chance to study the portrait or to do anything,
except when the Empress Dowager and the crowd of
attendants were present.

I had taken to the Palace only a small folding
easel, which was not at all suitable for regular work
on so large a portrait, but it was impossible to get a
better one in Peking. Her Majesty, who observed
everything, noticed that it was not convenient, and
suggested that I draw a design for a large easel and
give it to the Palace carpenters to copy. She thought
they would be able to make me one. I did so, and
they made me a very satisfactory working easel.
When the eunuchs found that this Palace easel suited
me, five others of different sizes were made. I asked
for what reason, and was told that everything for Her
Majesty was made in sixes. It would have been
establishing a precedent, making an innovation, to
have fewer than six easels for her portrait.

Her Majesty also ordered some large flat boxes,
with lock and key, to be made for my materials.
These boxes were covered in yellow, for they were to
be used for the Sacred Picture, and must be in the
Imperial color. I forgot to say the six easels had all
been stained a bright yellow! A table, surmounted
by one of these yellow boxes, occupied a prominent
place in the Throne-room during the whole time this
portrait was being painted. When I finished painting
each day, the Chief Eunuch, himself, removed the picture from the easel, and a number of others came and
took my brushes and palette, put away the easel and

closed the yellow box and locked it. Our head eunuch carried the key to the box.

When the afternoon sitting was finished, we went out for another of those delightful promenades around the grounds. The days were now growing visibly shorter, and the evenings were beginning to be cool. As we went through the gardens, Her Majesty stopped at all her favorite points and looked for a few moments at the view, as if to greet it again, after her absence. She loved the Summer Palace and it always seemed a pleasure to her to return to it. We had tea in one of the tea-houses where there were tables and seats. She ordered the eunuchs to make a sort of blancmange of lotus-root flour, which was delicious, and, as she said, most wholesome. When the Empress Dowager goes for a walk, portable stoves and all the paraphernalia necessary for cooking a light repast are taken along. It seemed wonderful to me to see the way the Chinese could cook, with apparently so few conveniences. After this we had tea. The finest tea in China is sent to the Palace. The first leaves of the plantations all over the Great Empire are reserved for Their Majesties. Her Majesty, who is a great epicure, has her choice of these chosen leaves. She adds to the delicacy of its already fine flavor by putting into her tea-cup the blooms of dried honeysuckle, the flowers of jasmine, or other fragrant blooms. The honey from these flowers slightly sweetens the tea, besides giving it a delicate, subtle flavor, quite unique. These dried blooms are brought in a jade bowl, with two long cherry sticks, with which Her Majesty takes the flowers and places them in her cup, stirring them into the tea with these graceful wands. The Chinese never use a teaspoon. Her Majesty drinks her tea from a jade cup, which is placed in a curiously fashioned, cunningly wrought, open-work, silver saucer. The Chinese take their tea boiling hot, and the jade does not get so hot as a porcelain cup.

We continued our walk through the gardens after leaving the tea-house, and when we were passing a bed of flowers Her Majesty spied some curious grass, which she ordered the eunuchs to gather. When it was brought to her she deftly wove several blades of it into a perfectly recognizable representation of a rabbit. She did it so quickly I did not realize she was trying to make anything until she tossed the finished result over to me and asked me what I thought it was. It was unmistakable.

When we reached our objective point, one of the highest eminences in the grounds, with the whole panorama of the Western Hills spread out beneath us, and the setting sun glowing over all in brilliant splendor, it was a glorious scene. She called me up to her side and made a graceful, sweeping gesture of the hand that said, "This is all mine, but you may share it with me." She had that sense of possession of nature's beauties which all artistic souls feel, for their appreciation makes what they view their own. She felt it was hers, because she loved it so, and she knew I would appreciate it, which few of her "entourage" did, as none of them were such passionate lovers of nature as the Empress Dowager, and custom had dulled their perception of the beauty of the scene. The exquisite pleasure the contemplation of this glorious view gave me, made me tremble with delight. As the day was fading and as I was thinly clad, Her Majesty thought I was cold, and, seeing I had no wrap, she called to the Chief Eunuch to bring me one of hers. He selected one from the number that were always brought along for these promenades, and gave it to Her Majesty, who threw it over my shoulders. She asked me to keep it and to try to remember to take better care of myself in the future.

CHAPTER XIII

WE began now to go out on the lake in the
steam-launches, instead of the picturesque
Imperial barge. The Empress Dowager is artistic
and conservative enough to like the old-fashioned
barge; but she is also intelligent enough to appreciate the advantages of other modes of locomotion,
and has no prejudices; in fact, she rather likes trying
new things. When the days were long, the air soft,
and the bosom of the lake engirdled with its chain of
blooming lotus, she preferred the barge; but when
the shorter and cooler days came, when the lotus were
no longer in bloom, she ordered the steam-launch for
our promenades. She seemed now to like its swift
and noisy progress as much as she had before enjoyed the softly gliding motion of the barge. Her
Throne on the launch was on the prow, just outside
and above the cabin, where the Princesses and Ladies
sat. Her Majesty always wanted the fresh air and the
view, and never went inside. The young Empress
and the Ladies sat within the luxuriously fitted-up
cabin with its lounges and tables.

The first day we went out in the launch the engineer seemed not to have it quite under control, and we soon ran aground in a field of water-plants near the island. There was great consternation among the eunuchs when it was found the launch could not advance, even by putting on full steam. The engineer didn't seem to know what to do. Her Majesty ordered the engines reversed, and this was tried, but it was some time before the launch moved. The Princesses and eunuchs became quite excited, but Her Majesty was perfectly unconcerned, and laughed at their fears for her safety. She said it would be no great matter for her to walk over to the island. It would only mean one pair of shoes the less! When the launch finally moved, the Chief Eunuch, not wishing to run the risk of another mishap, wanted to give word to the engineer to return; but Her Majesty would not hear of this, and insisted upon completing the excursion as she had at first planned it. We had several other mishaps, and the launch finally ran aground; and no effort of the engineers, no putting on of extra steam, was able to get us off again. Her Majesty kept her good humor, ordered her barge brought alongside, and we were all "transshipped." We finished our tour on the lake as she had planned it, but in the barge instead of the launch. She is too intelligent not to use any means at hand to attain her ends, and she is intelligent enough to see that these ends can be attained, by some means or other, before she fixes upon them.

The Emperor of China, with the usual Chinese tolerance,—and the Chinese are the most tolerant people in the world as to religious faith,—is not only the head of one church, but of all the churches in China. He is, as Emperor, the Great High Priest of Heaven, the High Priest of Buddhism and Taoism, and is, of course, a Confucian; though this is a philosophy rather than a religion. But though a philosophy, there are certain rites and ceremonies observed by the Confucians. All the great ceremonies of the different cults are celebrated in the Palace temples with rigid impartiality and equal pomp. Whatever may be the individual leanings of the Emperor, and, of course, he must have his own preferences, he participates in each of these celebrations. But his official, public exercise of religion, is limited to the worship of Heaven and Earth, to which he makes annual public sacrifices in the Great Temple of Heaven at Peking.

The afternoon of our first steam-launch excursion, finished in Her Majesty's barge, there was a splendid ceremony in the chapel at the foot of the hill crowned with the Temple of the Ten Thousand Buddhas, to the memory of Confucius, the great Sage, whose philosophy has directed the lives and laws of the Chinese people for nearly twenty-five hundred years. Though a philosopher like Plato, he is appreciated and his teachings followed by the masses, as well as the classes, in China. He is not a religious leader but an ethical teacher, and though many temples have been erected to his memory, they are like Halls of Science and not temples to a divinity. There are no images either of Confucius or the Sages in these temples. They are classic halls, bare of all church-like ornamentation. Quotations from the "analects," painted on scrolls, cut into wood, and carved out of stone, adorn the walls, not only of the interiors of the temples, but of the courts and verandahs of the buildings. At the place where the altar would be in a temple, there is a plain niche, painted in red with a tablet bearing an inscription in gold, "The Seat of the Perfect One." On either side are similar niches, containing the tablets of four other great Sages, among whom was Mencius. These semi-annual sacrifices are in commemoration of Confucius as an ethical teacher, a wise philosopher, a Sage. At this service in the Palace, the participants and celebrants were all in full Court dress. There was an address to the memory of the great Sage, with music and hymns; the latter were rhythmic verses, containing some truth inculcated by the Sage. There was an altar with a dragon table in front for offerings. There were sacrifices, incense, and music. The altar was rich with splendid vases, rare old bronze bowls, and incense-burners, and sweet with flowers and fruit. On the dragon table, which stood in front, were offerings of millet, meat, and wine. Tall cressets of open iron-work containing huge, burning pine-knots were placed in front of the raised platform, on which stood the altar, which was beautifully illuminated with tall candles in square, silver candelabra. The court in front of this temple, as well as the surrounding buildings, were hung with charming painted lanterns.

Their Majesties, with the Empress and Ladies, preceded and surrounded by eunuchs and officials, in full Court dress, went in ceremonious procession through the verandahed corridors, from Her Majesty's Throne-room to the temple. Their approach was accompanied by the slow beating of drums. When they reached the temple, three yellow cushions were placed on the paved floor for Their Majesties and the Empress, and red cushions for the Ladies. The music was played in rhythmic strains, while Their Majesties knelt and prostrated themselves three times; the Empress and Ladies doing likewise. The officials and other participants knelt outside in the court. When the prostrations were finished, a yellow chair was brought for the Empress Dowager. She sat during the rest of the service, but the Emperor, the Empress, and Ladies remained standing during the whole celebration. This consisted of a number of genuflexions and prostrations by the celebrants, and a moving about of the offerings on the dragon table in a ceremonious and reverent manner. The chief officiant read the address from a long scroll. After finishing it, he placed it on a casket on the altar. The first part of the ceremony took place inside the temple, then the celebrants went out into the court and intoned the six hymns and made renewed prostrations. I was not able to understand enough of the hymns, or to get them sufficiently translated to make out their meaning. They were all of uniform length. They were in praise of Confucius and were called " Odes to Peace." When all the verses were intoned, the scroll with the address, some of each of the offerings, were placed in the huge iron incense-burner, that stood in the center of the outer court, and set on fire by the chief celebrant, while one of the several flagons of wine that had made part of the offerings was poured over the blaze.

With the Empress Dowager

I had not expected to enter the temple with Their Majesties and the Ladies, but when we reached the door, the Empress drew me in with her. They seemed to realize that I enjoyed seeing these celebrations and to perfectly understand my not taking any active part in them. I always remained standing, but I listened reverently to the intoning of the hymns and the reading of the address. I conducted myself as I would at any religious ceremony, and they seemed to appreciate it.

When all was finished, Her Majesty told me to go up to the altar and examine the rare, old, bronze ornaments, the candelabra, etc. They explained to me that the address, which had been read, was burned, as it had filled its mission when it was read; that the ashes of a literary essay were a most fitting offering to the memory of Confucius, the great philosopher. When all was over, Their Majesties ordered the boats to come to the foot of the terrace, where the last part of the celebration had been made, and we returned to the Palace by way of the lake.

CHAPTER XIV

THE PALACE EUNUCHS

THE internal affairs of the Palace are managed by eunuchs, among whom there are all grades, all sorts and conditions. Some are clever literati given to study; some have the polished, insinuating manners of the courtier; some have a Mandarin rank of high degree; some are menials. There are actors and singers, cooks and gardeners, teachers and pupils, writers and readers. They occupy all sorts of positions, from Their Majesties' body-guard to gate-keepers. In this hierarchy, Their Majesties' Chief Eunuchs held the first place. Under each of these there are six eunuchs of high rank, all exceptionally clever, who have raised themselves to the positions they occupy in the Palace by their own efforts or by some special qualification.

Each of the hundreds of pavilions and palaces in the Inclosures has a corps of eunuchs, presided over by a head eunuch. These act as guards to the premises, as well as servants, and keep things in readiness for a visit from Their Majesties. There is a head eunuch who directs the large corps of Palace gardeners; another who presides over the dozens of cooks in the Imperial kitchen; one is at the head of each of the departments, and each of these head eunuchs, chiefs of the different departments, is under the jurisdiction of the Chief Eunuch, for Her Majesty's Chief Eunuch may be called the real Chief Eunuch of the Palace. He is not only older than the Emperor's Chief Eunuch, but is more capable. The two Chief Eunuchs, from their position near the sacred persons of Their Majesties, have unusual power. They may make or mar the career of the eunuchs beneath them; and they not only have this power inside the Palace, but from their exceptionally fine opportunities to present petitions, to speak for or against certain people, they also have a great deal of power with people outside the Palace. Her Majesty's Chief Eunuch has almost the power in Peking, among officials and courtiers, that "Son Eminence Grise" had at the Court of Louis XIII of France. He is courted and fawned upon, receives magnificent presents, and nobles of high degree wait upon his pleasure; but while he occupies this high position with outsiders, in the Palace I saw no evidence of his having any unusual power with Her Majesty, beyond that of one who has been in the life-long service of his master and who has the privileges resulting therefrom.

The peculiar position of a Chinese Emperor, which shuts him in his Palace like a Buddha in a temple, makes some sort of confidential private messenger an absolute necessity. There is much business of an unofficial kind, which must be transacted in a private way. The Chief Eunuchs are naturally called upon in such cases. When the Ruler of the Celestial Empire is a woman, the Palace becomes more of a gilded prison, a shut-in shrine, than even in the case of an Emperor. She cannot see officials, or even members of the Imperial clan, except in the Audience Halls. Thus a Chief Eunuch under an Empress would have even greater power than under an Emperor; and in this instance, Her Majesty's Chief Eunuch, Li Lien Ying, is really of exceptional ability!

In person he is tall and thin. His head is, in type, like Savonarola's. He has a Roman nose, a massive lean jaw, a protruding lower lip, and very shrewd eyes, full of intelligence, that shine out of sunken orbits. His face is much wrinkled and his skin like old parchment. Though only sixty years old, he looks seventy-five, and is the oldest eunuch in the Palace. He has been there since the age of ten. He has elegant, insinuating manners, speaks excellent Chinese— having a fine enunciation, a good choice of words, and a low, pleasant voice. If one may judge from appearances, he possesses ability in a marked degree. Of His Majesty's Chief Eunuch I can say nothing. I only saw him on the days of the Theater, or some festival, when His Majesty passed the day with the Empress Dowager and the Ladies, when he was always accompanied by his suite.

Her Majesty's second eunuch, Sui, who is of equal rank with Li Lien Ying, is as unlike him as two people could possibly be, both as to person, character, mental and moral nature. This one has none of the qualities of the intriguer—no Macchiavellian schemes would be forwarded by him. He is almost a giant in size, tall and heavy. He is forty-six years old, and

has a round, full face, without a line—a typical
Chinese face, as we know it from pictures, benevolent
and kind. He, also, is a good Chinese scholar, and,
of course, speaks it elegantly. Her Majesty will have
no one around her person who does not speak it well.
If it be true that Her Majesty, in choosing her ministers, tries to have them the opposites of each other, so
that she may thus hear the different sides of a question and arrive at more just conclusions, her two
Chief Eunuchs seem to have been chosen in the same
way.

There is a eunuch appointed to administer the
punishment, ordered by Their Majesties for the
eunuchs around their persons. For the higher
eunuchs, this is generally the deprivation of a certain amount of their annual wages, or the loss of
their buttons, for the buttons on the hats of Chinese
denote their rank, and to be deprived of a button, or
to have one of lower rank given, is considered a
disgrace. I once saw Her Majesty very angry over
the failure to carry out one of her orders, by two of the
high eunuchs, and she ordered them to be deprived of
two months' pay. The head eunuchs of the different
departments administer whatever punishment they
see fit, to those over whom they are placed. This punishment is generally corporal. Sometimes they abuse
their authority and are very cruel in administering
this, but, as a rule, the eunuchs seem to be of a mild
and peace-loving nature, rather than cruel and vin-
dictive—inclined to condone the faults of their inferi-
ors rather than punish them to the full extent of their
authority. There seemed to be a feeling of " esprit

de corps" among them—a spirit of mutual helpfulness.

Each of the higher eunuchs has a number of pupils among the lower grades, who call him "Master," and whom he trains in manners and teaches his own specialties. The higher eunuchs seemed to take the liveliest interest in the good conduct, and literary, or other, advancement of these pupils, and they push their interests with Their Majesties in every way possible—each one, of course, trying to advance his pupils beyond those of some other eunuch.

Her Majesty has a great horror of opium smoking. If a eunuch, however high his position, indulged in it, the severest punishments she ever ordered were administered. They were not only deprived of so many months' pay and loss of their buttons, but were sometimes banished from the Palace for a certain length of time, and even severe corporal punishment would be ordered. These stringent measures did not prevent some of them, however, from indulging surreptitiously in the narcotic, but they took the most extreme precautions to prevent its being found out. Her Majesty has unusually acute olfactories, especially for opium. This, it seems, can be detected by its odor, which hangs around the clothes, and, like the odor of the rose, one "can break the vase, it lingers there still." But it seems the eunuchs have special linen clothes, which they put on for smoking, and these are given to be washed, immediately the fascinating pipe is finished. Unless one is an habitual smoker, the drug has very little outward effect and, except by the odor, it cannot be detected.

With the Empress Dowager

The eunuchs are very fond of all sorts of pets, and have in their quarters dogs without number, cats and birds. While the younger eunuchs generally depend for their advancement upon their teachers, who report favorably on them to Their Majesties, they sometimes attract the attention of Their Majesties, and may be raised out of their places by Imperial favor. Among the eunuchs assigned to my service in the Palace, was one who was fortunate enough to attract the Emperor's notice. His Majesty had happened to notice him, carrying my wraps on one of the promenades with Her Majesty. He liked his face and manners and took him into his own service. The eunuch had a "button" bestowed on him and promised to mount very fast in grade. This eunuch had been in the Palace about fifteen years; and had His Majesty not happened to notice him, he might have lived and died in oblivion, and never had a button, for his "master" was dead and he had no protector to push his interests!

When one realizes that the Palaces of the Chinese Emperor are like towns, that their affairs are administered principally by the eunuchs, one can see there must be a good deal of intelligence among them, as well as great opportunities to add to their personal wealth.

I heard, before I went into the Palace, of the great power and unscrupulousness of the Chief Eunuchs; that it would be necessary to be very conciliatory toward them and make them many handsome presents. I did not find it so. I never made an effort to conciliate any of them, nor gave any handsome presents, and I found them all respectful, and I had every consideration shown me by them, and found them, on the whole, pleasant enough to deal with. Some of them were clever and interesting even, and they all had very good manners. In fact, I cannot too highly praise the manners of the Chinese, as a race. I quite concur in the opinion of a clever Frenchman, who said of China, "Aujourd'hui c'est là où les bonnes manières se sont refugiées."

CHAPTER XV

WHEN Her Majesty the Empress Dowager was
Empress of the Western Palace, Co-Regent
with the Empress of the Eastern Palace, who died in
1881, the Empress of the Eastern Palace was known
as the "Literary Empress." All State affairs were
left to the stronger executive ability of the Empress
of the Western Palace; while she of the Eastern Palace gave herself up to literary pursuits and led the life
of a student. She was a woman of such fine literary
ability that she, herself, sometimes examined the es-
says of the aspirants for the highest literary honors in
the University of Peking. She was also a writer of
distinction.

During the long Co-Regency of these two remarkable women, widows of the Emperor Hsien-Feng, one
led the life of a student; the other, the active, militant
life of the ruler. For the present Empress Dowager
has been the real ruler of the great Chinese Empire
for the last forty-five years. Had the Empress of the
Eastern Palace not been such an exceptional light as a
literary woman and had not Her Majesty, Tze Hsi,
possessed so many other and more remarkable quali-

ties, the latter's name might also go down to history as a "literary Empress," for the Empress Dowager has literary qualities of no mean kind. She writes a graceful poem, is able to express herself in elegant Chinese, as well as in the ruder, more forcible Manchu language. She can write in literary style, fine idiomatic Chinese, and this is a rare accomplishment for a woman. The written Chinese language is quite different from that spoken by even the most cultivated. Imagery and figure abound to such a degree, literary form is so important, that many fine scholars are unable to write the language acceptably, except for practical purposes. Aside from Her Majesty's literary acquirements, she has an enlightened taste, is a great reader of the classics, and a fine critic. She also loves poems of heroic adventure. One of her favorite historical characters is the Chinese Jeanne d'Arc, the warlike Maiden, Whar-Mou-Lahn, who went forth to battle in masculine guise, had many heroic adventures in her twelve years' service, and, through them all, remained a virgin pure.

The Empress Dowager has a wonderful verbal memory. Memory, so highly esteemed by the Chinese, is most carefully cultivated, and is generally better developed with them than with us. Her Majesty's memory is, however, considered exceptional, even among the Chinese. She can repeat pages, not only of the classics, but of her favorite authors. One of the widows of her son (the Emperor Tung-Chih), who came regularly every week to pay her respects to Her Majesty, is a very clever woman and a great favorite of her august mother-in-law. This lady also possesses a remarkable memory. On her visits to the Palace I used to hear Her Majesty and this Empress quoting from some of their favorite classics or poems. The quotations would pass from one to another, sometimes for a half-hour without stopping, and, at times, they would repeat in concert some favorite phrase. I will never forget how they looked: Her Majesty sitting at her Throne table with her flowers or some light occupation, her daughter-in-law standing beside her, each of their faces lighted up with pleasure as they repeated line after line.

When the Empress Dowager went to her own apartments for her "siesta," her reader would come bringing volumes of her favorite authors. Some days I could hear his voice rising and falling in regular cadence during the whole time she was resting in her apartments. When she was particularly interested in what had been read to her she would have the book taken out when she went for her daily promenade and would sit and read as she was carried along in her open chair, or was rowed along on the barge. This did not often happen, however, for she took such keen delight in all its manifestations, she preferred to read in Nature's book when out of doors.

She is a great lover of the theater and prefers the classic, the old plays, to the modern Chinese drama. She had one new play staged, while I was in the Palace, with which she seemed to be much pleased. She studied the play for several days before it was given for the first time, and, at the first representation, she followed every line with intense interest. She sent her eunuchs several times to the stage to suggest changes in the rendering of certain parts and in the interpretation of certain lines. The Theater generally begins with a short play, which is often a light farce. She seemed sometimes to enjoy these very much and would laugh heartily at the good hits, which were often original additions by the actors, allusions to some passing event. Contrary to my preconceived idea as to the Chinese, they are witty and appreciate humor in others. The Empress Dowager has a fine sense of humor. She not only sees the point of a joke, but she can turn one very cleverly herself.

She is very particular about the way Chinese is spoken, a great stickler for purity of expression and elegance of style. There are as many dialects in China as there are Provinces in the Great Empire; and although the literati and gentry speak, what is called Mandarin Chinese, some of the most highly educated of the literati from the Provinces speak it with an accent. Her Majesty, who has a musical ear and great discernment as to sounds, gets very impatient when listening to Chinese spoken with an accent. It is said, other things being not quite equal, she will give the preference, in an appointment, to an official who speaks perfect Chinese and who has a good voice, especially if his office brings him often into the Presence. However, particular as she is, bad Chinese in a man of merit is not a bar to advancement, for Li-Hung-Chang, whom she appreciated so highly, and to whom she gave such preferment, is said to have spoken very indifferent Chinese.

Whether it be, that Her Majesty's musical and exquisitely modulated voice, so fresh and silvery, so youthful, adds to the charm of her Chinese, when she speaks it, it sounds like beautiful rhythmic poetry. She speaks it so graphically, with such expression and graceful gestures, that it charms one even who does not understand the language.

One day when she was out for a walk, one of the directors of the gardeners was brought up to explain something to her, some change in the laying out of new flower beds. She listened a few moments, but I saw her frown and begin to look impatient. After a few more words from the poor man, who was evidently overcome by timidity and probably speaking worse Chinese than usual, Her Majesty turned to the Chief Eunuch and said, "Let him tell you and you can translate to me; I can't stand any more of that language," and she walked away, still frowning.

Another day, I heard the Empress Dowager tell one of the Ladies at Court (her daughter-in-law), who was also a great purist in the matter of language, about her own Chinese having been misunderstood by one of the eunuchs. There are many Chinese words almost exactly alike in sound, which are only differentiated by the inflection or tone. Thus there must be great accuracy of enunciation, and there must also be great accuracy of ear. Her Majesty had given an order to one of the eunuchs. The stupid fellow had misunderstood the inflection and had done the exact opposite. She was so amused and astonished, when she found that *her* tone had been misunderstood, that she did not reprove him for his stupidity.

One day, she corrected one of the Princesses for the pronunciation of a word, and she said (in an aside) it was not strange this Princéss did not speak better, for her father's Chinese was " execrable," thus showing that even Princes do not always speak the language correctly.

One of the most precious gifts the Empress Dowager makes, and which is sacredly treasured by its recipients, is a scroll with a single great character written upon it by Her Majesty's own hand. This is considered one of the most difficult feats of a Chinese writer. These characters are sometimes four feet long. One day we were invited to go into the Throne-room to see Her Majesty make some of these characters. When I went into the Great Hall, Her Majesty and the Ladies were already there. She was stirring a great bowl of India ink, for she is very particular as to its consistency and fluidity. When the ink suited her, she took from a eunuch standing near, who held a number, a huge short-handled brush, which she could hardly clasp in her small hand. She tried two or three, before she found one that pleased her, and, turning to me, said, " You see I also have my choice in brushes." I asked Lady Yu-Keng to tell her that I thought her large brushes were more suitable for my hands and that my smaller ones would have been more appropriate for her. She laughingly replied she preferred the Chinese brush, and that her hands, small as they were, were able to wield it very satisfactorily, which was no vain boast.

When all was ready, and the huge scroll spread out before her on a table, she dipped her brush into the bowl of ink, held by the eunuch, and began the first stroke of one of these famous characters, in which she is said to equal the most proficient writers in China. I was amazed to see the firmness of her wrist and the beautiful clearness of her stroke, which deviated not a hair's breadth from the line she wished to follow. She made six great characters on six of the scrolls. These characters meant "Peace," "Prosperity," "Longevity," etc. When she had finished these, she said she feared her hand had no longer the firmness necessary for doing another.

While she was writing, the young Empress, the Princesses, and the eunuchs stood around, watching her with intense interest. They seemed to take great pride in her firmness of touch and her accuracy of line.

The Chinese written character must be made in a certain way. It must begin at a given part. The strokes must follow a given direction. The transversal strokes must be placed with mathematical precision. Nothing is left to the caprice or individuality of the writer. Any one, knowing the Chinese written characters, can tell you whether these complicated hieroglyphs were begun at the proper place or made in the proper way. They may look perfectly correct to the uninitiated observer who has a most accurate eye, and still not be so considered by the connoisseur.

The firmness of Her Majesty's touch is also very apparent in her painting, for she is very artistic, and paints flowers in a charming way; in fact, she is remarkably clever with her fingers. She does not embroider now, as she formerly did, nor does she paint so much, for she says her eyes are not so good as they were, though she does not and has never

THE EMPRESS DOWAGER WRITING A "GREAT CHARACTER"

worn glasses. There are a great number of artificial flowers made in the Palace, as no Manchu lady's coiffure is considered complete without flowers. Her Majesty is very particular about the way these flowers are made, and when they were brought to her for inspection, with a deft touch she would give a defective flower the required form.

She often makes new designs for the flowers, having them woven into quaint figures, or having a number of small blooms made into a representation of some large flower. She sometimes had her diadem made of the snowy blooms of the fragrant jasmine, set with leaves and other small flowers, representing jewels, and she would wear this instead of her real jewels.

She is a great believer in one of the rules that Confucius lays down for the attainment of "Illustrious Virtue"; she "cultivates her person." She is always immaculately neat. She designs her own dresses, and has her jewels set according to her own directions. She is very artistic in the arrangement of her flowers and jewels, and sees that they harmonize with her toilet. She has excellent taste in the choice of colors, and I never saw her with an unbecoming color on, except the Imperial yellow. This was not becoming, but she was obliged to wear it on all official occasions. She used to modify it, as much as possible, by the trimmings, and would sometimes have it so heavily embroidered that the original color was hardly visible.

She is a great epicure, and often designs new and dainty dishes. She has perfumes and soaps for her own use, made in the Palace. Although there are quantities of French and German soaps and perfumes bought for the Palace, she prefers an almond paste that she has made and often uses the soap made in the Palace. The maids would make these under her supervision. I have frequently seen them bring the mortar in which they were stirring it to Her Majesty, that she might see its progress, and she would energetically stir it herself. She is also a great lover of perfumes, and herself combines the oils of different flowers so as to produce most subtle and delightful perfumes. The Chinese say " colors, odors, and perfumes are good for the soul." The Empress Dowager's soul was certainly well cared for in this respect.

The Chinese are so near to nature, so simple in every way, that their influence over animals and birds is extraordinary, and seems to us almost magical. They are very fond of all animals, and especially so of birds. They train and teach these latter in wonderful ways. I have often seen a Chinese go near a singing bird's cage and tell it to sing, and it would pour forth its little heart in melody. Birds never seem to have any fear of them. In the afternoons, in early spring, or on a fine day in winter, one may see hundreds of well-dressed and dignified men each carrying a covered bird cage, taking the birds out for the air. When they arrive at some open space in the city, or beautiful spot in the environs, they uncover the cages and hold them aloft, or simply sit with them on their knees, and the bird will sing as if its little throat would burst. They have absolutely no fear, and, though caged, seem to have a perfect understanding with their owners and obey their voices. They are often let out of the cages when taken out for exercise, but they will return to them at the call of their owners; and these birds are not hatched in cages—they are taken from the forests and trained.

Two of the religious precepts of the Chinese—"Hurt no living thing," "Protect all living things"—are carried so far, they will allow an animal to live in misery rather than put him out of it by a speedy death. They love all animals and fear none. They say if you do not attack an animal, however dangerous he is, he will not harm you.

The Empress Dowager seemed also to possess this almost magical power over animals. Her dogs never paid the slightest attention but to her voice, and would obey her slightest gesture; but, fond as she was of them, she rarely caressed them; and she was so particular about her hands that, when she did stroke or fondle one of her pets, she would immediately after have a cloth wrung out of hot water brought to wipe her fingers. I never saw a dog in her arms but once, and this was a puppy which she took a fancy to when visiting her kennels one day, and she brought him back to the Throne-room in her arms and played with him for some time.

On one of our promenades in the park I saw a curious instance of her wonderful personal magnetism and her power over animals. A bird had escaped from its cage, and some eunuchs were making efforts to catch it, when Her Majesty and suite came into that part of the grounds. The eunuchs had found it impossible to entice the bird back into its cage; nor would it come upon a long stick with a perch attached, which they held up near the tree where it rested. The eunuchs scattered at the approach of Her Majesty, and she inquired the cause of their being here. The Chief Eunuch explained what they were doing, and the Empress Dowager said, "I will call it down." I thought this was a vain boast, and in my heart I pitied her. She was so accustomed to have the whole world bow to her, she fancied even a bird in the grounds would obey her mandates, and I watched to see how she would take her defeat. She had a long, wand-like stick, which had been cut from a sapling and freshly stripped of its bark. She loved the faint forest odor of these freshly cut sticks, and in the spring often had one when she went out. They were long and slender, with a crook at the top. I used to think she looked like the pictures of fairies when she walked with these long, white wands. She would use them for pointing out a flower she wished the eunuchs to gather, or for tracing designs on the gravel when she sat down. To-day she held the wand she carried aloft and made a low, bird-like sound with her lips, never taking her eyes off the bird. She had the most musical of voices, and its flute-like sound seemed like a magical magnet to the bird. He fluttered and began to descend from bough to bough until he lighted upon the crook of her wand, when she gently moved her other hand up nearer and nearer, until it finally rested on her finger!

I had been watching with breathless attention, and so tense and absorbed had I become that the sudden

THE EMPRESS DOWAGER IN THE GARDENS OF THE SUMMER
PALACE—CALLING A BIRD

cessation, when the bird finally came upon her finger, caused me a throb of almost pain. No one else, however, of her entourage seemed to think this anything extraordinary. After a few moments she handed the bird to one of the eunuchs, and we continued on our promenade.

I saw another instance of her magnetic power, this time with a katydid. One of the Princesses, seeing one on a bush, tried to catch it, but in vain. Her Majesty held out her hand toward the beautiful insect, made a peculiar sound like their own cry, and advanced her outstretched finger until it rested upon it. She stroked it gently for a few moments, and then removed her fingers, and the katydid made no effort to fly until she put it down!

CHAPTER XVI

THE GREAT AUDIENCE HALL—SOME OFFICIAL CUSTOMS

WHEN His Majesty the Emperor reigned alone, he was in the habit of holding his Audiences as early as three o'clock A.M. It is said, however, that this custom was owing as much to his personal shyness as to his love of early rising, for at these Audiences he would allow but two candles on the Throne-table in front of him, and the Great Hall was lighted elsewhere only by the beautiful Chinese lanterns, which shine with but a dim brilliancy and are not very effective as lights. Thus his face could not be seen if an official should so forget the Proprieties as to raise his eyes to the Imperial Person.

Their Majesties' Audiences are held in the Great Audience Hall, a detached building apart and quite distinct from all the other buildings of the Palace inclosure. The inscription over its great doors points out that it is the " Hall where Industry is to be applied to State Affairs." In all the Palaces the Audience Hall is nearest the outside walls and entrances, so that the officials who are privileged to have Audiences must only pass through the outer courts to reach the hall— Their Majesties' Palaces with their private apartments being at some distance beyond. At the Winter Palace, where there are so many walls within walls, each of Their Majesties' Palaces is surrounded with walls, and the Audience Hall is also in a walled-in inclosure near one of the Great Gates, but at the Summer Palace there are no walls except the exterior ones!

The interior of the Audience Hall, at the Summer Palace, is not by any means bare or austere. It is furnished in the same style as the Throne-rooms, with splendid ornaments, curios, tea-tables and chairs, and, curious anachronism, there are here three pianos! The walls are hung with ornamental scrolls, as well as with those bearing some gigantic character traced by an Emperor's hand or some condensed bit of philosophy of the Sages. One of these scrolls has an admonition to the Emperor to remember that "he is responsible to Heaven for the happiness and prosperity of his people."

There is a great dais in the center of the hall, on which stands the Throne, with its table, behind which is the three-, five-, or seven-leaved screen. The ancient dais was lower than those now used, and the antique Throne, with its capacious size and cushions, was more like a lounge than the modern Throne. This seems to indicate that the administration of justice by the Emperor was in ancient times less formal and more patriarchal than to-day. In former times the Emperor could lounge upon his Throne at his ease when seeing his Ministers, and they could approach nearer the Sacred Person, as the dais was not so large nor so high as that in use to-day.

Heads of departments and Princes with honorary

official positions have Audiences on certain days of the month, to report upon affairs of their Boards or to pay their respects to His Majesty. Every day Their Majesties hold Audience and see the Prime Minister and Grand Secretary, and there are frequent meetings of the Grand Council. The Prime Minister, Prince Ching, has the last Audience of the day, and business reported on during the other Audiences is then discussed.

All telegrams and despatches go to their respective Boards, and are, except in cases of extreme gravity, only reported to Their Majesties at the Audiences. Af' *c* eleven all State business is supposed to be finished by Their Majesties. They are then free from State worries and cares until the following day. During the times of the rebellion in the Province of Kwang-Si, when the Russian evacuation of Manchuria was expected, and at the time of outbreak of hostilities in Manchuria (the three grave events occurring during my stay in the Palace), telegrams and despatches were constantly being sent to Her Majesty out of Audience hours. They were brought to her Throne-room, and sometimes even during her walks in the gardens they would be handed her. These despatches were sent over to the Palace from the Wai-Wu-Pu on their arrival. Of course, it was by Her Majesty's express command that her privacy was thus infringed upon. No official would otherwise have dared transgress the prescribed rules. The despatches were received at the entrance of the Palace by the eunuch whose province it was. He placed them in the yellow-covered, silken-lined box, in which they were presented to Her Majesty on bended knees.

Some Official Customs

In front of the Throne dais, during the hours of Audience, there are five cushions placed on the floor for the members of the Grand Council to kneel upon when they are memorializing Their Majesties. The Prime Minister's cushion is nearest the Throne. A cushion to kneel upon is a privilege only granted members of the Grand Council. Any other official, when making communications to Their Majesties, must kneel upon the bare marble floor, and must kneel beyond the space occupied by these five cushions. He is thus placed at a disadvantage. The distance at which he is from Their Majesties may prevent his hearing some of their words, especially the Emperor's, whose voice is very low and without any carrying quality. The official may overcome this difficulty and shorten the distance by paying the eunuch who conducts him to the Audience Hall, to remove some of the cushions, so that he may kneel nearer the dais. The Prime Minister's and Grand Secretary's cushions may on no condition be removed, but the other three are subject to the will of the introducing eunuch. If this latter be sufficiently paid, and there is a fixed price for each cushion, he will remove the three of the lower members of the Cabinet.

When the official who has been granted an Audience is conducted to the Audience Hall by the eunuch appointed for the purpose, the latter throws open the great doors, falls upon his knees at the threshold, and announces the name and position of the official, gives the hour and minute of his arrival at the Palace, and, before he rises, he has deftly removed the cushions for which he has received the

required sum.   After his name has been announced,
the official enters and kneels as near the dais as is
consistent with his rank and the sum paid the eunuch.
When the eunuch has introduced the official, he turns
from the door and must run away as fast as he can.
Officials and eunuchs stationed at some distance
watch his departure.   Should he linger or transgress
this law, capital punishment is the result.   This is to
avoid eavesdropping and the possible transmission of
State secrets.

When the official granted an Audience hears the
last echo of the steps of the departing eunuch, he falls
upon his knees and begins the relation of his business.
Their Majesties question him, if necessary, to elicit
further explanations.   When the Audience is finished,
the official rises and walks out.   The Chinese never
back out of the Presence, and it is not considered a
breach of etiquette to turn their backs upon Royalty!

The officials who are obliged to go often to Audiences resort to an amusing subterfuge to protect their
knees from the marble floor.   They strap heavily
wadded cushions around their knees before they go
in, and they can thus kneel in comfort.   The long
Chinese gown worn by the men, of course, hides these
knee cushions.

His Majesty assumed the cares of State at an early
age, when he was still filled with boyish spirit.   Many
of the heads of departments are old men, and some
of them doubtless most tiresome in reiterating facts
and dwelling upon details.   When the young Emperor
first took over the direction of affairs and held his
Audiences alone, he would get very impatient at

THE OFFICIAL AUDIENCE OF THEIR MAJESTIES

hearing several of these old men go over tiresome details. As it is not "according to the laws of propriety" for the official to raise his eyes to the Sacred Person, while the old man rambled on, with prosy detail, the young Emperor would slip off the Throne and quietly descend from the dais, and when the poor official raised his eyes to make his obeisance to the Emperor, he would see only the vacant Throne! His Majesty had been in the rear of the hall behind the screen for perhaps five minutes smoking a cigarette or otherwise diverting himself!

I noticed a curious fact as to the quality of the sacredness of the persons of Their Celestial Majesties. This sacredness seems to belong to them as rulers and not as individuals. In the Audience Hall when administering justice, they are not approached nor addressed, except upon bended knee. In the Palace, in their own privacy, when they give an order or any command touching upon official affairs, this order is received by the attendant, be he courtier, high official or great prince, on his knees. When any official communication is made to Their Majesties, in private or elsewhere, it is made kneeling, but when Their Majesties are in their private capacity and spoken to on ordinary affairs, they are addressed almost familiarly, and the courtier or simple attendant stands while speaking to them. If, however, in the midst of a familiar conversation an order is given, the attendant immediately drops upon his knees to receive it.

The kow-tow (pronounced ker-toe and meaning literally to bow the head) is used as a form of thanks, and is not a manner of greeting. The actors kow-tow to Their Majesties at the beginning and end of each performance at the Theater, first to thank for the honor they are to receive in being allowed to act before them, and at the end to thank for the privilege granted. The officials "bow the head" to thank for an Audience or any favor or gift they have received or are to receive from Their Majesties. The kow-tow is not only made by people at the Palace and at Imperial Audiences: it is sometimes used by equals to each other as a proper manner of thanking for some great favor. To make the kow-tow, the person kneels three times and each time bows his head three times, touching the ground with it. The kow-tow could not be made by a foreigner without looking most awkward and appearing most servile, but the Chinese do it with dignity, and it is neither ungraceful nor degrading-looking. It is a time-honored manner of giving thanks, a Chinese tradition surviving from a time when the courtiers were perhaps like slaves, but at present it does not imply any slave-like inferiority on the part of him who performs it.

CHAPTER XVII

THE SUMMER PALACE AND ITS GROUNDS

THE Summer Palace, the Empress Dowager's favorite residence, is really a superb domain. Its naturally picturesque situation among the beautiful Western Hills, sixteen miles from Peking, has been improved wherever possible, by the devices of art. The many buildings that constitute an Oriental Palace have been most picturesquely grouped on the banks of its great lake. The eminences and natural undulations have all been made the most of as sites for Palaces and temples, and the grounds are laid out with all the art the Chinese landscape artist has at his command.

The buildings of the Palace proper, where Their Majesties and their suites live, are all massed in one great town-like group at the southeastern end of the lake. In this group are the Theater, with its courts, and the Great Audience Hall. Palaces, temples, summer-houses, tea-booths, dot the whole surface of the great park, and all the vantage-points have been utilized for constructions.

A beautiful white marble terrace runs the length of the southern side of the lake. Pavilions at intervals vary the monotony of this line or give accent to the natural indentations of the banks. Picturesque landing-places, with their marble steps lapped by the waters of the lake, also lend their variety to this terrace surmounted by its beautiful lotus balustrade.

The highest of the hills in the park of the Summer Palace is crowned by the Great Temple of the Ten Thousand Buddhas. This is approached by hundreds of steps, which lead up from the broadest part of the marble terrace over the lake. Beautiful Palaces are built along this terraced height. Picturesque pai-lou (memorial arches) are built at such beautiful points, that Nature herself seems to have designed these positions for them.

A fair, verdure-clad island lies peacefully on the bosom of the lake, and the Palace and temple built thereon seem a part of the natural formation of stone out of which they rise. A graceful seventeen-arched bridge of white marble connects this island with the northern bank of the lake.

The canal from Peking, which feeds the lake, winds in and out of the grounds in such graceful meanderings as to seem some fair mountain stream. The outlets to the lakes are spanned by the graceful camel-backed bridges that only the Chinese architects build. Nature and art are everywhere so blended, so harmonized, it is difficult to tell which is which. The simple lines and beautiful proportions and harmonious colors of the one-storied Chinese buildings make even these seem almost a part of the landscape.

Chinese architecture—and one grows to admire it very much when studied in its own environment—is tent-building, carried to its greatest perfection and made enduring by the use of materials that last. The grouping of the Chinese buildings is on the same order as the congregation of tents of some roving tribe of Nomads. The downward curve and upturned tilt of their roofs is but the natural slope of the canvas and its uplifting by the tent-poles. These slender tent-poles have developed into the supporting pillars of the verandah, and the raised canvas door of the tent has grown into its buoyantly curved roof. The ornamental eaves are but the solidified silken fringes and embroidered valances of the tents of old. The curious roof ornamentations of the modern Chinese house replace the weights that held the tent-canvas steady. These weights, from rough stones, have now become carven images, cunningly wrought. The Chinese even erect their houses as their ancestors raised their tents. The builder places the columns and puts on the roof before the walls are built. Except the pagoda—and this even seems like so many superposed tents—the Chinese building remains to-day, in spite of its elaborate roofs, its lacquered pillars, and elaborate ornamentation, like some splendid tent, grown into greater fixity and beautified by some magician's wand. It is admirably suited to the calm pastoral landscapes in which it rests, and seems a part of Nature itself, and is never out of keeping with its surroundings!

Wherever available, in the grounds of the Summer Palace, flowers are planted, and they succeed each other almost the whole year round, for the Chinese are wonderful gardeners. The extensive grounds are, however, not given up entirely to flowers and beautiful constructions; there are great fields of grain.

With the Empress Dowager

Wheat and millet, and even vegetables, are raised in these pleasure grounds. It was curious to me to see how picturesque so prosaic a thing as a field of turnips might become, when properly placed in a large pleasure domain. By the planting of these useful crops, a great deal of fertile land is utilized, without any detriment to the landscape, and the utilitarian spirit, so strong in the Chinese, is satisfied.

There is one terraced hillside in the grounds of the Summer Palace, called the "Flowery Mountain." In the season of the peonies, which the Chinese call "The King of Flowers," this is really a flowery mountain—one mass of blooms of exquisitely blended colors and faint evanescent perfume. The China Aster is also brought to great perfection by the Chinese gardeners, and in the time of the chrysanthemum the grounds fairly blaze with this autumnal glory. The Chinese do not go in for the cultivation of the chrysanthemum of extraordinary size. Her Majesty does not care much for these; but her gardeners arrive at some wonderful combinations of colors and some most curious shapes. The year I was in the Palace, Her Majesty was delighted with a beautiful green variety, that the gardeners had succeeded in getting, and that year there was also a new variety whose petals were like threads, they were so thin and hair-like.

The Temple of the Ten Thousand Buddhas is so called from its being built in glazed yellow tiles, each representing a niche, in which is seated a Buddha, of which there are many more than ten thousand. The interior is composed of three chapels. In the central one thrones the Great Buddha. There was another

OLD RUINS IN THE SUMMER PALACE

famous Buddha in this temple, which was invested with peculiarly sacred qualities, but it was hurled into the lake below and broken into a thousand pieces when the foreign troops were in possession in 1900. Her Majesty seemed to feel the depredations to the temples, by the foreigners, more keenly than anything else. The Chinese are so perfectly tolerant in matters of religion, they cannot understand our attitude toward any other religion but our own, and our contempt for any other kind of worship except that in which we ourselves indulge.

The Chinese are said to hate the foreigner. They certainly have not much reason to like him; nor to admire our much vaunted civilization. The European Christian soldier in China has burned, destroyed, and killed with as much barbarity as the heathen, and in many instances has given the latter points in cruelty.

On the slope behind the terraced hill of the Ten Thousand Buddhas are the ruins of the old Summer Palace, destroyed by the European troops fifty years ago. After this, the site of the dwelling Palaces was changed, and they were massed on the southern side of the lake. Her Majesty has nearly hidden all trace of the 1900 devastations to the Summer Palace, but these old ruins of the former Palace still remain, and they are not a blot upon the landscape. On the contrary, they have become picturesque with time, and give the one note of somberness to this smiling demesne that is needed to accentuate its charm. There is a small lake not far from these old ruins, built around with smiling pavilions and a curious tower-like construction which is used as a private temple.

There are landing-places and small boats. It looks like a charming bit of old Venice. We never went here, however, but once. There are some unhappy associations connected with this beautiful spot, and Her Majesty did not seem to care to visit it. The promenade in the direction of the old Palace also seemed to sadden her, for she had passed the early years of her married life in these now crumbling ruins.

From the highest elevations in the grounds of the Summer Palace, we could see the road from Peking! Sometimes Her Majesty and the Ladies would watch from some of the summer-houses, the carts and chairs and vehicles as they passed along. Several times we saw the Emperor and his suite returning from some ceremony in Peking, over the road cleared for his passage. Her Majesty, herself, would be the first to descry him, and she would say, " The Emperor comes." Then the Empress and Ladies would all look, for it was not against the Proprieties for them to look at His Majesty at such a distance. These views of the high road from the eminences of the Summer Palace were all Her Majesty and the young Empress ever saw of the outside world and common humanity; for neither at the Winter nor Sea Palaces could they get any views from a distance, nor was there any opportunity of seeing beyond the walls. When Their Chinese Majesties go abroad—and this is generally only from one Palace to another—quaint, triangular flags are placed along the Imperial route, warning the people that Their Sacred Majesties are to pass, and that the road will be reserved for them between certain hours. No vehicles or pedestrians are allowed for some time before and after the Imperial passage. In the City of Peking, the inhabitants, even on the streets where the Imperial cortège is to pass, are shut into their houses and not allowed to go out of their doors during the time, and at the intersection of the transversal streets huge curtains are hung, shutting them off from the Imperial way. For these progresses of Their Majesties, the roads are covered with yellow sand.

CHAPTER XVIII

THE FESTIVAL OF THE HARVEST MOON—WORK ON THE PORTRAIT

WE think the Chinese so unemotional, so little given to pleasure or amusement; but there are more popular festivals in China, indulged in by all classes of people, than in any country in the world, except perhaps Japan. The people, from the highest to the lowest, enter into these celebrations with whole-souled earnestness and real enjoyment, and all the popular festivals, as well as the religious ceremonies, are celebrated in the Palace with apparently the same zest as among the people.

The Mid-Autumn Festival, popularly known as the Festival of the Harvest Moon, which is at its full at the time of the celebration, was, of course, observed with due ceremony at the Palace. For these festivals there are always representations at the Palace Theater, and one of the plays on such days is the dramatization of the Legend of the Festival. The legend of the Harvest Moon is this: One day an Emperor received the visit of a fairy. When she left she gave the Emperor an herb, saying, should he eat it, he would be endowed with Immortality. The Emperor was called out, soon after the fairy's visit, and forgot the gift for a time, and the herb lay upon his table. During his absence from the Throne-room, a young handmaiden entered and, seeing the root on the table, with childish curiosity, tasted it, and, finding it good, ate the whole of it. When the Emperor again thought of his precious gift from the fairy, he hastened back to the Throne-room, to remove it from the table where he had left it. What was his horror to find it gone! Learning that the little handmaid was the only person who had been in the Throne-room, he called her up to find out what she had done with it. When he found she had eaten it, he ordered her killed, that he might thus again obtain the herb. Before the eunuchs could accomplish their task, the charm began to work, and she felt the wings of Immortality; and borne up by them, she flew to the skies and took refuge in the Moon, where she still lives with the pet white rabbit she had in her arms at the time she flew away from the earth. She is now an Immortal, and in the Moon she compounds the Elixir of Immortality. The rabbit, also, shares her immortality, and ever watches at the lunar threshold.

The drama, with this little maiden as heroine, was played by Her Majesty's actors on the day of the Moon Festival, and the finale of the plays that day was one of the most beautiful spectacular tableaux I have ever seen. The Chinese obtain most artistic effects in their illuminations, and by the most simple means. The stage represented a lake covered with luminous lotus, with the full moon floating above. Throned on a gigantic lotus flower in the center of the lake sat an immense, golden Buddha, impassible and serene, ingeniously illuminated lotus flowers and luminous birds, emblems of Immortality, hovered over the lake, and the whole tableau was supposed to represent Nirvana, when the soul is absorbed into Nature and forms a part of it. It was really fairy-like.

The Ladies dined in Her Majesty's loge, and this beautiful, illuminated tableau was scarcely finished before we were obliged to hurry away to join Their Majesties, who had already started for the gardens where the ceremony was to take place. The procession, with the Emperor and Empress Dowager and Ladies in full dress, as usual for a ceremony, was accompanied by hundreds of lantern-bearing eunuchs. It wound, in and out, through the verandahed corridors and the paths of the garden like some great glow-worm, until it came to the marble terrace beneath the Temple of the Ten Thousand Buddhas, on the great terrace over the lake.

Here, in an open space bathed in the rays of the softly glowing moon, with the glory of the setting sun still in the west, in front of the great Stone Pailou stood a beautifully illuminated floral pai-lou and an altar decorated with the usual pyramids of fruits, floral offerings, and flagons of wine. The pai-lou to the Moon was entirely of chrysanthemums, with an inscription "To the Glory of the Chaste and Pure Celestial Orb" in white blooms, like gleaming stars, across the top.

Their Majesties first made the bows and prostrations to the Moon, and placed floral offerings on the altar. Then the young Empress and Ladies did likewise, while the eunuchs recited a poem in melodious and rhythmic cadence. The Chinese "recitative" is very musical, much more so, to the foreign ear, than their music. This poem to the Moon was recited by two voices in alternating rhythm with wonderful effect. When the recitation was finished, an "auto da fe" was made of the offerings, to which were added sticks of sweet incense and paper cut in curious designs. Over all was poured some of the inflammable wine from the flagons on the altar, and the flames leaped high above the huge incense-burner that stood on a great bronze tripod in the center of the moonlit terrace. It was a wonderfully picturesque sight—the brilliant circle of splendidly gowned Ladies, with the Emperor and Empress Dowager in their midst, around the flaming censer, whose leaping flames glinted and glowed upon the jewels and gold embroidery of their costumes. The lantern-bearing eunuchs formed a faintly glowing circle around this shining center; and over the whole fantastic picture the brilliant Harvest Moon shone with unwonted splendor, as if to show itself worthy of the obeisances it had just received from this brilliant group.

When the flames no longer leaped from the censer, when only the white smoke of the incense curled through the interstices of its cover, Their Majesties turned away, and the lantern-lit procession followed them to the banks of the lake, where the whole Palace fleet, brilliantly illuminated, lay moored beneath the marble terrace. The eunuchs, holding aloft their gleaming lanterns, stood along the terrace and knelt on the steps leading into the water, while Their Majesties descended them. On two of the boats, at either side of the Imperial barge, the eunuchs held their lanterns to form the characters "Peace" and "Prosperity." The waters of the lake were now glowing with the reflections of the myriad lanterns and dancing under their many-colored lights. A faint glow still illumined the western sky, while the reflection of the resplendent Moon gleamed like liquid diamonds across the lake! When we reached the Imperial landing-place, its great arc-lights on the two tall, painted poles sent their reflections shimmering, in long, wavy lines, far out into the lake, and almost rivaled in their splendor that of the celestial orb itself.

Although I took part in all these Palace festivals, my work on the portrait was advancing, but I longed for more opportunity to quietly study it and for a little more freedom in working. I felt I needed more time also for my painting. I ardently desired to be able to work some when Her Majesty did not pose, and I finally decided to ask her to allow me to remain at my painting when she and the Ladies went for their morning walks after a short sitting. It was a deprivation for me to give up even one of these delightful walks, when I saw such a charming side of the Empress Dowager's character, but I felt it must be done. She reluctantly consented to excuse me on a few occasions, but she seemed to feel it was not hospitable on her part to leave me alone; and when she did so she would remain out a shorter time than usual. She seemed so concerned at my working while the others enjoyed themselves, that I soon ceased to ask to be left at work; I could only try to make the best of the time I had at my disposal.

Work on the Portrait

My desire to have more time for my painting and more opportunity for studying the work was not the only cloud in the heaven of these delightful days. As the portrait progressed I found myself constantly running up against Chinese conventionalities as to the way it was done. They wished so much detail and no shadow. Had Her Majesty been alone to be considered, she was artistic and progressive enough to have, in the end, allowed me more liberty; but she, also, was obliged to conform to tradition, and no fantasy could be indulged in painting the portrait of a Celestial Majesty. It was necessary to conform to rigid conventions.

I had such a fine opportunity to do something really picturesque in painting this great Empress and most interesting woman, and I found I was to be bound down by the iron fetters of Chinese tradition! I could neither choose an accessory, nor even arrange a fold according to the lines of the composition. I was obliged to follow, in every detail, centuries-old conventions. There could be no shadows and very little perspective, and everything must be painted in such full light as to lose all relief and picturesque effect. When I saw I must represent Her Majesty in such a conventional way as to make her unusually attractive personality banal, I was no longer filled with the ardent enthusiasm for my work with which I had begun it, and I had many a heartache and much inward rebellion before I settled down to the inevitable.

The Empress Dowager, however, knew nothing of my discouragement, and seemed perfectly contented with the progress of the portrait then on hand—so pleased, in fact, she asked me if I would not like Mrs. Conger to come and see it. I, of course, replied that I would, and an invitation was accordingly sent, through the Foreign Office, inviting Mrs. Conger to come to see the portrait.

As Her Majesty was to receive her in the Throne-room where I painted, it was decided I could not work on that day. I fully expected the portrait would be exhibited in the Throne-room, the only place where it had a proper light; but, to my disappointment, Mrs. Conger was asked to look at it in the small room where it was kept when I was not working on it. When we went in, the Chief Eunuch ceremoniously removed the yellow covering over the "Sacred Picture," which hung flat against the wall in a very bad light, with annoying reflections. The small room was also uncomfortably crowded with Her Majesty and suite, so that it was impossible to see the whole canvas at once. Mrs. Conger was, however, so pleased with the likeness and lifelike expression in the eyes, the upper part of the picture being in a fairly good light, that the comment stopped here.

This first portrait represented the Empress Dowager sitting on one of her favorite Cantonese carved Thrones. The figure was life-size. In one hand she held a flower, and the other lay over a yellow cushion. The tip of one small embroidered shoe, with its jeweled, white kid sole resting on a dragon footstool, showed under the hem of her gown. The head was a three-quarters view, with the eyes looking at the observer. A jardinière, with her favorite orchid, stood behind the Throne at the right. It was painted in full light.

Work on the Portrait

The canvas was four by six feet in size; and there was thus no place for any of the emblems or insignia of Her Majesty's rank, save that she was clothed in her official costume of Imperial yellow.

This was the conventional reality, and I had dreamed of painting Her Majesty in one of her Buddha-like poses, sitting erect upon an antique Throne of the Dynasty, with one beautifully rounded arm and exquisitely shaped hand resting on its high side, contrasting in their grace with its severe lines. I should have exaggerated her small stature by placing her upon the largest of these Dynastic Thrones. Her wonderfully magnetic personality alone should have dominated. At the left of the Throne, I should have placed one of those huge Palace braziers, its blue flames leaping into the air, their glow glinting here and there upon her jewels and the rich folds of her drapery; the whole enveloped in the soft azure smoke of incense, rising from splendid antique bronze censers. Across the base of the picture, under her feet, should have writhed and sprawled the rampant double dragon. The Eternal Feminine, with its eternal enigma shining from her inscrutable eyes, should have pierced, with almost cruel penetration, the mystery of her surroundings. Her face should have shone out of this dim interior, as her personality does above her real environment. I should have tried to show all the force and strength of her nature in that characteristic face, exaggerating every feature of it, rather than toning down one line.

With all these possibilities that the Empress Dowager's person and surroundings would suggest to the most unimaginative of artists, and with the conventional traditions, which I was obliged to follow, no wonder I became discouraged. But I had always the solace of her personality—the fascinating study of herself to delight and console me. New phases of her character and personality were constantly opening out before me. She dominates everything and everybody in the Palace, and is far and away, the most interesting personality there, not because she is the first figure at the Court, but because she is really the most interesting one, and she would be that in any position. No wonder that when she smiles the Court is gay—her smile is so entrancing. No wonder that when she frowns the Court trembles, for she excites sympathy in all her moods.

CHAPTER XIX

A GARDEN PARTY AT THE SUMMER PALACE

NOT long after this, Her Majesty gave a garden party for the ladies and gentlemen of the Legations. These garden parties occupy two days, for ladies and gentlemen are not received at the same time by Their Majesties of China. The Corps Diplomatique and attachés were entertained the first day, and the ladies of the Legations the following day. The entertainment was the same for each. The gentlemen were formally received in the Great Audience Hall by Their Majesties, after which a repast was served them in a pavilion near. When this was finished, they were taken for a tour of the gardens and lakes, and they left the Palace about two o'clock. None of the Ladies of the Court, except, of course, the Empress Dowager, were present at the receptions of the gentlemen of the Corps Diplomatique. The ladies of the Legations were received the following day.

I was rather embarrassed as to what I should do, at this first formal reception, for the ladies of the Legations, since my arrival in the Palace. Being a foreigner, I thought it looked incongruous for me to receive with the Chinese Ladies. My uneasiness

165

seemed to be divined by Her Majesty (she was always wonderful for her tact); she said, as I had been presented first in private Audience, it would be well for me to be presented also in public Audience. She suggested that I should go to the Foreign Office, meet Mrs. Conger on her arrival, and come into the Throne-room with her. When the eunuchs announced that the ladies had arrived at the Foreign Office, Her Majesty ordered my red Palace chair to take me there.

The Foreign Office is only a few hundred yards to the left of the Imperial entrance to the Palace. Mrs. Conger was one of the first ladies to arrive. When the other ladies came, all walked over to the gate of the Palace, and, after entering, went to a pavilion at the right of the Audience Hall, where they arranged themselves in the order in which they were to be presented.

The verandah and large marble platform of approach to the Audience Hall were shaded with tent-like silken awnings and covered, for the day, with red carpets, the latter a concession to foreign taste; for Her Majesty, though having many beautiful carpets stored up, has none in use, and only in winter and for certain functions are the courts carpeted. She never uses them in the interior.

A double line of Princesses, led by the Princess Imperial, descended the steps of the Audience Hall and met the ladies on the marble platform. The Princesses then turned and preceded them into the Audience Hall. Here they separated and stood in a picturesque group on either side of the Throne dais.

A Garden Party

Here, in the dim obscurity, sat the Empress Dowager on the Dynastic Throne, with the Emperor seated at her left. In front of Her Majesty stood the official table, with its cover of Imperial yellow reaching to the floor. To the ladies standing below the dais only the heads and shoulders of the Empress Dowager were visible above the table, with its pyramids of fruits and flowers.

The ladies made three reverences on entering, and each advanced and went up on the dais at her presentation. Her Majesty's interpreter, the elder Miss Yu, stood at her right, a little behind, and repeated the Chinese name and title of each lady presented. Her Majesty, who has a royal memory for faces, recognized each lady who had been presented before, but treated all with equal cordiality. This cordiality was sometimes construed by the ladies, on their first presentation, as a special mark of interest in themselves; but it was the Empress Dowager's invariable position toward all the foreigners at these diplomatic receptions. Like all well-bred hostesses, she was most particular to show no difference even to those ladies she liked best.

When all had been presented, the eunuchs removed the official table behind which the Empress Dowager received the formal presentations, and she descended from the dais. One of her yellow satin chairs was brought and she sat down at the right side of the Audience Hall. The ladies were then, collectively, presented by Her Majesty to the young Empress and the Princess Imperial, and tea was ordered. While the ladies were drinking tea, standing around the

Empress Dowager's chair, she said a few words to each, informally.

When the tea was finished, the ladies, conducted by the eunuchs and accompanied by the Princesses, went through the court of the Theater, past the Palace of the young Empress, through Her Majesty's court to her Throne-room, where luncheon was served. This was in alternate courses of foreign and Chinese food. There were foreign wines and table waters, as well as Chinese, and quantities of sweet champagne, without which, the Chinese imagine, no foreigner can eat.

After luncheon, at which the Imperial Princess and Princesses acted as hostesses, the visiting ladies went to the marble terrace overlooking the lake. Here they were met by the young Empress and the secondary wife of the Emperor, for they were never present at the table when the foreign ladies were entertained, any more than Her Majesty herself.

The Empress Dowager's barge did not lead the Palace fleet that day. There were three big house-boats, each of which ponderous affairs had a large cabin with a yellow-covered seat for Her Majesty, which, though she never used, was never occupied by any one else. Anything covered with yellow is sacred to Their Majesties, and is never used except by them.

We were rowed across the lake, first to the island, where the Palace and small temple adjacent were visited, after which the ladies took the boats again and continued the tour of the lake to the Marble Boat. This Marble Boat was built over the lake as a summer-house for one of the Emperors, and is on the plan of the Palace house-boat, but with an upper, as well as

THE SECONDARY WIFE OF THE EMPEROR
In Summer Coiffure

lower deck. It is one of the things in the Summer Palace most talked about by foreigners, and it is a curiosity, though not a thing of beauty. It was never made the objective point of any of Her Majesty's promenades, nor visited, except when foreigners were invited to the Palace. On the lower deck of the Marble Boat, where was the best view of the lake, light refreshments, sweets, and fruits were served. When the tour of the lake was finished, the ladies made their adieus to Their Majesties and the young Empress and Princesses, and left the Palace grounds for the Foreign Office, where they took their own chairs and carriages for Peking.

In spite of Her Majesty's cordiality and the efforts of the Princesses and Ladies, these garden parties were not always as pleasant as they might be. There seemed an absolute lack of harmony among the ladies of the Legation. Each seemed to watch the other with a jealous eye, in constant fear that some one might overstep her place. Some did not hesitate, even, to show their private animosities on the steps of the Throne, or before their hostesses at the table. They seemed to act on the principle that the Chinese, not understanding the language, would not understand anything else. It was unfortunate that this most punctilious of people, the Chinese, should have had this apparent lack of friendliness to judge the European ladies by. They received all with equal favor and perfect etiquette, and it was a pity that the lack of harmony among the foreign ladies should have led them to commit what seemed to be breaches of etiquette, which the Chinese could not have failed to observe. I was astonished to see how observant the latter were and how accurately they gauged our standing.

Their comments on our costumes were also very interesting. Her Majesty seemed to like foreign dress, especially when in pretty colors, for she reveled in color. She said the foreign costume was very becoming to well-made and well-proportioned people; but she thought, while it showed off to advantage a good figure, it was unfortunate for any one who was not so blessed. She thought the Chinese costume, falling in straight lines from the shoulder, was more becoming to stout people, for it hid many defects. One universal comment, among these Chinese ladies, on us, was that we look old for our years. The well-bred Chinese repress, from early childhood, all outward evidences of emotion. They lead such simple, wholesome lives—" Early to bed and early to rise "—that there are rarely any lines visible in their faces until they reach an advanced age, when they seem to go suddenly from ripe womanhood into extreme old age.

They have a particular aversion to blond hair. They did not tell me so, as I have blond hair; but on the stage all the demons are represented with blond hair, and the more blond it is, the more wicked the demon. One day, one of the Ladies suggested to me that there were some very fine vegetable hair dyes for turning the hair black without injuring it; in fact, the growth was increased thereby. She said if I used this, my hair " might in time become black; at least, it would grow much darker."

CHAPTER XX

I HAD several days of good work on the portrait
after the garden party, when Her Majesty decided
it was sufficiently advanced for the characters, giving
her name and titles, to be placed across the top of the
canvas. As she has sixteen appellations, represented
by sixteen characters, and as they were all to be placed
upon the picture, together with her two seals, official
and personal, it required some manœuvering to get
them into the space required. This lettering was looked
upon as a very important detail; there were numbers
of models of the characters made before the proper size
and style was arrived at. The seals, about three inches
long, had to be placed at either end of the sixteen characters, and there was a great deal of deliberation as
to the color in which the characters were to be painted.
Red was finally decided upon. The two seals were to
be painted, one in red characters on a white ground,
and the other in white characters on a red ground.
As I had not known these appellations were to be
placed across the top of the canvas when I began the
portrait, I had not allowed for them, and putting them
on took away from the space above the head and de-

171

tracted from the general effect. This was another discouragement. I left the discussion of the lettering to Her Majesty and the writers, and I decided to give the canvas over entirely to the latter for a few days, in order that they might place the characters thereon, and that Her Majesty might have time to decide upon their color at her leisure.

Her Majesty had told me, a few days before, she wished me to paint a "number of portraits" of her, so I decided to begin another now, and I hoped to be able, as this was not to be an official portrait, to have a little more liberty in painting it. Her Majesty decided that it should be painted in her ordinary dress and without the Manchu coiffure, which she only wears at her Audiences, as it is very heavy and very tiring to her head. The day I began the portrait she had on a gown of soft, embroidered blue. Her hair, in a coil at the top of her head, was beautifully dressed, with the jasmine flowers so quaintly arranged, a realistic butterfly poised above them; her jewels so discreet and picturesque, I asked her to pose and let me paint her as she was then. Her coiffure, without the Manchu head-dress, is much more becoming to her than with the huge, wing-like construction which made her look top-heavy; for when she wore it, being in official costume, she was obliged to wear a great profusion of jewels and ornaments. In this portrait she was seated upon her Throne, but not in a traditional attitude, and I began it full of hope; for, at least, I had more choice as to the surroundings and accessories, which were not obliged to be "according to tradition." As it was only to be seen by her intimates, I asked her to let me paint her two favorite dogs lying beside her footstool, the blond " Shadza " and dusky " Hailo." Her Majesty gladly consented, and " Hailo" was ordered to be decorated in his " gala costume." This consisted of two huge chrysanthemums tied in his hair over his ears. " Shadza," the Pekingese pug, resented any such accoutrement and was painted in his natural state. She took the liveliest interest in the painting of the dogs' portraits, and seemed to think it much more wonderful to paint these little animals, so that they were recognizable, than to make a likeness of herself. I was obliged, of course, to do them very quickly. She sat behind me all the time I was painting them, and the rapidity with which they grew much astonished her.

I discovered about this time I was not the only painter in the Palace. Her Majesty has a corps of painters always there. These painters decorate the thousands of lanterns used in the Palace ceremonies and processions. They paint the scenery for the spectacular plays at the Theater, and the flowers used for the decorations of the screen-like walls I have already alluded to. Some are very clever flower painters, and one even paints portraits, but they have never seen the Empress Dowager except from afar! Though Mandarins of the Third rank, the painters were obliged to withdraw from the court where they worked when Her Majesty and suite passed by. It was amusing to see these dignified, handsomely gowned officials being hurried out of the court on Her Majesty's approach by the eunuchs who precede her. Their paintings were submitted to her by one of the eunuchs, by whom she sent her instructions to them.

With the Empress Dowager

I saw these painters first, at the time of the chrys-anthemums. There were some new varieties in one of Her Majesty's courts that she wished painted. One day, on going into this court, I saw a group of bebuttoned officials studying the flowers. They gravely inclined their heads with the customary dignity of the Chinese, and I found later they were "confrères."

It was interesting to me to see their methods—so different from ours, but arriving at a very artistic result. I never spoke to them; but, as I was an outer barbarian, I took advantage of my position and watched them work from my windows, though I took care to keep myself hidden behind the curtains, in true Oriental style. They worked in the court quite near my pavilion. The chief painter selected the flower to be copied, and the others stood around while he painted, petal by petal, with most laborious and minute attention. While he worked, the others took notes and made studies of the same flower. When this laborious first study was finished, it was copied with a freer hand by one of the painters, and this copy was copied until they finally arrived at a dashing study, which seemed to be done "de premier coup."

When the chrysanthemums were in their full glory, one day when Her Majesty had allowed me to remain at my work while she and the Ladies went for their walk, she brought me, on her return, a curious new variety. When she handed it to me she said, "I will give you something nice if you guess what I have named this flower." It was one of those new

varieties with hair-like petals and a compact center, like the bald head of an old man. I told her
I was afraid I could n't guess, but I thought "it looked
like an old man's head." She was delighted, and said,
"You have guessed. I have just given it the name
of the Old Man of the Mountain."

We were still having daily walks in the gardens,
and there was always some delightful little incident
to make them pleasant and memorable. One day,
when we were out and were resting, while Her Majesty
was sitting alone before the "Peony Mountain," the
young Empress and Ladies stood in a group at a little
distance. We were near some arbor-vitæ trees, and
the young Empress picked a piece that looked like a
"peacock's feather." She told me to kneel and let her
"decorate" me. She stuck the curiously shaped
branch in my hair so that it hung over the neck and
looked like the "peacock feather," which is given as
a reward of merit to the highest officials, and is always
worn upon their hats. When she had placed it, she
told me to rise, and called me "Your Excellency
Carl," which is the title of those who possess the decoration of the peacock feather. I kept it in my hair
and soon quite forgot my "decoration." When we
were walking on, Her Majesty noticed it. She had
been preoccupied and sad that day, but when she saw
it she smiled, and said, "Who decorated you with the
peacock feather?" I told her the young Empress had
done so. She said that was her prerogative, but she
added, "If you were a man you would win it, and
probably a yellow jacket also, for you are fearless."
Why did she think me fearless? Could she have

heard that the foreigners in Peking seemed to think it was almost as much as taking my life in my own hands to go and live entirely alone among the Chinese at Court, and put myself in Her Majesty's power, after the Boxer trouble?

Another afternoon we went into the Great Audience Hall when we were passing it, and I had an opportunity of studying in detail the interior of this magnificent hall. I examined closely some of the rare old niellée bronzes and wonderful Chinese cloisonné, for here are some of the finest specimens in the Summer Palace. In the back of the hall were three pianos, two upright and a new Grand piano, which had but lately arrived at the Palace. Her Majesty wished us to try the Grand piano, and one of Lady Yu-Keng's daughters, who had studied music in Paris, played a few airs. Her Majesty thought the piano a curious sort of instrument, but lacking in volume and tone for so large an instrument. She asked me to play also, and then said she would like to see how the foreigners danced, and suggested my playing some dance music. The Misses Yu-Keng waltzed, and she thought it very amusing to watch them. She could not, however, understand how ladies and gentlemen could enjoy dancing together, nor what pleasure they found in it. She said the Chinese pay others to dance for them, and would not think of doing so themselves for pleasure. It seemed to her the charm was rather in watching the graceful movements of the dancer than in executing those movements one's self. I wondered what she would say, could she see one of our crowded European ball-rooms,

PAILOU IN GROUNDS OF SUMMER PALACE—ON THE SHORE OF THE LAKE

with hundreds of couples on the floor at the same time, making violent efforts to steer through the crowd. I fancy she would not have found pleasure even in watching these dancers.

CHAPTER XXI

A EUROPEAN CIRCUS AT THE PALACE

CHINESE ceremonies and celebrations were not all I was destined to enjoy while at the Summer Palace. There began to be talk of some "foreign entertainment" soon to be given, and when I found this foreign entertainment was to be a circus, a real European circus, I was delighted. I had been out in China two years, and had not had much European entertainment during that time, and—shall I confess it?—I dearly loved a circus if the horses and animals were fine. This circus was then in Tientsin, and some one had suggested to Their Majesties it would be an interesting thing to see. A young Manchu was sent to Tientsin to investigate. When he returned, flaming posters were submitted to Their Majesties by the Chief Eunuchs. When the Empress Dowager saw the vulgarly colored picture of a summarily clad young woman of the show, I was watching her face and I saw a look of contemptuous scorn pass over it. She brightened up, however, when she saw the pictures of the animals at their tricks, and the men on horses, and it was decided that the circus should be brought up from Tientsin! The animals and performers were to be domiciled in one of the parks near by, but the

A European Circus at the Palace

tent was to be stretched within the inclosure of the Palace.

Sites for the ring were discussed, and it was finally decided to have the tents pitched at the extreme western end of the lake. There was a large open field here, planted in turnips! As the turnips were ready to be gathered, it was decided that the crop should be pulled up and this place prepared for the tents.

One day we went out into the turnip field, and the Empress Dowager herself pulled the first turnip; then the Empress and all the Princesses pulled some, and when they found a curiously shaped one, it was given to Her Majesty. It was a strange sight to see the Great Empress Dowager, sitting there at the side of the field, on her yellow camp-stool, smiling and interested, with the turnips piled around her, and the gaily dressed Empress and Princesses in their silken gowns flitting in and out of the field, apparently enjoying, to its utmost, the simple task of pulling these prosaic vegetables. The eunuchs and attendants stood in crowds around to take the turnips when pulled. They were not allowed, however, to pull any themselves. When a small square was denuded, Her Majesty and the Ladies returned to the Palace, and an army of workmen came and pulled up the whole field and began to prepare the ground for the circus tents.

As the performance of the circus was to be on the first day of the month, the Imperial players were at the Theater. When the morning Audience was finished, Their Majesties and the Empress and Ladies went to the Theater and listened to two or three plays. After luncheon, taken in the Imperial loge, Their Maj-

179

esties started for the landing-place, followed by the young Empress and Ladies. The lake was gay with beautiful barges, great house-boats, and numbers of flat boats for the eunuchs. The barges and house-boats were picturesquely decorated with flying banners, pennants, and tasseled wands. Two steam-launches, puffing away, gave an air of modernity to this most Oriental fleet. One of the steam-launches was splendidly decorated with yellow banners, with gorgeous yellow silk scarfs festooned around the cabin and the Imperial flag flying above it. The Empress Dowager and the Emperor descended the marble steps to this gaily decked launch, and started off alone for the other end of the lake, the Imperial banners and colors flying.

The Empress and Princesses went in the Empress's State boat; the visiting ladies followed in another of these ponderous but picturesque affairs. In size they are as large as an ordinary Chinese pavilion. The Empress's cabin was carpeted and splendidly upholstered in cloth of gold, with the usual tea-tables and lounges. It had one of those gallery-like prows with silken awnings, where the Princesses stood. The young Empress sat within, on one of the gold-covered couches. As she had been brought up with several of the Princesses as playmates, the young Empress generally waived ceremony with them; but she knew how, when necessary, to maintain a sweet dignity that was charming and perfectly in accord with her exalted position. To-day was a State occasion. She sat alone, and the Ladies remained outside on the prow. She asked me to come in and showed me the interior and some of the curiously inlaid tables. She knew I was interested in all these things. She made me sit at her side, and when I demurred she said she knew it was not the foreign custom to sit on cushions on the floor, as was the habit of the Ladies when in her presence, and that I must sit beside her. This was the consideration they always showed me at the Palace, which I fully realized was not due to any special liking for me, but simply to their exquisite breeding—their desire to make me feel comfortable and at home.

When we arrived at the other side of the lake, the Empress and Ladies stood while Their Majesties landed. They were welcomed by a great burst of music from the bands. A number of Princes and Officials stood waiting to receive them and conduct them to the handsome loges that had been prepared for them.

It was a picturesque procession that started from the landing-place—the Empress Dowager and the Emperor, under the big, embroidered, yellow silk, State umbrellas, preceded and surrounded by gorgeously attired attendants and splendidly gowned officials, the young Empress and Ladies, in gala attire, following after, with their eunuchs and attendants. The day was perfect, and glorious sunshine added to the brilliant effect. The side of the tent toward the Imperial loges was open. There was a railed platform before the pavilions that had been erected as "loges." These pavilions were luxuriously fitted up: Their Majesties' loges were hung with the Imperial yellow. A yellow satin chair (with a smaller one at its left) was placed in the center of the raised platform, under the silken awning, and

Their Majesties could sit here or within as they chose. The Empress and Ladies stood in groups on either side of this platform.

About two hundred officials had been invited to see the circus, and, contrary to the usual custom, there was no screen between them and the Imperial party. On the right were two bands of foreign music, or rather of Chinese musicians who played foreign music on European instruments. These were the bands of Yuan-Shih-Kai, Viceroy of Tientsin, and of Sir Robert Hart, the Inspector-General of Imperial Customs. Sir Robert's band was formed about eighteen years since, when, as music is his hobby, he decided to try to have some Chinese taught European music on European instruments. He has now a well-equipped band of twenty trained Chinese musicians under a competent European conductor. They play on both brass and stringed instruments. His efforts have been so successful that his example has lately been followed by several high Chinese Officials, first among whom was Yuan-Shih-Kai. The latter's band is military, with fifty musicians, who play only on brass instruments. The two bands played alternately during the intervals of the performance.

For the first time during my residence at the Palace, I now had an opportunity of seeing the Imperial Princes and many of the great nobles and officials. Though they were often asked to the Theater at the Palace, the screen between them and the Imperial loge was never removed, except at the end of the performance, when they bowed their thanks and when the Ladies retired to their own loge. The gentlemen,

A European Circus at the Palace

however, could be well seen at the circus; and though the Chinese Ladies did not glance in their direction, I took advantage of being a foreigner, and when I was behind the others, and could do so without being seen, I closely scanned their faces and attire. Several of the Princes of the Imperial Family came up to the platform where Their Majesties sat and made their bows to them, afterward slightly saluting their relations among the Ladies and Princesses.

Among these young Princes at the circus was a son of Prince Kung and an adopted son of the Imperial Princess. This young man not only had a remarkably fine figure, tall and slender, with broad shoulders, but his face was very handsome. His bow, on coming up to pay his respects to Their Majesties, was as graceful as that of a young chevalier. His regard was so ingenuous, his expression so clever and withal so modest, his whole demeanor so gracious, I was much struck with him. His dress was elegant, and his jewels chosen with discretion. There was none of that overloading of belt ornamentation that the young dandies of the Imperial set were then affecting. His father was one of the great Princes of China, and if this young man develops and carries out the promise of his youth (he was then only seventeen), I fancy he will be heard of also. Like most of the young Manchu Princes, he held a position in the Imperial household, such as Master of the Horse or Captain of the Archers.

It was not much of a circus, but none of the Imperial party had ever seen one before, and the setting was so gorgeous, it was unique as a circus performance even to me. The Empress Dowager and the Emperor had splendidly jeweled opera-glasses, which a eunuch held ready for their use. The Emperor, disliking to be looked at, held his own glasses before his face most of the time. It seemed to me he used them principally for the purpose of screening himself. The animals pleased both Their Majesties; but aside from the dwarfs, of which there were two, the rest of the performers seemed to have but a mediocre interest for them. Her Majesty was particularly interested in the dogs and trained animals, and His Majesty in the horses and fancy riding. I was standing near him, and he looked keenly at me several times to see how the performance struck me; and one of his head eunuchs asked me in English—the Emperor would not try it— whether I thought it was "good or bad." Their Majesties sat through the performance, the Empress Dowager only retiring to her loge once during the time, which was while one of the summarily clad young ladies was gyrating on a trapeze. There was a magnificent tigress which the circus master had trained, and which was his "pièce de résistance." The Empress Dowager would not allow this to be taken out of its cage, and though it was brought out in front of the Imperial platform, it was too cat-like to interest her. She has a great antipathy to anything feline. When the performance was finished, the Imperial party left in the same state in which it had arrived, Their Majesties accompanied to the launch by the Princes and high Officials, the music of the two bands playing simultaneously. The Ladies of the Palace and Their Majesties, themselves, have so little novelty in their lives, I think, on the whole, the innovation of the circus was generally appreciated.

CHAPTER XXII

PALACE CUSTOMS

THE Empress Dowager is an early riser, but the joint Audiences which Their Majesties now hold are never at the extraordinary hours in vogue when His Majesty ruled alone. When there is a press of business, and many heads of departments to be seen, the Audiences begin very early, but they rarely extend past eleven o'clock—the usual hours being from half-past seven to eleven.

When the Empress Dowager sleeps, a maid watches in her room, two eunuchs stand on guard in the ante-chamber to the room, four watch at the door of the ante-chamber, and her body-guard of eunuchs fill the building where her private apartments are situated. The maid and eunuchs who watch in the night are changed every second day. Only the High Eunuchs are in-trusted with the duty of guarding her bed-chamber and Throne-room. At the Summer Palace, Her Majesty's bedroom is not more than fifteen feet square; the bed, like all in North China, is built into an alcove in the room. Shelves run around the three inclosed sides of the alcove, and on these are placed Her Majesty's favorite ornaments—small jade curios, books, and, of course, clocks. In this bedroom I counted fifteen timepieces on the bed shelves, and all running. Their ticking and striking, not at all simultaneous, was enough to run a nervous European woman wild; but Her Majesty takes so much out-door exercise, she seemed to have no nerves. There were no flowers in her bedroom, but the ante-chamber, leading into it, was always full of flowers, pyramids of apples, and "Buddha's hands."[1] The bed alcove is separated from the room by satin curtains, suspended from a handsomely embroidered valance, with two long embroidered bands to loop them back.

Her Majesty is a light and irregular sleeper. When she wakes and finds it impossible to go to sleep again, she rises, is dressed, and often goes for a walk in the grounds, at what we would call the most unseasonable of hours. She says Nature is beautiful at every hour of the twenty-four, with a different charm for each moment. As she loves it in all its phases, she likes to see it at every hour of the twenty-four, at least once a year! When she wakes and goes for a walk at night, the eunuchs who are on duty in her Palace accompany her with lanterns, but she never takes these night walks, except by moonlight, and when the night is beautiful.

Whether she has slept well or ill, she rises at six o'clock; for the morning is devoted to business, and she never misses an Audience. On rising, she takes a bowl of hot milk, or lotus-root porridge; then her maids and tiring-women begin her toilet for the Audience. This is the "grande toilette" for the day, for full dress is worn by the Chinese in the morning, and in the evening they wear simple gowns. When her toilet is finished, the young Empress and Ladies, having "assisted" (from without) at her "lever," she comes out into the Throne-room and receives their morning greeting. The Emperor then comes to pay his respects to the Great Ancestress, and together they go in State, accompanied by all the Ladies of the Court, to the Great Audience Hall. The Ladies of the Court remain outside the Great Hall until the Audience is finished, when they accompany Her Majesty to her Throne-room. The business of the day is then over. Her Majesty lays aside her robes of State and gives herself up to duties connected with the Palace.

While I was painting the portraits, she would pose on returning from the Audience; or, if the Audience had been too tiring, she would first go for a walk. Then would begin her various self-imposed household duties. She would overlook the baskets of flowers and fruits sent into the Palace daily, select some to be sent as presents, and send others to the eunuchs of the kitchen to be cooked. Then she would look at new rolls of silk, just arrived from the Imperial looms, or examine new articles of toilet, fresh from the workshops of the Palace tailors. Sometimes she would play a game, of which she seemed very fond, and of which I know no counterpart. It was played on a large square board, covered with white silk and painted in fantastic designs, representing the Earth and Fairyland. The object of the game was to get an ivory chessman, representing "man," into Fairyland. The length of the move was decided by throwing dice. There was no box for throwing the dice: they were taken in the hands and thrown into a jade bowl. The numbers uppermost were then counted and the move made. She would play this game with the Princesses; and sometimes two of the High Eunuchs, who were proficient, would be called in to make out the number. The game was played for money, but, if Her Majesty won, the others did not pay. If, however, they won, she paid, and at once. She was ever a cheerful giver. She had wonderful luck, and it was a rare occurrence for the others to win. I only happened to see it three times. The Princesses were always pleased to play this game, for they had a chance of winning and they never lost. One day I saw her get quite angry with one of the Ladies playing. This Lady could not bear to lose, and would get sulky and cross if she did. This annoyed Her Majesty, until finally she reproved her sharply. She asked her why she played a game if she were not willing to take her chances as they came, and meet loss or gain with equal equanimity.

The Empress Dowager only eats two solid meals a day—luncheon and dinner. These were exactly similar. The dishes, so far as I could see, were identical; but they were so numerous, and of such variety, one could make a change of menu by eating different dishes. The hours of these two meals were very irregular; in fact, Her Majesty had no fixed hour for anything except rising and attendance at the Audience Hall. "Early rice," as the Chinese call luncheon, was served the Empress Dowager at any time between half-past ten and half-past twelve. She was likely to order it at any hour after she returned from the Audience. "Late rice," or dinner, was ordered with the same irregularity. She was very fond of nuts and

PRINCESSES OF THE COURT

fruits, and ate them between meals, when she drank tea, hot milk, and certain fruit juices.

The young Empress and Ladies of the Court were not bound to these irregular hours. They ordered their meals in their own pavilions at the hours they wished. Sometimes they had but just finished their own meals, when the Empress Dowager would order hers, and, when she had finished, invite them to eat at her table. Then it would be a matter of etiquette to eat with, at least apparent, relish. At this meal at Her Majesty's table, her place remained vacant. When I was in the Palace and we were invited to eat at her table, the Ladies sat; but when I was not there, the Ladies stood to eat, if she were still in the building, thus observing a very old convention. The Empress Dowager was very rigid about the observance of all traditional customs, and a stickler for Court etiquette, but she was also very considerate of the Ladies. When she had eaten, she would leave her Throne-room, or would conceal herself behind some screen, so that they might sit and eat in peace. I have seen her return to the Throne-room while the Ladies were eating, but she would do it stealthily, not allowing the eunuchs to precede her, so that the Ladies might not be obliged to rise on her entrance.

When the Empress Dowager dined, she sat at the head of a long table absolutely groaning under the many dishes placed thereon. Huge silver platters stood on side tables with sucking-pig, steamed goose, whole fowls, etc. Before serving the latter, they were brought to her to look at, just as the butler, in Europe, shows the pheasant and set dishes to the mistress of the house. Her dishes were of yellow porcelain, with curiously chased silver covers of pyramidal shape and quaint design. When she arose to go to the table, a eunuch standing near would shout, "Remove the covers," the word would be repeated along the line of waiting eunuchs, who would spring forward and whip off the covers of the many dishes on the table as if by magic. At Her Majesty's place were two spoons, a saucer and bowl, a pair of chopsticks, and a small folded square of soft cloth, corresponding to our napkin. When she sat down, she attached to the front of her dress, by a quaint, golden pin, a large silken napkin,—for she was immaculately neat and had a horror of a spot on her clothes. She was an epicure and thoroughly appreciated any new dish the Palace cooks sent forth, and, like all epicures, she ate very slowly and seemed to enjoy her food. She never drank wine or anything else at meals. I only saw her drink wine on two occasions, when some new vintages had been received at the Palace, and then it seemed more to judge of their merits, as a connoisseur, than anything else. When she finished her meal and left the table, the eunuchs brought hot cloths for her hands and a golden "rince-bouche." After this, one of the maids would bring her a silver basin, soap, and towels, and she would indulge in an elaborate hand-washing.

After "Early rice" came the hour of her siesta. She would retire to her bedroom, and her reader, bringing several volumes from which to choose, would come to read to her. She would remain in her room for an hour and a half, whether sleeping or being read to. When she awoke, she would make another careful toilet, the Ladies would join her, and she would go for a long walk before taking "Late rice."

On the first and fifteenth of the month, the Imperial players were at the Theater. On these days, the Emperor, instead of returning to his own Palace, would accompany the Empress Dowager and the Ladies from the Audience Hall to the Theater. The Imperial Hymn was played on Their Majesties' entrance into the court of the Theater, and when they had entered the Imperial loge, the players would come in a body on the stage and "kow-tow." Then the actors, splendidly gowned, would make the customary wishes for the Imperial Peace, Prosperity, Longevity, after which there would be a posture-play in costume, and then the plays for the day would begin. On Theater days Their Majesties would lunch and dine together in the Imperial loge. They did not sit at the ends of the great table, but at right angles to each other—the Emperor at the head of the table, and the Empress Dowager at his left. His Majesty was not much of an epicure. He ate fast, and apparently did not care what it was. When he finished, he would stand up near Her Majesty, or walk around the Throne-room until she had finished.

The Empress Dowager was very rigorous in the observance of all fasts, as well as feasts, prescribed by the rites. On fast-days, no meat nor fish was eaten at her table. The meals consisted entirely of vegetables, bread, and rice; but there was always a great variety of these dishes, and they were temptingly prepared. Meat dishes and fish were always prepared for me when I was invited to eat at the Imperial table on fast-days, until I learned that the Empress Dowager and the Ladies were fasting, when I asked to eat only what was prepared for them when I dined with them at Her Majesty's table.

On Festivals and Theater days, Princesses of the Imperial Family, wives of Manchu Nobles, and high Officials were invited to spend the day at the Palace. Sometimes their children would accompany them, little girls and boys under twelve. I never saw a boy over seventeen in the Palace; and only once, one sixteen years old. This was a son of Prince Ching. When these young people came to the Court, they observed the same rules of etiquette as their elders, and behaved with great decorum. Her Majesty is very fond of children, but very particular as to their manners. When a little girl did not make a graceful bow, Her Majesty would not correct her, but would ask the young Empress, an authority on etiquette and very graceful, to bow. Her Majesty would then tell the little girl to notice how the Empress bowed and try to do it in that manner. The child, or her parents, generally followed this suggestion, and the grace of the bow was improved on the next visit to Court!

On one occasion, a lady of high rank, married to a kinsman of the Empress Dowager, was invited to the Palace with her family. She had two little girls, and when the family went up to bow and repeat the salutation to Her Majesty, the younger daughter, only five years old, refused either to make the bow or repeat the salutation, but sat down on the floor and cried! The Empress Dowager waited patiently for the mother to correct the little girl, for she is very fond of children and disposed to condone their faults. The little girl would not, however, listen to reason and continued to show temper. Her Majesty could not allow such a breach of the "Proprieties," even in a child of this age, and the high rank of the family of the little girl made it the more imperative that she should conform to the rules of Propriety and observe the etiquette of the Court. When Her Majesty saw that all efforts at bringing her to reason were fruitless, she ordered the child to be taken away. Whereupon the mother began crying, and begged her not to be offended with the little girl. She replied, "Do you think a person of superior intelligence could be offended with a baby? I send you out of the Palace to teach you a lesson, which you must teach your child. I do not blame her; I blame you and pity her; but she must suffer as well as yourself. You must teach your child that 'it is by the rules of propriety that the character is established' (Confucius)"; and she was inexorable. The family left the Palace and was not invited again for some time.

1 " Buddha's hand," a very fragrant fruit of the family of lemons, which is shaped like a hand, with long, curving fingers. Pyramids of this fruit are used for their perfume.

193

CHAPTER XXIII

HER Majesty was looking tired and anxious these days; the Audiences were unusually long, and despatches were arriving all during the day. She would often go to the Gardens immediately after her Audience for solitary walks, unattended by the Ladies, and when she went out for the walk, accompanied by the Empress and Princesses, she would sit distraught and abstracted before the finest views and those she loved most. She seemed absent-minded, and when some eunuch with the official message would kneel before her, awaiting her order to deliver his message, she would recall herself with an effort. One day when we were out, after days of this anxiety, and she was sitting alone in front of the "Peony Mountain," the Empress and Princesses standing in a group at a little distance, she looked a pathetic figure. Her strong face looked tired and worn. Her arms hung listlessly by her sides and she seemed almost to have given up, and I saw her, furtively, brush a tear away. The days were so like each other at the Palace, the Chinese dates being different from ours, I lost my reckoning until I had a Tientsin paper, and I saw that the date on which the Russians had promised to evacuate

Her Majesty's Anxiety

Manchuria had passed and they were making no move toward doing so; and that there were rumors of war between Japan and Russia. This, then, must be what was weighing upon the mind of the Empress Dowager. A few days later a telegram was handed her in the Throne-room while she was posing, that seemed to greatly agitate her. It was from Kwang Hsi, and reported the ineffectual attempts of the authorities to put down a serious rebellion there. Thus, there were interior as well as exterior troubles to make her anxious. She seemed to take these State troubles to heart; and it was touching to see her anxiety, which she made but little effort to conceal when surrounded only by the Ladies. The Emperor, on the contrary, preserved his usual calm exterior, and if he was racked by anxiety, showed no evidence of it. This may have been because he had schooled himself to hide his feelings. Be that as it may, his face had always that enigmatic smile lurking around the corners of his mouth. I fancied, though, his eyes looked more resigned and sadder than usual.

The date of the Empress Dowager's Birthday (November 16) was approaching, and preparations to celebrate it were beginning. She was determined to keep this celebration very simple. She issued edicts prohibiting the high Officials and Viceroys from sending the extravagant presents which always pour in at the celebration of the birthday of any one of her age in China. She recommended great economy in expenditures for the celebration, saying it would be improper and unworthy at this time of National distress, when the Foreign Indemnity was not yet paid, to make a large outlay for her Birthday. The celebration of a birthday in China is a great event, almost a religious ceremony, and is observed with great rejoicings by all classes. The poorest in the land, if they are not able to keep any other festival, always celebrate with as much pomp as possible the birthdays of their parents. This is one of the duties enjoined by the Book of Rites, and, in spite of Her Majesty's expressed wishes on the subject, the Emperor could not allow her Birthday to pass without a fitting celebration.

The Emperor beseeched Her Majesty "on bended knee" to allow him to have her Birthday celebrated with the same pomp as usual—to permit him to add another honorific title to the sixteen she already possessed—but though she was very proud of her titles, which the Ministers and Emperor had conferred upon her at different times, she was inexorable on this point, for the adding of a new title would necessitate an annual grant of twelve thousand dollars in gold. She also insisted that everything must be on a smaller scale than usual. She was, one could well see, in no happy frame of mind. There was none of the enthusiasm she had shown over the preparations for the Emperor's Birthday. Then she was in gay good humor. She then evidently fully believed that things were going well for the State, that China would soon obtain her full rights in Manchuria again; then everything seemed brighter for the Nation's outlook than now. It was her duty, however, to go through these Birthday celebrations, which, curtail as she would, must, nevertheless, be very elaborate, owing to her age as well as to her high rank. The Empress Dowager's

Her Majesty's Birthday

wishes as to the adding of a new title were observed, and it was not conferred, but the preparations for the Birthday went on, on a magnificent scale. Presents came pouring into the Palace, and even more elaborate festive decorations than those used for the Emperor's Birthday were being put in place.

Her Majesty was to receive the prostrations of the Emperor and Empress,[1] Princesses, and members of the Imperial Family, on a Throne in the Palace, that was built half-way up the terraced hill crowned by the Temple of Ten Thousand Buddhas. She did not receive these prostrations in the Great Audience Hall: this was set aside, by tradition, for the Emperor, alone. Had she been reigning for him, she would have received them there, but as she was reigning with him, she received them in the other Palace. The elevation of this Palace permitted all who were allowed to enter the Precincts to offer their congratulations, to get a glimpse of Her Majesty. As the weather was getting cold, the marble steps leading up to this Palace, the courts, and even a large part of the terrace over the lake, were covered with carpets of gala red.

The congratulations and prostrations were to begin at 2 A.M., the hour of her birth. There were three pairs of huge silver candelabra standing at either side of the Throne to hold the enormous wax candles of Imperial yellow, entwined with golden dragons, which weighed fifty pounds each. They stood five feet high. Lanterns with the ever-present character "Sho" and others inscribed "Wan-Sho-Wu-Chiang" (no limit to Imperial longevity) stood on each step of the long flight leading up to the Palace. The whole terrace below, all the

197

temples and buildings in the grounds, were brilliantly illuminated with splendid lanterns, elaborately ornamented with tassels of red silk, with the characters for longevity emblazoned thereon in vermilion.

With the few changes necessitated by the different season of the year of the Empress Dowager's Birthday, everything was carried out as for the Emperor's except on a larger scale, as she was celebrating more years than His Majesty. The Palace was filled to overflowing with the many ladies invited to be present. Some came from the heart of distant Manchuria, the cradle of the Dynasty. The winter Court dress of the ladies, worn for Her Majesty's Birthday, was of satin, lined and trimmed with fur, with sable collars. Like the summer Court dress, the winter gown was elaborately embroidered in the golden double dragon. The picturesque summer coiffure had also been replaced by winter hats of fur with jewels across the front and an elaborate crown, studded with precious stones. Brilliant bunches of flowers were worn on either side of the coiffure, in winter as in summer.

The celebration of birthday festivities in China is always accompanied by rites and worship of the ancestral tablets, and Her Majesty was obliged to go into Peking several times during the celebration. The ceremonies, themselves, were also very tiring. All this effort to keep up, and to properly carry out her part of the ceremonies, added to her real anxiety, made the forced celebration of her sixty-ninth Birthday far from a happy event to the Empress Dowager of China, who found the Empire she was trying to guide, in so perilous a position—war threatening on its confines, foreign complications of all kinds to deal with, and rebellion within.

[1] It has been said by foreigners, that Her Majesty the Empress Dowager obliges the Emperor and Empress to make the prostrations before her on her Birthday as an indignity to them and to show her authority. The truth is, that every son in China kneels before his parents on their birthdays, and should the Emperor fail to do so, the whole of China would be horrified and cry out against his unfilial conduct. Her Majesty is not only the wife of his uncle, the Emperor Hsien-Feng, but the sister of his mother, and, more than all else, the Empress Dowager is the Emperor's adopted mother. The duties of an adopted child to his adopted parents are the same, in China, as to his own parents. In the Viceroy Chang-Chih-Tung's famous ode to the Emperor, he speaks of this filial piety as one of the Emperor's greatest qualities: "Who does not admire the filial reverence and piety with which he waits upon his august mother? Setting a brilliant example to all, he inquires early and late after her well-being and watches over her meals in person. Let us now add a new ode, extolling to the skies our Emperor's fidelity to his Imperial mother."

CHAPTER XXIV

THE WINTER PALACE

THE Summer Palace was always the Empress Dowager's favorite Palace, but after the Boxer rising and the subsequent occupation of Peking by the Allies, when foreign troops were stationed in both the Peking Palaces, and so much damage done them, she would have preferred to have lived the whole year round at the Summer Palace. As it is, she occupies it from eight to nine months of the year, going out to it at the first opportunity in the spring, and leaving it only when it is so cold as to make it impracticable. There is a system of heating it by furnaces beneath the floors, but Her Majesty never used these, and the small Chinese porcelain stoves, sorts of braziers, were quite insufficient for heating the immense halls. This, however, would not have influenced her, as she never minded the cold, but it was very difficult for the officials to take the long trip to the Summer Palace during the winter, and this consideration alone caused her to move into the Winter Palace when the weather became very cold. The members of the Cabinet and the Princes had summer homes in the immediate vicinity of the Palace, but there were thousands of officials who were obliged to come out every day from Peking.

The Winter Palace

The time had now come for the Court to move in definitively to the Winter Palace, and shortly after the Birthday festivities, Their Majesties took up their residence in the Capital. Before I left the Summer Palace, the young Empress suggested that I should go to the Winter Palace the next day in time to assist in receiving Her Majesty on her arrival there, for, as usual, I left the Summer Palace the day before the Court, and went in to the United States Legation. At every change of residence of the Empress Dowager, the young Empress, Princesses, and Ladies of the Court precede her by a few hours, and stand upon the threshold of her own dwelling Palace to receive her when she arrives. Full Court dress is worn for this reception, and it is, as is everything touching Her Majesty, a ceremony!

The day of the Empress Dowager's entrance into her loyal City of Peking for the winter, in December, 1903, was a typical Peking winter day; the air was crisp and clear, the atmosphere positively sparkling, and like champagne. One seemed to breathe an elixir. For her "progresses" from one Palace to another the Empress Dowager always had, what they call in England, "Queen's weather."

The City of Peking is composed of three walled towns—the Chinese, the Tartar, and the Imperial City. Within the Imperial City lies the Winter Palace, its battlemented, turreted walls surrounded by a moat. After passing through one of the great gates, in the wall surrounding the Imperial City, and crossing the stone bridge that spans "the Grain-bearing Canal," we soon came in sight of the splendid walls and lofty gates of the Palace inclosure. The red outer walls of the Palace, faded by Time and weather to a charming gray-pink, with their beautiful corner constructions of airy-looking turrets reflected in the still waters of the moat beneath, were most picturesque. We were carried along the raised road beyond the moat until we came to a marble bridge (formerly a portcullis), that leads into the gate of the Palace in front of the Manchu Banner quarters, at the foot of the Coal Hill. Our chairs, by special arrangement, were allowed to enter the inclosure proper, of the Winter Palace; but even after entering the exterior gates, one winds in and out between high walls, through massive gates and heavy wooden doors studded with huge iron nails and ornamental copper balls. Against the high wall on either side of this approach, wooden sheds were built as sleeping-places for the guards and soldiers. Each shed had a front of lattice-work, with paper pasted over the interstices. Within was a cemented platform, which the Northern Chinese use as beds. These have a place underneath for building a fire, for they keep warm at night by sleeping on hot beds and use very little cover.

Just beyond the last of these guard-houses, our official "green chairs" were put down between two high walls, with forbidding gates in front of us. Here we took the red Palace chairs which were awaiting us. We were swiftly carried through still other gates and past a very labyrinth of walls. The courts were all paved in large flagstones of white marble, and surrounded by high walls with heavy doors. We finally reached a charming court, where, standing un-

The Winter Palace

der the overhanging branches of a beautiful cedar, we found the young Empress and Princesses, in full Court dress, already awaiting the coming of Her Majesty. It was a pretty group that stood there, gowned in their splendid Court costumes, the sunlight glinting upon the jeweled crowns of their fur caps, and giving a touch of nature to the brilliant flowers in their hair. My plain, foreign, tailor-made gown was the only dark spot in this bright group of gorgeously attired ladies.

Presently the cymbals and flutes sounded the weird notes of the "Imperial Hymn." The great wooden doors of the court were thrown open and the Imperial procession came in sight. Splendidly gowned eunuchs advanced in two lines, walking with rigid bodies and stately step. At a sign from the young Empress, a hush fell upon the chattering group of Princesses and each took her proper place. Then the Imperial chair-bearers crossed the threshold, with Her Majesty sitting erect in one of her "open chairs," for as soon as she gets into the Palace grounds she leaves the closed palanquin, in which she is obliged to travel abroad and which she very much dislikes on account of its stuffiness. The Ladies, as if moved by one impulse, made the formal bow at her approach, and repeated the usual Imperial salutation "Lao-tzu-tzung-chee siang," which I repeated with the others. Her Majesty had her chair stopped in the center of the Court and got out, and I went up to salute her. She shook hands, and said she hoped I would be happy in the Winter Palace, but that it was a dull, depressing sort of a place, with too many walls and gates, after the open brightness of the Summer Palace. After a few minutes' conversation she went into the Throne-room, followed by the Empress and Ladies.

Her Majesty's Throne-room at the Winter Palace fronted on a court which was surrounded by well-built walls with curiously shaped doors and windows and ornamental yellow and green tiled designs at intervals. In the center of the wall in front was the immense gateway, with wooden folding-doors, which had just opened for her passage. The verandah of the Throne-room had two rooms projecting upon it, making of it a rectangular space with walls around three of its sides. This verandah was quite different from any at the Summer Palace, where they run the whole length of the buildings, back and front.

Entering, I was struck by the beauty of the great central hall—the harmony of its proportions, the somber splendor of its color. It seemed to me the most satisfying, the most picturesque of all the restful, harmonious Chinese interiors I had seen. Its dull red walls, splendid coffered ceiling glowing in color and glinting in gold, its central dome, with elaborately carved pendatives, was painted in brilliant primary colors, subdued into a rich harmony by the demi-obscurity, for it had no "lantern" and received its light from the windows below.

The curious feature of the domes in several of the palaces in the Violet City, so effective from within, giving elevation and space to the interiors, is that they are not visible from the outside of the edifice. The beautiful straight line of the roof, with its upturned

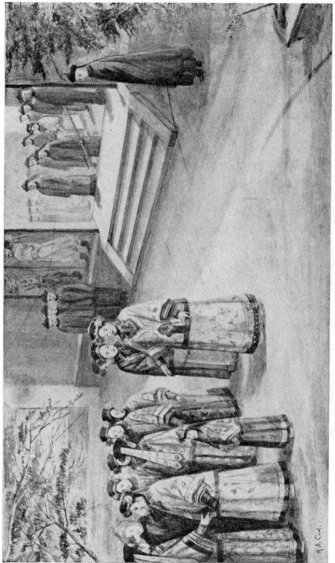

COURT IN THE WINTER PALACE—"HER MAJESTY COMES"

The Winter Palace

corners, remains intact in its purity and retains its restful simplicity.

The hall was paved with great blocks of highly polished black marble, which dimly reflected the glowing splendor of the walls and ceiling. In the center of one side was a low dais, richly carpeted, on which stood a great antique throne and footstool of red lacquer, framed in ebony and inlaid with cloisonné—the three-leaved screen behind was of bronze, with landscapes in low relief. On each leaf a poem in golden characters gave the needed touch of brilliancy to the somber massiveness of the dull bronze.

Great wooden doors, with huge gilded dragons in high relief, opened into apartments on the right and left of this splendid hall. These portals were always thrown wide, and heavily padded satin portières hung from the lintels. The front and rear of the hall was almost entirely of glass, with the pillars that supported the roof standing clear between the windows—the lower half of plate glass, the upper, of transparent Corean paper.

The apartments to the right, where, at a sign from Her Majesty, I followed the Ladies, were her day-rooms. Her sitting-room, projecting on the verandah, brilliantly lighted by two sides of windows, was in dazzling contrast to the somber splendor of the Throne-room. The sun pouring through the windows, the gay flowers and growing plants, the fruits piled high in great painted bowls, the divans, beneath the windows, with satin cushions, the touches of femininity, the subtle perfume, even the small shrine to Buddha—everything bespoke the characteristics of its august mistress, who, in her hours of ease, loved sunshine and flowers, and reveled in beauty and perfume.

On entering, Her Majesty approached the small shrine, lighted three slender tapers of fragrant incense, and placed them upright in the perfumed ashes of the golden censer at the feet of Buddha. She rearranged the offerings, placed a picture of the Mother of Buddha behind the Image, and then stood in reverent attitude a few seconds before turning to her waiting tirewomen to have her outer garments removed.

As I had now learned that my interest in her surroundings pleased her, I looked around the room. It was as lofty as the Great Throne-room, but the rear wall was divided into two stories, and a hidden stairway led to the upper rooms. In an alcove, under the second floor, was built the bed where she took her siesta in the afternoon, screened from the sitting-room by beautifully embroidered satin curtains. The walls of carved teakwood had a rare frieze of panels of flying birds and bats in mother-of-pearl. There were scrolls bearing quotations from the classics; and, of course, many beautiful and curious clocks adorned the dragon tables, the window-seats, and carved chests !

In prominent places, each flanked by good-luck pennants, hung two steel-engravings: the first representing Queen Victoria in regal array; the second, the Queen and Prince Consort, surrounded by their children and grandchildren. I was surprised to see them here in Her Majesty's living-room, though I had heard that the Empress Dowager had a great admiration for the Queen, and that she thought there were many points of similarity in their reigns. They had each been widows the greater part of their lives, and had each ruled over great empires. She said she noticed in the Queen's face the same lines of longevity that she, herself, had. She probably dreams of as long a life as the great Queen of England had.

The Empress Dowager was astonished that I had seen so many members of the English Royal family, and the Queen herself, when I had never had an "Audience," and was still more so when she learned that the Great English Empress took her daily promenade outside her Palace Walls in "an open chair," and could be seen by any one who happened to pass that way.

Her Majesty told me I might go up the hidden stairway, leading from her bed-alcove to the floor above, where was her private chapel. Here, on special occasions, services were held by lama priests. It was a beautiful haven, in whose dim, religious light one might meditate or pray.

Its high altar, with a great golden Buddha of fine design, had tall, golden candlesticks, shining with pearls and rubies. Richly wrought and enameled vases held bouquets of jeweled flowers, and censers, damascened with gold, sent up spirals of perfumed smoke. The floor was covered with a splendid silken rug of Imperial yellow, and small, exquisitely executed, paintings of the saints and personified attributes formed a dado around the walls.

Curiously shaped windows, with bits of translucent

shell set into the elaborate lattice-work, shed but a dim light, and out of mysterious depths shone the splendid jewels of the altar ornaments, the dull gold of the Great Buddha, and the gleaming dado of red-and-gold clothed saints! This was Her Majesty's favorite chapel. She had followed me up and showed it with pride. She appreciated its perfect artistic quality as much, I am sure, as she loved its religious element.

Here she could come, from the privacy of her bed-alcove, mount the hidden stairs when she willed, unnoticed and unattended, and here seek that peace which seemed so far away those troubled days of January, 1904, when all looked so dark for her country.

Her Majesty's Throne-room is in the first of three large halls in the northeastern corner of the inclosure, which, with their courts, extend to the exterior walls of the Palace. The buildings are raised about eight feet above the marble-paved court and are approached by handsome, white marble steps. Leading up to the second, for the first time I saw a "spirit-stairway" used in secular architecture. This "spirit-stairway" consists of a block of marble placed in the center and reaching from the top to the bottom of the stairway. This block, instead of being cut into steps, is elaborately carved with the double dragon. It lies in the middle of the stairway like a beautiful heavy carpet thrown over it, too stiff to take the form of steps. The "spirit-stairway," not to be touched by mortal feet, is used in the approaches to all the fine temples; and when, as in the case of the Temple of Heaven at Peking, the stairs are high, the effect is as beautiful as it is original and unique.

CONFUCIAN TEMPLE—SPIRIT STAIRWAY IN CENTRAL FLIGHT OF STEPS

The Winter Palace

The hall with the "spirit-stairway" is the handsomest of the three in the Empress Dowager's inclosure. Its interior, a height of fifty feet, has a splendid coffered ceiling, and its walls are of wonderfully carved wood, with cloisonné medallions, which give great richness and splendor. A balcony surrounds this lofty hall, with openings from it into rooms over the side apartments, which are of but the usual height. This great front hall, with a dais and throne, screen and ceremonial fans, showed it was for more formal receptions than the beautiful domed room we had first entered. Opposite the Throne dais stood a "cistern" of splendidly carved jade to hold water for cooling the temperature in summer. A handsome music-box, which had been sent as a present to the Dowager Empress by Queen Victoria, and several other presents from European Royalties, stood around. The apartments on the right were for His Majesty's use when he came to the Theater, which was near. On the left were Her Majesty's night apartments. Two doors led through the openwork screen which separated the hall from the entrance at the rear. Here there was another magnificent block of jade, about five feet high, elaborately carved in designs representing the manner in which the jade is mined and taken from its native mountains.

From the central hall, a raised marble platform led into the third of the buildings. Here, again, the central hall occupied the entire height, while the sides were divided into two stories. This was one of the Emperor's Throne-rooms, and he had graciously given it for my use while painting the Empress Dowager's portraits. I had been told I was to have a " magnificent place for working" in the Winter Palace, and so far as magnificence went, I had it here. But, lofty and spacious as the hall was, it was very dark, and there was also a disagreeable reflection from the shining, yellow-tiled roof of the Palace in front. The court was very small, and the reflection from the roof was consequently unavoidable. My heart fell. It was a dreadful disappointment to find that my " studio," to which I had so looked forward, was so unsatisfactory as to light !

The Empress Dowager's quarters at the Winter Palace are separated by high walls and guarded gates from the Emperor's. The pavilions of the Emperor's inclosure are on a more magnificent scale even than those of the Empress Dowager. The Audience Hall of the Winter Palace is in the Emperor's inclosure. In Her Majesty's inclosure, there is a Theater, but the Imperial "loge" is small, indeed, when compared with the splendid hall at the Summer Palace. Tradition seemed to be more rigidly observed here than at the Summer Palace, and everything seemed to be referred to the Emperor; whereas Her Majesty seemed to be the first figure at the Summer Palace, and there, traditional laws were often in abeyance.

CHAPTER XXV

THE Legation quarter of Peking lies in the Tartar City, just under the walls of the Imperial City. The United States Legation, in 1904, occupied a Chinese Temple on the canal, at the left of the "Water Gate," the opening of which was exacted by the Allies in 1900. Before this time, there was no gate between the Chien-Mên and the Hata-Mên.

It was a picturesque jaunt in the early morning that I had from the United States Legation to the Palace. My cart rattled down the road, running parallel to the canal, past the splendid inclosure of the English Legation to the "Glacis," and across the Marble Bridge, that traverses it, to the narrow street under the great red walls of the Imperial City. The walls all over China are wonderful feats of architecture, the culminating point of the science of the Chinese builder. The "Great Wall," long counted one of the wonders of the world, is one of many in China, and only remarkable on account of its size and great length. Nearly every town and city in China has massive, well-constructed walls, which, with their splendid gate-towers, make them really remarkable works of architecture. Even the palaces and parks of the rich have fine walls,

211

the monotony of their line varied by the turreted summer-houses which surmount their angles. These walls, quite overtopping the cities and houses they inclose, with their watch-towers permitting their defenders to see at great distances, must, in medieval times, have been a splendid protection against the attacks of enemies or the inroads of barbarians.

The main thoroughfares of the Tartar City are very wide, with a raised causeway, about two feet high, in the center. When Their Majesties go abroad, this is covered with yellow sand and is used as an Imperial roadway. Ordinarily any cart or chair, irrespective of the rank of the occupant, may use it. It is always kept in excellent condition, and seems to be a survival of the raised roads that Marco Polo speaks of in describing the grounds of the Palace of Kublai-Kahn. The lower roads on either side of this raised causeway are generally in a lamentable state. Itinerant cooks ply their odorous trade of frying grease-balls, etc.; barbers shave their clients and act as manicures and chiropodists, in full view of the passer-by; venders of old iron, clothes, vegetables, etc., spread out their wares in the middle of the road, in reckless disregard of the wandering fowls, dogs, and even pigs, which roam about. Pools of stagnant water and piles of refuse add their quota to the malodorous confusion. Still the streets are not unpicturesque. The elaborately carved fronts of the shops, the graceful signs, with their red pennants, the gaily colored lanterns swinging to and fro, the great umbrellas unfurled here and there over the itinerant venders, all have a certain sort of charm.

Peking

After entering the gate of the Imperial City, the roads are gay with carts, official chairs, and handsomely caparisoned horses. We sometimes met attachés of the "Wai-Wu-Pu" and different Yamens hurrying to and fro with despatches, or caught a glimpse, in the depths of his green chair, of one of the great ministers, the thin white-bearded face of Prince Ching, or the heavy Jewish-looking physiognomy of Na-Tung, the new minister, who seems likely to grow in favor. Sometimes we passed a bridal procession, with its gay, red-embroidered chairs, or some splendid funeral, with the great red catafalque, covered with magnificent embroideries (for red is used alike for wedding chairs and for funeral decorations)—its massive, long poles held by hundreds of red-gowned bearers and accompanied by the motley crew of figurants, who are always hired for funeral celebrations in China; the catafalque, followed by white-covered carts, carrying the mourning white-garbed women of the family. Sometimes we passed a crowd of yellow-gowned lama priests and monks returning from some celebration in the Palace—sometimes, great droves of camels laden with coal from the mountains or produce from afar. During the annual visit of the Mongolian Princes to Peking we met them with their fur-dressed and leather-booted followers, their quaintly caparisoned horses, and splendidly bedecked camels, for they were domiciled in Palaces, within the Imperial City.

All this we could see as we went on our way to the Great Gate of the Palace, itself. Within the walls and at the gate of the Empress Dowager's Palace, with the usual Chinese tolerance, the consideration of the great for the poor, beggars are allowed to come at certain times each day, to receive remnants from the Imperial kitchen. The poor are also permitted to examine the garbage of the Palace, before it is carted away. There was always a motley crew of ragged beggars around this gate, who received, apparently, kind consideration from the soldiers and guards. At least, they were allowed to ply their trade and to follow their avocations in peace.

I found the light, in the magnificent hall which had now become my studio, so obscure, even in front of the great plate-glass doors, that it was almost useless to attempt to work. After trying to do so for two or three days, I told the head eunuch it was impossible. I did not wish to trouble Her Majesty with my annoyances, for she had enough of her own cares, and seemed to grow daily more and more anxious and depressed over the constantly growing rumors of war in Manchuria; but it was impossible to work longer where I was, and I decided I would have one of the ends of the hall, which projected beyond the overhanging eaves of the verandah, fitted up for my work, and in order to have sufficient light, even here, it was necessary to have the upper paper windows replaced by plate glass. The eunuchs demurred. They said this would necessitate great changes, with heavy expense, besides establishing a precedent, as no other part of the Palace had plate-glass windows at the top! The next time the Empress Dowager came in, I told her it was impossible to work as it was. She, herself, remarked how dark it was, and noticed the reflection

Beginning the Portrait for St. Louis

from the yellow roof opposite. And when she heard
what I wished, she ordered it to be done at once, saying she would "speak to the Emperor" about it. An
order of Her Majesty's was always promptly carried
out, and two days after, to my astonishment, the plate-
glass windows were placed as I wished. I had the
divan that was built under the windows removed,
and all the furniture taken out of this end of the
hall. The eunuchs hesitated about removing an immense elephant clock of wonderful mechanism, as
it had not been moved for a hundred and fifty
years, but I finally accomplished even this! Even
without the furniture, this end of the hall was but a
small space in which to work; but I had a fairly good
light, and a quiet place to paint in, for the first time
since I began painting the Empress Dowager. Here I
was sufficiently far away from Her Majesty's apartments, as well as from those of the Princesses and
Ladies, to be able to work in quiet, without interruptions. A set of European furniture had been placed in
the great hall, when it was decided to give it to me, and
though this did not please me, in an artistic sense, it
being absolutely out of keeping with its environment,
I found the well-cushioned easy-chairs a real comfort
when I wanted to rest.

As soon as I was comfortably settled in my new
studio, the Empress Dowager began to talk of having
another large portrait begun—large enough to represent her with all the paraphernalia of Royalty (the
ceremonial fans, the three-fold screen, the nine phenix,
plants of heavenly bamboo) and pyramids of apples—
all emblematic, or symbolic. I told Her Majesty it

would be best to make a small study for this picture, and that the size of the portrait could be determined on after this was finished. She readily assented, and I began the small study. There were a number of beautiful thrones in the Palace, any one of which would have suited the lines of the composition. I selected one of the superb, antique thrones of red lacquer, a magnificent work of art, but the Empress Dowager did not care for this throne. It was not a matter of whether the lines or color suited the picture, the point was to have everything "Ho-shih" (proper), as the Chinese say. With the Chinese, propriety is a religion, and a thing that is "proper" must conform to tradition, for tradition and propriety are synonymous. The question of the throne was left in abeyance for the moment, as Her Majesty said there was one she would like to have painted, which she would have found before I began the big picture.

I finally began the sketch. Her Majesty was dressed in one of her official winter gowns. Its fur lining rendered the already heavily embroidered satin stiffer than ever, and any stray folds that might perchance have appeared, were pulled out by a heavy fringe of pearls around the hem. She had on her famous pearl mantle over an official jacket. In her coiffure she wore her long tassel of pearls, and many curious ceremonial jewels. She had on fur-lined undersleeves, which hid half her beautiful hands. The effect of her tiny finger-tips, with their long curving nails and jeweled shields, the palms not being visible, was most unfortunate. Added to this, she held them

PRINCE CHING

tightly together in her lap, and the lines were obscured by a large, pale-blue handkerchief in one hand.

My heart fell. Thus I would lose one of her chief beauties. I begged Lady Yu-Keng to ask her to pose her hands differently. She said she could not do such a thing; so, in my inelegant Chinese, I told Her Majesty I did not like her hands as they were. "But I like them like that," she said, looking at me with a charming expression of amused astonishment, amazed that it was possible for any one not to like what she liked; and she kept her hands as they were, and I was obliged to begin the picture with the hands in that position.

The first sketch was quickly made, and Her Majesty expressed herself as pleased with it. Then came the discussion as to the size of the portrait. I made my measurements, and thought five feet by eight was large enough, but when she saw what size it was going to be, she thought six feet by ten would be better. The Palace carpenters were accordingly called in, and I gave them as accurate directions as I could, for making a stretcher. The Chinese workmen are clever, patient, and apt at carrying out suggestions, and the stretcher was satisfactorily made. But the canvas was to be put on this stretcher, and this they seemed to have no idea of, so I was obliged to try to do it myself. Owing to the size of the canvas, I was compelled to stand on a stool six feet high (they had no ladders), with the huge stretcher before me. An army of eunuchs stood around to assist me, presided over by a head eunuch. I used the iron pincers and pulled the canvas, myself. It

was held at the corners by eunuchs, also on stools;
one eunuch held the tacks, another the hammer, etc.
Each order I gave was repeated in a loud voice by
the head eunuch, and at every failure to comprehend
my directions, the working eunuchs were rebuked and
threatened with the "bamboo." Finally, I accomplished the difficult task, and the great canvas was
stretched. Her Majesty was greatly exercised when
she learned I had done it myself. She said that I
should have made the eunuchs "stretch four or five,"
until they learned to do one properly. But I had n't
sufficient canvas for such experiments, and could get
no more in China.

CHAPTER XXVI

SOME SOCIAL CUSTOMS—MANCHU AND CHINESE

I MET the wives and families of all the Princes, nobles, and high Manchu officials in Peking, for they
came to the Court at stated intervals, besides on many
special occasions, when they were invited by Her Majesty. The most frequent of these visitors to the Palace were Prince Ching's wives and daughters, the
wives of the Emperor's brothers, his father's secondary wives and their daughters, and the sisters of the
young Empress, one of whom is the clever Princess
Schun. The widow of the Grand Secretary Yung Lu,
who lost, in one year, her husband and a promising
son, and who was nearly crazed by grief, also came
often. She was not very brilliant, nor the kind of
woman to appeal to Her Majesty; but her grief seemed
to touch the Empress Dowager, and she received special
marks of favor when in the Palace, and came and went
as she willed. A step-daughter, whom she had herself
brought up through a very delicate childhood, was the
wife of the Emperor's brother, Prince C'hun. Should
they have a son he will probably be the next heir to
the Throne.

On their marriage the brides of nobles of a certain
rank go to the Palace to be presented to the Empress

219

With the Empress Dowager

Dowager. This ceremony corresponds to the presenta
tion, on their marriage, of ladies at the English Court.
These brides are always magnificently dressed in embroidered gowns of rich colors, and wear, for the first
time, the Court coiffure of the married ladies, the magnificent golden filigree, jeweled construction, which I
have already described, and for this occasion they wear
a profusion of jewels. The Manchu ladies use much
more discretion in wearing jewels than the Chinese
ladies. The latter will sometimes wear as many as fifteen bracelets on each arm, and the number of jewels
they put in their coiffure seems to be limited only by
the space they have at their disposal.

The brides come to the Palace in red satin bridal
chairs, accompanied by their husband's mother and his
married sisters, if he has any; if not, by his nearest
women relations. On their arrival in the Precincts
they first go to the Throne-room and make their bows
and prostrations before the Empress Dowager, to thank
her for the gifts she has sent. Sometimes Her Majesty
would speak to them at some length, seeming to give
them advice. After making their obeisances to her,
they then make their salutations to the young Empress. They spend the day at the Palace, take
luncheon with the young Empress and Princesses, and
leave about three o'clock. These brides were generally very young girls, though sometimes I was surprised to see that they had well passed the first bloom
of youth, for I had thought that all Oriental women
were married very young. The young Empress was
always charming to the brides, and seemed to watch
over their pleasure, and try to make them enjoy this

rather trying day, when they were the observed of all observers. Among these brides, the winter I was in Peking, was the wife of the Emperor's youngest brother, a charming young girl with sweet manners, far more attractive in every way than Yung Lu's daughter, the wife of Prince C'hun.

The Chinese look upon a daughter, at her birth, as a misfortune, one of the ills that must be endured, and while loving her individually, a daughter is not welcomed into the family nor allowed the privileges of a son. It is, however, quite different with the Manchus. A daughter not being able to sacrifice to the ancestors, even Manchus prefer a son; but a daughter is a welcome member of the family, and she has a distinct and independent position of her own. One of the Chinese ministers to Washington once told me that the only unmarried woman in the world whose position is analogous to that of the " American Girl," in her own family, is the Manchu girl.

As long as the Manchu girl remains unmarried, she is a veritable power in the household. She ranks as high as her brother, and always takes precedence of her brother's wife, even if that wife be double her age and married before she was born. She precedes her mother even, as she is of the Blood and her mother of " another family." Not only has she these social privileges, but she has well-defined legal rights. Her father cannot make a disposition of his property without his eldest daughter's consent. She can go into her brother's house, dismiss his servants, and generally direct his affairs. Her word has more weight as to the bringing up of her brother's children than his wife's, as she is a sister, a born relation, and the wife is only an acquired relation. When she marries, however, she becomes a member of the family into which she marries; but even then, such is the ascendancy of the girl in the Manchu family, even after her marriage into another family, she often goes on dictating to her brother's family and her own as before, if she does not find her own household duties and her own family sufficient occupation to keep her from doing so. Such is the force of consanguinity among the Manchus, and the position of the daughter in the family.

The unmarried Manchu girl has not only this liberty in her family, but she has more liberty in the outside world than any other Oriental woman.

They are not so restricted in their social intercourse as any other Oriental women, and while they are not so literary as the Chinese, they have more social qualities and are brighter conversationalists, being both witty and gay.

They are not forced to marry against their inclinations and some remain single to the end of their days, or marry late in life if they so desire. These unmarried ladies are not only looked up to by their own families, but they are not regarded as being objects of commiseration by the world at large. On the contrary, they are rewarded with triumphal arches and splendid monuments if they have passed a long and exemplary life of maidenhood. Although the brides that came into the Palace were generally young, one who came to make her bow to the Empress Dowager, while I was there, was a lady of forty-two summers.

Some Social Customs

She had brought up two or three families of brothers' children and directed their households; but she finally succumbed to the charms of a wealthy official, who had lost his wife two years before and who had a number of children on which she could continue to practise her theories as to their bringing up. Had she held out longer and died a maiden, she might have had an arch built to her memory after death and gone down to posterity.

Only ladies, young girls and boys under seventeen were ever guests of the Empress Dowager in her Palace. The Manchu nobles and high officials were invited on certain days to the Theater, but there was always the high intervening screen between them and Her Majesty's and the Ladies' loges. The Princes and nobles who have official positions, see the Empress Dowager in the Audience Hall, and she is now over sixty. She has more liberty than before, but generally their Audiences are with the Emperor alone, and they never come into the Ladies' Precincts. At the performance of the European circus in the Palace grounds I saw, for the first time, nearly all the Princes and Manchu officials.

The Manchus are a taller race than the Chinese and more athletic-looking. They are fond of exercise, indulge in archery, riding, etc., and do not look down upon a military career, as do the Chinese. It is said that polo playing, which the English got from India, originated among the Tartars, and that it is still played in Manchuria. I never saw polo played by the Manchus, but I have seen some daring riding done by the young nobles that would seem to show they could

223

play polo if they would. The Manchu nobles have an inherited military rank, and they also receive military advancement for proficiency in archery and riding. The warlike spirit that prompted the Manchus and their progenitors, the Nu-Chih Tartars, who not only conquered China, but, as " the Huns," almost overran Europe itself, is no longer so militant as it was. The modern Manchu is becoming almost as peace-loving as the Chinese themselves, but there are still qualities which show their descent from a race of warriors.

They wear the ordinary Chinese costume, and though it is said "the shaven head and wearing of the queue" were instituted as marks of degradation for the Chinese when they were conquered by the Manchus, the Emperor himself and all the Manchu nobles shave their heads and wear the queue! They wear satin boots with white kid soles. Their hats, in summer of finely woven straw, and of fur in winter, have the crown covered with a tassel of red silk, surmounted by the jeweled button denoting their ranks. From this button stands out, almost at right angles, a jade-mounted aigret, mixed with the peafowl feathers, if they have attained that rank. In winter, they wear splendid sable short coats. Except these sable topcoats, fur is never worn on the outside of a garment in China, but is used only as a lining.

When I saw the Manchu nobles at the circus at the Summer Palace, they wore the splendid summer Court costume, embroidered in the double dragon, reaching below the knee. They were tightly belted in around the waist, and very full and ample across the shoulders, giving the men the appearance, at least, of broad shoulders, and enhancing their already fine figures. One could see that the Emperor was the " glass of fashion and mold of form " of the young nobles; for they all aimed, as much as possible, at his slenderness of figure and even imitated his carriage. The young dandies, however, wore a much greater profusion of ornaments than His Majesty ever indulged in. The belt buckle, the handsomest ornament worn, was of carved jade, ruby quartz, or of beautifully chased gold set with precious stones. They were then wearing a profusion of ornaments dangling from their belts—embroidered cases for fans, chop-sticks and knives, and many other ornaments besides the watch, an indispensable adjunct to every Chinese gentleman's costume. This is worn hanging from the belt in a handsome, embroidered case with an open front, so that the elaborate case, generally studded with jewels, beautifully enameled, or curiously incised, could be seen. This case had a sort of fob attachment made of silken cord, woven into quaint designs and finished generally with a wonderfully carved piece of jade, ruby quartz, or some other curious stone.

Manchu ladies wear their gowns long and loose, hanging from the shoulders, and never show the line of the waist, nor the outline of the figure; but the men belt in their gowns tightly, and are very proud of a small waist.

Among the social customs in China, which obtain also among the Manchus, is "concubinage." But it exists in such a form that in its actual state, it might more properly be called "plurality of wives." The concubine, or secondary wife, as I will call her, is taken from the bosom of her family, and her position in her husband's family is considered as secure as that of the first wife. Though the first wife only has a legal standing, custom gives the secondary wife equal rights, and she is no more likely to be put aside than the first wife. There are, I suppose, men in China who put away a secondary wife, if they are wealthy enough to have taken one or several, but they would be socially and generally ostracized.

The man marries in China as soon as he reaches manhood. Some young girl who is of the same social standing and has the requisite qualities for his wife is chosen for him by his parents. This is the legitimate wife. She is the first and remains first always, taking precedence of any and all others that may be chosen. The secondary wife is often of the same class as the first wife. She is generally chosen by the man himself, and is taken from some good family who may be poor, and she is an honest young girl.

She is received, on her entrance into the household, by the wife and the man's mother, if she be alive, and her position in the family is assigned to her. While she must pay court and due respect to the first wife, she has her own servants and her own rights, and leads her own independent life. The first wife has entire authority, in certain matters, over the secondary ones, but they generally live amicably together. As the first wife is married several years before any second wife is taken, and as she is also generally their superior in age, this entitles her to their respect, aside from her legal standing and her position as first in the household. The secondary wives stand in the presence of the first wife until she asks them to sit. Should they have any children, the latter call the first wife "mother," and though the mother has her part in bringing up the child, it calls her, if she be a secondary wife, by her first name, and, in important matters, her authority over the child must give way to that of the first wife. But the first wife rarely abuses her authority over the children any more than over the other wives, and does not interfere except for, what she thinks is, the child's good.

In theory, according to our ideas, and with American or European women, this would be a sad state of affairs, but practically, as it exists in China and with Chinese women, it seems to work well. The arrangement of the houses in China is also well adapted for this kind of life. There are a number of courts surrounded by pavilions, each court and its pavilions forming a unit—a separate dwelling-place—this unit being a part of a great whole.

The wives live in harmony together, and seem like a family of sisters. The first wife apparently takes pride in the good conduct and handsome appearance of the others, and there seems to be very little jealousy among them.

If this be the position of the secondary wife in the families of the gentry and nobility, one may imagine how much more exalted it is in the Imperial family and how the secondary wife of an Emperor would be considered. To have their daughter chosen as the secondary wife of an Emperor is looked upon as an honor in the highest Manchu families. Of course, they would prefer to have her the first wife, for she has more power, but none of them would demur at an alliance of the secondary kind for their daughter, for she may thus become the mother of an Emperor, and she does become, by this marriage, a member of the Imperial family, and is treated as such. She ranks higher than any of the Princesses or Ladies of the Court, and takes precedence of all except the first wife, or a secondary wife, of the Emperor, who may have been married before she was. Her place is at the side of the first wife, the Empress. In the Palace she is called by the same title as the first wife, a Manchu word meaning "Mistress." She cannot wear the Imperial yellow, it is true, but she does wear the Imperial orange, which no other Lady at Court can wear.

These secondary wives are not taken for some physical quality from among the masses; they are not in the Palace as the result of a caprice of the Emperor. They are from the highest families in the land. They are generally chosen by the Emperor's mother, if she be alive, with as much care as the first wife, and her position is inferior, only from an official standpoint, to that of the Empress. She may even become Empress herself on the death of the first wife and those who precede her. The Emperor of China has no "harem," but he may have as many wives as he wishes. His wives never live together in the promiscuity of a harem, where all individuality is lost. Each wife has her own establishment and her own position, and is not dependent on her physical charms for her maintenance in that position, any more than is the first wife. Should she be the mother of children, she may advance beyond the others who have none, excepting always the first wife; and even should she have no children, she has always her separate establishment and is considered a member of the family. The Emperor Kwang-Hsu has two wives, both designated by the same title in the Palace. In this account of my experiences I only allude to the first wife, because it would be confusing to speak of two Empresses where there is also an Empress Dowager, and also because the first wife, in this instance, is so much the stronger character and the more interesting personality.

CHAPTER XXVII

PRESENT-GIVING IN CHINA

PRESENT-GIVING is really carried to great excess all over China, and whatever obtains in China obtains at the Palace. The Palace is spoken of in Peking as the "Inside," that is, the heart of the Empire. From this "Inside," customs and habits flow and pulse over the rest of China, as the blood does from the heart, by a thousand arteries reaching to the very confines of the Empire, and it also receives the impress of what passes on outside among the people. Whether it be, in the instance of present-giving, that the custom has grown from the "Inside" to the "Outside" or vice versa, I know not, but it is universal in China. However, it probably reaches its greatest excess in the Palace.

Births, marriages, and deaths are all marked by presents, and there is a very riot of present-giving at the New Year! Every one then exchanges them, from the lowest to the highest. Next comes the anniversary of the birth. This is celebrated with an unheard-of pomp in China. The more exalted the rank and the greater the age, the more splendid is the celebration and the more magnificent the presents. The Emperor's Birthday was the first I saw celebrated, and I

Present-Giving in China

was astonished at the number and elegance of the presents that flowed into the Palace on this occasion. But at the Empress Dowager's Birthday all this was far surpassed; and her presents exceeded in number and elegance His Majesty's, for she was celebrating more years than the Emperor, and the number and value of birthday presents increase in proportion to the years. Their elegance and number are also regulated by the rank. The presents the Grand Secretary and the Prime Minister receive on such occasions would quite astonish a Westerner, and, of course, far surpass in number and magnificence what would be offered to the president of a department, as his would exceed, in elegance, those offered to secretaries of the Board.

Every festival, every ceremony, and all anniversaries are marked by presents, in the Palace. There is scarcely a day that presents are not sent into the Palace, that some are not sent out, and rarely a day when some presents are not exchanged by those " Inside." The Empress Dowager and the Emperor receive the greatest number, and, of course, they give the greatest number. This seemed to me the greatest extravagance of the Empress Dowager. At every change of season, she presents the young Empress, the Princesses, and Ladies, without reference to her favorites, with silks, dresses, shoes, and ornaments appropriate to the season, and not only do the Ladies receive these articles of wearing apparel at the changes of the season: she gives them many presents at each festival. Besides this, she gives nearly all the expensive Court dresses that are worn at the Palace, which cost, with

231

their embroideries, from three to six hundred dollars each. She presents the Ladies with coiffures and many jeweled ornaments as well. On the occasion of a wedding among the Manchu nobility, which must be announced to the Court before it takes place, Her Majesty presents the bride handsome rolls of silk, embroideries, and jewels. On the occasion of births among the courtiers, she sends handsome ornaments to be worn by the new-born child. Even on the death of certain people, she sends handsome presents to the family, or something to be worn by the departed, if it should be a widow, who had led a long and exemplary life of widowhood, and had devoted herself to charity and good works.

When the ladies of the Legation were first received at the Palace, the Empress Dowager naturally followed the Chinese Imperial custom of giving each lady a present. This precedent having been established and seeming to have given pleasure, when the ladies were received the next time, which was after the Boxer rebellion, she gave them presents again. Unfortunately, this act was construed into a desire on her part to wheedle the foreigners, and curry favor, so that she might receive better treatment at the hands of the Powers. The truth is, she loves to play the Lady Bountiful, and she never mixes up the social with the political, and I am sure she had no " arrière-pensée " but was simply indulging her usual bent. After the first few Audiences (when the presents were really of value), Her Majesty gave small and unimportant presents at the garden parties, which were made the subject of ridicule. Her Majesty had heard that the ladies did

Present-Giving in China

not wish to receive such handsome presents as she had first given, and she hence gave inexpensive souvenirs. Finally, the Ministers asked the Chinese Foreign Office to request the Empress Dowager to give no more presents at the Audiences, and the custom was abolished; though Her Majesty continued to give presents in private, and she still sends, on the four great Chinese festivals, flowers, fruits, and confectionery to all the ladies of the Legation, as well as to every lady who has ever been received at the garden parties, and on the departure of any Minister from Peking, she sends his wife some parting presents.

But though present-giving has been stopped at the Audiences of the foreign ladies, it goes on with the same excess in the Palace and among officials in China. At each of Their Majesties' Birthdays, in spite of their protests and edicts to prevent it, presents pour into the Palace! Every official who has ever been presented in Audience, or who has the right, by his official position, to send anything, does so. Edicts from the Throne to prevent it will remain as ineffectual as those with reference to the binding of the feet of the Chinese women (which Her Majesty has for years been "recommending" in edicts to be abolished), for it has become so thoroughly a part of Chinese life as to be almost indispensable. Present-giving in China is one of those "unwritten laws" whose tyranny is hardest to break away from. Though the system of present-giving is a great tax on the officials, as well as their subordinates, in this instance the change must come from the people.

As I was an inmate of the Palace for so long, of

233

With the Empress Dowager

course I came in for my share of presents from the Empress Dowager. At every festival I was remembered, as well as the Princesses and Ladies of the Court, and when presents were sent to the ladies of the Legation, she sent similar ones to me. Many of the presents she made me showed a real consideration for my comfort and displayed much forethought. When the weather became cool, and the Ladies of the Court put on wadded dresses, Her Majesty sent one of her maids to my apartments to get one of my tailor-made dresses. She had the Palace tailors copy this in wadded silk. It was wonderful how well they did it, too, for, as I knew nothing about it, I could give no advice. She ordered a few changes made in the severity of the tailor-costume, thinking it was too hard in its lines. She had a long, soft sash to tie at the side, which, she decided, made it look more graceful. When the Princesses put on furs, Her Majesty, herself, designed for me a long fur-lined garment which she thought would be comfortable to paint in. She had some trouble in arriving at a result which pleased her, which would be warm enough, and which, at the same time, would not interfere with the freedom of movement necessary for me to work with ease. At the time of the Chinese New Year, she sent me two curiously fashioned fur-lined dresses. She had the skirts copied from old pictures. They were not unlike our pleated skirts, with an embroidered panel down the center of the front. The jackets were a sort of compromise between European and Chinese, and the costumes were not only pretty but very comfortable.[1]

THE AUTHOR IN CHINESE COSTUME

Present-Giving in China

For wearing with these she ordered a sable hat, for the Chinese ladies wear some sort of coiffure on the head, winter and summer. This had an embroidered crown of pale lavender satin, with long satin streamers embroidered in gold with good-luck emblems. The brim could be worn either turned off the face or pulled over the ears and tied under the chin with lavender strings. She said she had some trouble in finding a design which she thought would suit me. This hat she had also had copied from old prints. I learned later she had tried three sorts of sables before she got a color which she thought would be becoming to my unfortunate blonde hair! On the front of the brim she placed a Princess Button. This is worn only by Ladies of the Court, and represents the Flaming Pearl of the Dynasty. It was established by the founders of the Dynasty and is the distinguishing jewel of the members of the Imperial family. It consists of a large pearl, surrounded by three alternating rows of seed-pearls and corals, which are supposed to represent flames! This Flaming Pearl, symbol of the "Unattainable," is the eternal quest of the double dragon!

Her Majesty also presented me with a number of other charming things that I shall always treasure as coming from her, and as evidence of her consideration for "the stranger within her gates," or as spontaneous offerings from her naturally generous nature—ever desirous of giving pleasure. I wish I might have preserved the flowers and curious grasses which she, herself, gathered and gave me on our many promenades around the beautiful grounds of the Summer Palace, but which, alas! are withered and gone!

[1] Her Majesty said my individuality was not lost in these costumes, and that I was clothed in attire suitable to the Chinese interior. She had now devised a costume for me which was really in harmony with my new environment. Our rough tweeds and somber garments, out-lining and defining the figure, looked mesquin and out of place in these great halls. The bright colors and simple lines of the gowns of the Chinese ladies are much more in keeping with their interiors. Her Majesty's artistic taste had divined this, and she had made several attempts to devise something for me that was in harmony with the Chinese "milieu" and at the same time comfortable.

CHAPTER XXVIII

SOME WINTER DAYS AT THE PALACE

THE big, official portrait for St. Louis was advancing. I was able to accomplish much more now that I had a place where I could work uninterruptedly, and quietly study the painting when I was not working. Her Majesty came, with her usual retinue, to pose, but it was not at fixed times, and was often when I did not expect her. She was looking more and more anxious these days; but she came to pose whenever it was necessary, and was very particular as to all the details in the portrait. She often had the jewels and ornaments changed, and her pearl mantle was made over, after she saw it in the first sketch, as she did not like its form.

The throne, about which there had been a question when I began the portrait, and which had been a present to Her Majesty from the late Emperor Tong Chih, her son, had been "lost" during the Boxer troubles, but Her Majesty thought it might be reproduced from descriptions and from sketches by the Palace painters who had seen it; but I could not consent to work either from memory or other painters' sketches, and I was finally obliged to paint, "faute de mieux," one of the carved teakwood thrones of which

237

With the Empress Dowager

Her Majesty is so fond. This throne did not suit the straight lines of the composition so well as almost any other in the Palace would have done, but Her Majesty wished it.

I found the representation of the nine life-size phenix, in vigorous colors, on a blue cloisonné screen placed almost touching the throne, very difficult to represent, so that they did not seem to be real birds flying around her head. The vases of flowers and ornaments were also placed at exactly equal distances on either side of the throne, but it was necessary to paint them this way. It would not have been "proper" otherwise. The figure was in the exact center of the three-fold screen, and so near it, it was impossible to ge any atmosphere in the background. There was not a fold in either gown or sleeves; but I had now resigned myself to convention and tradition, and I copied mechanically what was placed before me, and made no more efforts at artistic arrangements, nor tried any experiments in execution. I worked like a good artisan, finishing so many inches a day.

The weather was now too cold for anything but the short constitutional, and, besides, there was no place in the Winter Palace to tempt one to promenades— only the walled-in courts and the shut-in walks, between high walls. Even Her Majesty's promenades were confined to going to the Audience Hall in the morning, and walking through the courts, from one Throne-room to another.

Every day we saw the Empress Dowager for some moments in her Throne-room before I went to my work. On Theater days, I made her my morning salu-

tation in her loge at the Theater, and when the light
faded and I could paint no more, I would go into the
young Empress's and the Ladies' loge for the last
play and the spectacular finale, when there were
always some good illuminations and pretty effects.
Her Majesty and the young Empress seemed now to
perfectly understand that I wanted to work, and must
work, in order to finish the large portrait for the St.
Louis Exposition. They saw I appreciated the amusements and ceremonies, etc., but that I did not wish
them to interfere with my work. When there was a
special festival, or some fine ceremony, I was always
called in, but otherwise I might go or not, as I wished.

I lunched generally with the Ladies, with the charming young Empress as gracious hostess, and dined at
night at Her Majesty's table. Two huge copper braziers
had now been placed in the Throne-room, and though
so picturesque with the blue flames curling above their
openings in the top, they made but little impression
upon the temperature of this lofty room. The curtains
over the immense doors that opened on the courts
were constantly being raised for the passage of some
eunuch, and it was very drafty. But one could at
least warm one's hands by the braziers, and they were
so beautiful and picturesque, I was reconciled to being
a little cold; besides, I soon became accustomed to the
temperature. The Chinese Ladies wear heavy fur-
lined dresses in the house, and cannot stand the rooms
very warm.

At dinner, a large carpet was now placed under the
table, which was an improvement over the cold
marble floors. This was done for my comfort, for

the Chinese Ladies wear two-inch-thick cork soles to their fur-lined shoes. Down the center of the table, during the winter, there were several silver chafing-dishes, with burning charcoal beneath their steaming contents. Soups, vegetables, and meat stews were thus kept boiling hot on the table. One night I suggested to one of the eunuchs to place the claret-bottle near the fire before serving it, that the chill might be taken off. One very cold day, soon after, the eunuch brought in a large teapot, and began pouring the boiling claret out of this! The Chinese drink their wines hot, and he thought he would improve on my suggestion of "taking off the chill," and he naïvely remarked "it was better for me to drink it thus on such a cold day!"

When there was no Theater, and it became too dark to paint, I would join the young Empress and Ladies in their sitting-room at the left of Her Majesty's Throne-room and there await dinner. The young Empress would then teach me Chinese. She was very particular about my accent and seemed to take a real interest in my progress. The Chinese language is very difficult for a beginner, even for one who has a good ear, for the "tone" or inflection with which you pronounce the word may change its meaning. Sometimes one after the other of the Princesses would repeat the same word in different tones and make me repeat it and then give the meaning of each tone. They would sometimes make puns on words, or give me a string of difficult words for the accent and to improve my enunciation, as the French teach the children, " Trois gros rats dans trois gros trous." When

Some Winter Days at the Palace

I would finally get quite tangled up with these words I would retaliate with "Peter Piper picked a peck of pickled peppers." This would end the lesson for that day, for they would all try to say it and get so hilarious that there was no effort at further study, and dinner would be announced in the midst of the fun.

Sometimes the young Empress and the Ladies would play cards in the evenings. Her Majesty seemed only to like her fairy game! The cards were narrow slips of pasteboard with curious devices on each, but little more than an inch wide, and there were one hundred and fifty in a pack. I never succeeded in getting into the merits of the game. Sometimes when the Ladies felt industriously inclined, they would weave a kind of braid. The threads, gold, silver, or silk, were attached to the center of a wooden table and were weighted at the ends. They would weave these in and out into cunningly fashioned braids and ribbons. The Princesses did a great deal of beautiful embroidery, making their own shoes, which are of exquisitely embroidered satin, but they could not do this at night, for only candles are used in the two Peking Palaces, the Summer Palace being the only one in China lighted by electricity.

One night at dinner the young Empress asked me to come earlier than usual the next morning, as there was something she wished me to see. Several eunuchs were waiting at the gate of the Palace to conduct us to the young Empress when we arrived at nine o'clock the next morning, and I then learned this was her Birthday. I hurried in and found the Imperial Princess and all the Ladies of the Palace, besides a number of visit-

ors, standing in front of the young Empress's pavilion.
They told me she had asked them to wait to present
their congratulations until I came, and said that I was
to go in first. I did so, and there, on a throne, sat the
young Empress in full Court dress, wearing the Court
coiffure, with its veil of pearls, which was most becoming to her narrow patrician face. She was looking
very sweet and gracious and held out her tiny hand to
me on my entrance. I bowed low over it and kissed
it, and wished her from the bottom of my heart " ten
thousand" years of happiness and all kinds of "felicitous omens." I then started to move out, but she told
me to remain in the room at one side and watch the
Princesses and Ladies as they came in. Each made
the prostrations before her and presented a jade
"ruyie," [1] which she received with due ceremony—the
same ceremony as for the Emperor's and Empress
Dowager's Birthday!

But these winter days were not all given up to the
Theater and festivals. There were some days of sadder import. Days of mourning were often celebrated
at the Palace. The anniversary of the deaths of some
Emperor or Ancestor was of frequent occurrence. It
seemed to me they celebrated the anniversary of the
death of every Emperor of the Dynasty! On these days
there would be sacrifices at the ancestral tablets and
religious ceremonies early in the mornings. The Empress Dowager and the whole Court would wear mourning for the day and there was never any sort of amusement. White, which is full mourning, is not worn on
these anniversaries after the third, but violet and blue
(second mourning) is put on. The flowers worn in the

Some Winter Days at the Palace

coiffure were also in violet, white or blue, the mourning colors. One night at dinner the young Empress, who acts as Mistress of Ceremonies in the Palace, told me the following was a day of mourning. She asked me if I would wear one of the mourning colors, as it was the anniversary of the death of the Emperor Tung-Chih (the Empress Dowager's son).

The next day I put on a black dress, our mourning, and wore violet flowers in my hair. When we entered, Her Majesty was sacrificing at the small shrine in her sitting-room. She was dressed in dark violet, heavily trimmed with black, and had not a flower of any kind in her hair—only a few pearls. She looked very sad and was more earnest and reverent at the sacrifice than usual, but when she had finished her sacrifice, she bade us "Good morning" and inquired after our health, with her usual consideration. We soon left the Throne-room for my working-hall, and I did not see her again until after our dinner with the Empress and Ladies, when we went into the Throne-room to make our adieus. As I had not been wearing black for some time (as Her Majesty said she did n't like it), she now noticed that I had it on and she asked Lady Yu-Keng, in an aside, "why." She was told that when I knew what anniversary it was, I had put it on on that account. She seemed much touched, took my hand in both hers, and said, "You have a good heart to think of my grief and to have wished to sympathize," and tears fell from her eyes on my hand, which she held in hers.

Poor lady! Private sorrows and sad memories were not all she had to grieve her now. I had noticed

243

her growing anxiety for many days! She seemed to feel all the gravity of the political situation of China. As the rumors of war between Russia and Japan grew, her anxiety increased and she was looking sad and careworn. She seemed to be full of doubt and fear, and quite unlike her usual self. I fancy she thought of the unprepared state of her country and feared that it might be drawn into this struggle. She seemed to be in doubt as to the course that was best to be taken. Even should the Empire not be drawn into the conflict, two hostile nations were to meet within its borders. The struggle was to take place in Manchuria, the cradle of the Dynasty. That beautiful, smiling country would be ravished by war, and the awful possibility of the ancestral tombs being desecrated, loomed up before her. The desecration of the tombs of one's ancestors in China is supposed to bring dire consequences upon the family, and a pious Chinaman would face any material loss rather than run the risk of these tombs being desecrated. She felt it all, and was sad. indeed.

1 Also spelled jiu.

CHAPTER XXIX

RELIGIOUS RITES IN CHINA

THERE are three great religions in China—Buddhism, Taoism, and the worship of Nature. The worship of Nature, in which is embodied their highest idea of an Invisible Deity, is the purest form of religion in China. Its Temples are situated in a magnificent Park in the Chinese City of Peking. The Temple of Heaven, the most imposing of the group, spherical and triple-domed, rears its proud height here and is visible from afar. Its triple dome tiled, without, in the sacred green of Nature and vaulted within in Heaven's own blue, is surrounded by groves of century-old arbor-vitæ. In other parts of the great Park are the scarcely less splendid Temples to the Earth, to the Sun and Moon and to Agriculture, and grandest, most unique of these Temples, is that to the Invisible Deity. Its foundations are the Earth, its walls are limitless Ether, its dome Heaven's own vault! On its great open altar this Nature-worship has its culmination and reaches its highest fulfilment. This altar is the Holy of Holies, the tabernacle of the group of Temples consecrated to the worship of Nature.

It is built in the center of a great marble paved

space with the secular arbor-vitæ radiating therefrom in long concentric avenues. It is of pure white marble, round as is the Earth. The Trinity in Nature and its Infinity are symbolized in its three superposed circles. Each of the circular platforms is surrounded by an exquisitely carved balustrade and approached by flights of nine steps each, to the north, south, east, and west. The central point of the great upper circle thus represents the center of the Universe, accessible from every point of the compass.

Here in this symbolic center of the world, in this great Temple, whose walls are Space, whose towers are Infinity, on this great triple altar, canopied with Heaven itself, the Emperor of China, "Son of Heaven," glorifies the Invisible Deity and sacrifices for the prosperity of "the Great, Pure Kingdom" and his people. This worship of the Invisible Deity has no Priestly Hierarchy. The Emperor of China is its one High Priest. He alone is worthy, as the Son of Heaven, to perform its unique ceremonies, on its one great Altar, in its single great Temple of China.

The Emperor prepares himself for the great ceremony of the semi-annual celebration on this altar by a rigorous fast of three days, spending the final night before the celebration in a vigil in the Great Park of the Nature Temples, where there is a Purifying Palace set aside for his use. This glorification of the Invisible Deity at the summer and winter solstices is the most solemn act performed by the Emperor in his quality of Son of Heaven.

The Emperor is not only the one High Priest worthy to sacrifice on the great altars to the Invisible

TEMPLE OF HEAVEN — PEKING

Religious Rites in China

Deity, the Priestly Hierachy of the whole of this Cult of Nature is vested in his Sacred Person. He alone offers sacrifices in the Temples of Heaven and the other Great Temples, at times set aside in the Book of Rites, and on special occasions. When famine devastates the land, when drought or any other National Calamity is visited upon the Empire, the Emperor prays in these Temples for its cessation, for he is not only the High Priest, but as "Son of Heaven" is the expiator for the afflictions visited upon his people by Heaven, and he publicly holds himself responsible for the misfortunes of the Empire. According to the Book of Rites, he says in time of trouble, "I will purify myself by sacrifice that these calamities may be lifted from the Empire and the people. I alone am responsible."

The great semi-annual celebration to the Invisible Deity is not only the most solemn of the religious rites the Emperor performs; it is at the same time the most formal of his official acts as ruler of the Great Empire. He prepares himself, by fasting and subduing the body, for the religious rite; for the official ceremony as Emperor of China, he is accompanied by all his ministers and the highest nobles of the land and surrounded by splendid pomp and Imperial pageantry.

Though in his triple quality of Emperor, High Priest, and Expiator, he personally sacrifices only in the great Temples to Nature the Emperor has all the religions of his Empire under his protection and is their nominal Head. He assists indiscriminately at Buddhist or Taoist ceremonies, and encourages with impartiality both cults. But these religions have priestly hierarchies, and complicated Rituals, and the Emperor is only the "Ex-officio" Head and High Priest. All the festivals and fasts of both are celebrated in the Palace.

The Chinese are not a religious people, though so moral a race. They are rather followers of a philosophy than members of religious bodies. The two most popular religions of China, Buddhism and Taoism, have become more or less outward forms. They are empty shells which may once have contained the Spirit, but have now become mere conventional representations of ancient rites. The Chinese people are really Confucians, and Confucianism is a system of ethics, a philosophy rather than a religion. Whether they be Buddhists or Taoists, they are all followers of Confucius, and live by the rules the Great Sage has laid down for them. The doctrines of Buddha and Laotze have become so incrusted with error in China as to afford no moral or ideal help to their followers. The Chinese participate indiscriminately in either of these religious rites, many of which have become mere outward spectacular ceremonies, where there is a great deal of display and much form, but very little real worship. They get all their moral support from the writings of Confucius and all their ideals from communion with Nature. They are really philosophers and worshipers of Nature, and the Emperor's semi-annual sacrifice on the altar of Heaven and those at the Temples of Nature typify the real worship of the people.

All the religious rites in China have their origin in, or are in celebration of, some natural phenomenon

Religious Rites in China

or some periodical event in Nature. They celebrate the summer and winter solstices, the equinoxes, the New Year, the awakening of spring, when the sap (life-giving element) begins to mount. The Harvest Moon is the time of the going to rest of this life-giving element. Their complicated ceremonial is but the crystallization of some simple observance of Nature's fundamental laws. This ceremonial has been kept alive all these centuries, because of the vivifying spark of Nature which enkindled them. These rites are now observed without a thought of their origin, but Nature still remains their creative force. In spite of their conventions, the Chinese have kept very near to Nature, and I believe this is the secret of their wonderful vitality. They have been overrun and conquered by many different races, and their assimilation of these conquerors is one of the most astonishing things in the ethnic study of this wonderful race.

No conquering race has ever changed the Chinese. Tartars, Mongols, Manchus have all passed and become amalgamated with them. Their conquerors have adopted the Chinese philosophy and religion, their customs and habits, and even their system of government. And they have never been able to impose any really new system of government upon the Chinese.

These founders of Dynasties in China have all been "warriors bold" and reckless marauders with little philosophy and no literature to speak of. When the Manchus, the last of these conquerors, founders of the present Dynasty, established themselves in Peking, in 1646, they were a wild and warlike race. They, like all the other conquerors of China, conciliated their vanquished foes by all sorts of concessions, and they now rule by Chinese laws, and to-day are hardly distinguishable from the Chinese. They have never made, any more than the other conquerors, the slightest impress upon this calm and passive race; and they have become Chinese. "To-day the Emperor Kwang-Hsu is recognized as one of the best Chinamen_ in China." The Manchu men to-day wear Chinese dress. The Emperor, himself, shaves his head and wears the queue, the one visible sign of degradation that is said to have been imposed upon the Chinese at the time of the conquest. Oh! Irony of fate!

The Manchus are now as quiet and peaceful a race as the Chinese themselves. They dread war. They live by the laws of Confucius. Though not a race of thinkers or philosophers, they have come to have the same ideals as the Chinese, and this, without the natural amalgamation brought about by inter-marriage, for it is only within the last few years that the Throne has issued an edict, allowing inter-marriage between the Chinese and Manchu, and even, with this edict, up to this time there has been very little mixture, by marriage, of the races. The Chinese seem easily led and conquered, but their national vitality is very vigorous, and has kept them pure in racial characteristics after their thousands of years of national existence.

The Festival of the Harvest Moon, which typifies the season when the life-giving element in Nature goes to rest for the Winter, I have already described. It is intermixed with legends and practices that destroy its original meaning; but the ceremony to the awak-

ALTAR TO THE INVISIBLE DEITY
In the Park of the Temple of Heaven

ening of Spring has not departed from its original intention, and is simpler and nearer Nature. The awakening of Spring, the day when the sap is supposed to stir from its long sleep and to feel the first throes of renewed life, is commemorated in a pretty, homely ceremony at the Palace. The radish and young shoots of lettuce, the first vegetables to receive the benefit of the rising sap, are presented on a silver salver to Her Majesty by a kneeling eunuch. She partakes of them, and then gives them to the young Empress and Ladies to taste of. When Her Majesty raises the first radish to her lips, the young Empress, Princesses, and Ladies assembled in her Throne-room, repeat the wish for Imperial happiness, synonymous with "National prosperity." This wish is echoed by the high attendants in the ante-chamber, and reëchoed by the eunuchs kneeling in the courts without, and still echoed and reëchoed by every inmate of the Palace, until the waves of sound reach to the outer walls. Then Her Majesty makes a wish that the sap may rise in such abundance as to produce a fruitful season, that all the people of the Great Empire may enjoy peace and plenty.

Thus are these first fruits of the awakening Spring partaken of with a simple ceremony of praise and thanksgiving. Thus are these homely plants consecrated with wishes made for the good of the country and the happiness of its rulers. It was to me a beautiful ceremony, so simple that it brought these people with all their conventions and all their forms very near the heart itself of Nature.

The annual plowing of a furrow and sowing of the

With the Empress Dowager

first seeds of the year by the Emperor, the planting of a mulberry tree (to nourish the silkworms) by the Empress, are other touches of Nature which show how near the Chinese are to the heart of things. One of the honorary offices which is considered a great mark of Imperial favor, and which the highest ladies of the land receive with reverent gratitude, is to be appointed "Guardian of the Cocoons"; for the silk industry is one of the great sources of National prosperity in China. These ladies of high degree, guardians of the cocoons, go in annual pilgrimage to the mulberry groves, where the cocoons flourish, to make sacrifices and prayers for the health and growth of the cocoon. Being so near to Nature, the Chinese are naturally a pastoral people, a race of agriculturists; and agriculture, being thus honored by the Sacred Persons of Their Majesties, becomes a lofty ideal. Labor, which the Emperor publicly performs, loses all taint and grows into an Inspiration.

CHAPTER XXX

HER MAJESTY THE EMPRESS DOWAGER

THE current story that the Empress Dowager was a slave-girl and is of low origin is absolutely false. Her Majesty is the daughter of a Lieutenant-General of the Manchu forces, a position only attainable by members of the highest Manchu nobility. She belongs to the family of the White Banner, second only to that of the Yellow Banner, of which the Emperor of China, himself, is the head. At the time of the conquest of China by the Manchus, there was a fierce struggle between these two powerful families for the supremacy, and the Yellow Banner finally carried the day. The Empress Dowager was brought up with great care and highly educated by her father, a noble of great acquirements.

Like all young Manchu ladies of rank, she went to the Palace for presentation to the then Empress and Empress Dowager between the ages of seventeen and twenty. She immediately attracted them by her cleverness and wit, as well as by her charm and beauty, and, being of an honorable and high Manchu family, was at once considered as a possible wife for the Emperor. On presentation to the Emperor, she met also with his approval and was then chosen as one of the wives and given her establishment at Court. She was the fifth chosen, and hence ranked fifth on her marriage and was taken precedence of by the four others who were married before she was.

She became at once a favorite, both with the Dowager Empress and Empress, the first wife, as well as with the Emperor. She soon took precedence over the wife just over her and became fourth wife, for secondary wives can mount in degree. A brilliant woman, with exceptional qualities, takes her place in a Chinese family, as in the world, above that of her less endowed sister, unless this latter should be the first wife. Her place can never be taken, except in case of her death. The first wife of the Emperor Hsien-Feng died two months before he came to the Throne and was never Empress. There were two years of mourning, prescribed by the rites, during which time there was no official Empress. Then the first of his secondary wives was made Empress, and she it was who was the first wife when the present Empress Dowager went into the Palace as fifth wife.

Two years after her marriage, she gave birth to a son, and five years later, on the death of his father, this son became the Emperor Tung-Chih; the young mother, together with the Empress, the first wife, who had adopted him, were given the title of "Dowager Empress." They were appointed Co-Regents for the boy Emperor, and bore, respectively, the titles of Empress of the Eastern Palace and Empress of the Western Palace, with equal rank and power. She of the Eastern Palace was a woman of quiet tastes, given to literary pursuits, with none of the remarkable executive ability of her Co-Regent, the Empress of the Western Palace, the great Tze-Hsi, who still rules the destiny of China. Though so different, they lived amicably together, thoroughly appreciated each other's qualities, and are said to have had a sincere affection for each other, which never weakened during the whole of their long association, first as wives of the Emperor Hsien-Feng, then as Regents for his son, and afterward as Regents for the present Emperor Kwang-Hsu. The amicable relations of these two Empresses were only severed by the death of the Empress of the Eastern Palace in 1881, when posthumous honors were lavished upon her by the present Empress Dowager.

China was passing through troublous times when the young Tung-Chih, son of the Empress Dowager, came to the Throne. His father, the Emperor Hsien-Feng died at Jehol, far from Peking, where the Court had gone at the approach of the foreigners, who were aiding in quelling the Taiping rebellion. The times were critical. The integrity of China, the future, even, of the Empire, depended upon the action of its ministers and its rulers at this crisis. In the absence of the Court from Peking, some reactionary ministers, strongly anti-foreign, claimed they had been appointed by the late Emperor as Regents for young Tung-Chih. Had his mother and adopted mother, the two Empress Dowagers, joined them, anarchy might have followed; and, at least, there would have been serious foreign complications, for this anti-foreign party would never have come to terms with the foreigners, who were then in Peking. It was most important for the ruling Power, that is, the party which should become Regents, to have the support of the Empresses who held the Sacred Person of the young Emperor, under their care. They were approached by both parties. The young Empress of the Western Palace, absolutely unversed in Statecraft, and, up to that time, ignorant of all that was passing outside the Palace walls, showed wonderful perspicacity and rare judgment in her keen grasp of the situation at this time. She repudiated the antiforeign party and joined forces with Prince Kung, whose name was then synonymous with Progress in China — an enlightened Prince and the most pro-foreign of all the Imperial Family — and she and the first Empress were appointed Regents for the young Emperor. Prince Kung was the Minister who, thanks to this coöperation of the Empress of the Western Palace, carried the negotiations with France and England to a successful conclusion.

This first political act of the young Empress of the Western Palace brought her into immediate notice, and showed the progressive statesmen of China that they had an intelligent aid in her. The Grand Council and the Princes of the Imperial Family at once recognized her superior ability and they have always stanchly supported her throughout her career and remained true to her in all vicissitudes. In fact, she has known how to inspire loyalty and great devotion in all by whom she has been surrounded.

It was through her wonderful grasp of the situation at this time and the great executive ability she showed later, that the two Empresses brought the Emperor

Tung-Chih through his minority, and when he began to reign in his eighteenth year, internal troubles had been quelled and foreign complications avoided, and China was in a much more settled and prosperous condition than when he came to the Throne, twelve years before.

There was an interval of but two years in their long Regency for the two Emperors, when the Emperor Tung-Chih, having reached his majority, reigned. The death of her son, the Emperor, at the early age of twenty, after only two years of actual reigning, was a dreadful blow to the Empress of the Western Palace. She had, however, but a short time for grief. With heart bleeding and sore, she was obliged almost immediately to again assume the duties of Co-Regent with the Empress of the Eastern Palace, for her nephew and adopted son, the young Emperor Kwang-Hsu. The two Empresses had then another boy Emperor only five years old, to protect, prepare for reigning, and to govern for.

One has only to be cognizant of events in China since the Dowager Empress Tze-Hsi has ruled, to know the facts of her government. When she took up the Regency, China was seething with rebellion and there were foreign complications, requiring great tact and keen intelligence. She has steered the ship of State between the two extremes, though she has sometimes run it against the rocks of Scylla in trying to avoid the whirlpool of Charybdis, and she has always been a "moderate" in her political course. China having, for so many centuries, had no relations with foreign powers, her statesmen being so absolutely unversed in modern methods of diplomacy, has not made a brilliant record in her foreign relations, and she has so frequently been made the dupe of European diplomacy, it is not wonderful China has tried to defend herself by duplicity: using what she thought the same methods she saw were so efficacious in the hands of Europeans.

When the Empress Dowager gave up the reins of government to the Emperor Kwang-Hsu, in the year 1889, after twenty-eight years of Regency, the Great Empire was at that time in a prosperous condition. Its ports had been opened to foreign trade, a fine Customs organization had been established upon a firm basis, and China was at peace with the world.

The first part of the young Emperor's reign was uneventful. He was directed in most things by his ministers, and followed the moderate policy laid down by the Empress Dowager. He seemed to have no special views of his own and no designs of progress for China. Until the war with Japan with reference to the suzerainty of Corea, in 1894, he was a passive figurehead. The Japanese victories changed all this. Their victory gave China one of her most humiliating lessons; for the Chinese, who had given Japan the nucleus of its literature, its art and architecture, looked down upon the Japanese as a race of imitators and had a deep-seated contempt for them as a nation. This victory almost awoke the passive leviathan—that is, China—from its long sleep of national self-content. The young Emperor, smarting under this galling defeat, felt that China had only been conquered by Japan's use of modern methods of warfare and determined on sweeping reforms in the government. Full of youthful enthusiasm, he felt he could put the Great Empire on the road to progress and wished to institute sweeping reforms in all departments. He immediately abandoned the moderate policy of the Regency and surrounded himself by a number of hot-headed, self-seeking reformers, each pushing some new method of reform. The reformers wished, at one fell swoop, to change the system of education, the system of government—in fact to make such sweeping changes that this conservative nation would have risen in a mass had they been carried out. Besides the Radicals, who were the reform party, there were also a number of discontents among the ultra-Conservatives, who, seeing the Emperor's anxiety and desire for change, began to push forward certain schemes of their own. Finally, the ultra-conservatives and reactionaries decided they would join forces with the Radicals, hoping by so doing to change the National policy and the then existing state of government. In the turmoil that would follow this upheaval, each hoped to carry out his own designs, quite different in scope. Each party made the Emperor believe that progress was its aim. The coalition of these two diametrically opposed parties was for the purpose of persuading the Emperor to depart from the moderate opportunist policy which had been the motive power of the Empress Dowager's régime. The adherents of the Reform party were opposed to this moderate policy because it was too conservative. Those of the Reactionaries objected to it because it was too progressive. The power of the central government vested in the young Emperor seemed likely to be crushed between these two self-seeking factions.

With the Empress Dowager

China's wisest statesmen saw the peril, sought the Empress Dowager, beseeched her to return from her retirement and, for the salvation of China, to give the Empire again the benefit of her wise counsels. When she realized the danger she returned. Such is the ascendancy of the "ancestor" in China, the Emperor could not refuse to accept the counsel of his August Ancestress, thus forced upon him. He issued an edict in which he recalled " that Her Majesty the Empress Dowager has on two occasions taken the reins of government, with great success, at most critical times. In all she has done, Her Majesty has been moved by a deep regard for the welfare of the Empire. I have implored Her Majesty to be graciously pleased to advise me in government, and I have received her assent." The Emperor's authority was not wrested from him— he was not deposed. He still remained the Emperor of China; but the Empress Dowager's counsels were forced upon him, he could not but accept them, and she became once more the real Ruler of China. This was what foreigners call the "coup d'état" of 1898.

Her Majesty's keenness of insight and fine judgment (as far as Chinese questions are concerned), served her well again in this crisis. She dismissed not only the self-seeking Radicals, but the self-seeking ultra-Conservatives. Such of the Reformers as were caught were tried, convicted of treason, summarily and cruelly punished. Those who escaped, among them Kang-Yu-Wei, the ringleader of the Reformers, were outlawed. The leader of the ultra-Conservatives, the Emperor's tutor, was not beheaded, but was sent into exile; for a tutor in China occupies almost the position of a parent to his pupil, and this position exempted him from more cruel punishment. These summary proceedings on the part of the Moderates, led by Her Majesty, were considered by the foreigners, who were altogether in sympathy with the Reformers, as a reversion to anti-progress ideas, and hence were considered anti-foreign. It certainly was an "anti-reform" movement that caused the "coup d'état" of 1898, but had the adherents of the so-called reformer Kang-Yu-Wei, whose subsequent career has proven how self-seeking he was, carried the day; had his sweeping measures been inaugurated, it might have brought China into a state of anarchy and would certainly have been most pernicious to the Nation, for she was not ready for the drastic measures the Reformers advocated, and the great mass of the people would have rebelled against them.

The "coup d'état" and the consequent check upon the Emperor's dreams of progress was a great blow to him. He was not only chagrined at the failure of his efforts for reform, by which he hoped to show the world that China still counted as a power and to retaliate upon Japan, but he was also profoundly discouraged when he discovered the real nature and designs of his chosen instruments. He saw that he had been over-sanguine in hoping to realize at once his enthusiastic dreams for the immediate rehabilitation of China's prestige; he saw that his ardent desire for progress was not enough, and that to hope to reform in a few years the century-old traditions of his most conservative people was but the wild irrealizable dream of youth, and absolutely impracticable. Though he knew he had been led away by his wishes for reform to expect the impossible, the disappointment was none the less severe and was most depressing to his sensitive nature. The reaction took place. His never-too-strong constitution broke down under the strain, and this breaking down of his health lent color to the reports, which were immediately circulated among Her Majesty's enemies as well as among the foreigners, that the Empress Dowager was trying to kill the Emperor! She was reported to have imprisoned him, was said to be trying to poison him at one time and at another to starve him to death—the nephew she had brought up through a delicate boyhood and whom she cherished as her own son! Time has shown the truth of these reports, for, had she so desired, she would have had no difficulty in accomplishing his death. She had any number of instruments at her hand, fanatically loyal to her and ready to carry out any of her wishes.

She still "assists" the Emperor in ruling; and, according to Chinese tradition, she, being his "ancestor," must always take the first place. She sits upon the Throne, he upon a chair at her side. It would be improper, according to all Chinese law, were it otherwise. The foreigners speak of the Empress Dowager forcing the Emperor to stand in her presence and to sit upon a stool while she occupies the Throne. It is not Her Majesty who forces him to do this, it is an immutable thousand-year-old tradition in China that a son must take a lower place than his parent in his presence, be he Emperor or peasant. The Empress Dowager still reigns. The times are still too troublous for her to withdraw her experience from the councils of State, and though longing for the quiet and rest so necessary to a woman of her age, and though really anxious to retire, she feels the time has not yet come.

The Empress Dowager, having crushed the Reformers, and reseated herself upon the Throne, was, from the time of the "coup d'état," considered to be anti-foreign and responsible for all the attacks upon foreigners by ignorant Chinese that took place after that event. When, only two years after the "coup d'état," the secret society of the Boxers began their sanguinary attacks upon the foreigners, Her Majesty was considered responsible for them, was looked upon as aiding and abetting the Boxers; and, by the foreigners at least, she was considered to be the high priestess if not the originator of the order. But the Boxer movement had no such high origin. It started among the people, the humble people, in the Northern provinces of China, far from the Capital, and had been in existence for a number of years before the attack upon the Legations in 1900.

The open contempt of many of the foreigners living in China, not only for the Chinese as a race, but for their most cherished customs and traditions; the fact that the Chinese converts of the foreign missionaries may break Chinese laws and still not be amenable to Chinese punishment; the constantly renewed demands of the foreign powers for territory, for the punishment of high Chinese officials and hundreds of other acts that no body of foreigners in any country but China would dare to try to force upon the people,

finally aroused even this peaceable, long-suffering
Nation.[1] The worm turned. The secret society of
the Boxers took "China for the Chinese" as its
motto, and to "drive out the foreigner," or, at least,
curtail his rapidly growing power, became its object.
This society gained in force and grew in volume until
it reached the Capital. Here, from the obscure classes
among which it had its origin, it spread to the upper
stratum of society and had followers among the highest in the land. Certain Princes of the Imperial
Family even joined the ranks—among these latter
the father of the next heir to the Throne, the Prince
Tuan. These gave the movement an added force and
made of it a patriotic effort.

Then from smoldering discontent, it burst into
open acts of violence against the foreigners. The
final spark which caused the outbreak in the Capital
and the attack upon the Legations is said to have
been the report, which gained immediate credence
among the discontents, that the Foreign Ministers
were going to interfere with the Government itself,
and ask for a change in it; that they were to
insist upon the Empress Dowager's retiring from the
management of State affairs. This interference, by
the foreigners, with the sacred prerogatives of China,
as a Nation; this attempt at the removal of the
Person of one of its Sacred Rulers, aroused the
people to a wild fury. Without waiting to find out
the truth of this report, and thinking, in their blind
ignorance, that by getting rid of the representatives
of the Foreign Powers, they might then be left in
peace, the mob first attacked and killed the German

Minister, the Baron von Ketteler, as he was on his way to the Tsung Li Yamen, which the Wai-Wu-Pu now replaces. Then followed the general attack on the Legations.

The movement then became a veritable torrent, rushing madly along, dashing aside all opposition and overwhelming right and reason.

The Emperor and Empress Dowager, powerful and autocratic as they are, could not stem the current, and only by going with it could they ever hope to bring judgment and reason to the surface again. No ruler in the world can or ever has been able to stop an uprising of his people when the latter felt they had right on their side or had been downtrodden or oppressed. Their Celestial Majesties were obliged to wait until the popular fury had somewhat abated before they could even attempt it. No sane person could believe that the Empress Dowager, with her natural intelligence and after thirty years of government and knowledge of foreign methods, did not know that this attack on the foreign representatives by the Chinese people would bring on severe reprisals. But she was powerless to do more than she did at the time. Their Majesties could not go against the people in their maddened state of mind. They hoped by joining the Imperial forces to the wild insurgents that these seething masses might be brought to reason. The mob was given a semblance of right by a declaration of war on the part of the government after the forts of Taku were taken by the foreign war-ships (which was really the first act of war of this unfortunate episode).

With the Empress Dowager

When I saw the position of the Legation quarter and especially that of the British Legation, where all the foreigners finally congregated—open to attack on every side, lying under the very walls of the Palace and the Imperial City—I felt convinced that had there not been some restraining force within their own ranks, the Chinese could have wiped out the foreigners in less than a week. Bad firing on their part could only have averted, for a short space, the inevitable result to the Legations. Had there not been some power that was acting as a check upon the Chinese, no European would have been left to tell the tale; and this restraining force I feel confident came from the Emperor and the Empress Dowager themselves.

The Empress Dowager (with the Emperor) was at the Summer Palace, as usual, during the summer of 1900. Though urged by her ministers and the Princes to remain there, where she was out of danger or could easily escape at its approach, she insisted on returning to the Capital and went into the Winter Palace a week before the Allies reached the city. She hoped as a " dernier resort " that the presence of the Sacred Persons, Their Majesties, in the city might serve as a check upon the soldiers and people, now maddened by their own fury; for the Imperial troops, instead of checking the insurgents and leavening the masses by their right and reason, had, instead, become imbued with the same spirit as the Boxers themselves ! But the Empress Dowager, on this occasion, counted too strongly on her popularity and upon the respect that the people felt for

266

the "Sacred Persons," for even after their return to the Capital, even Their Majesties' presence—even the issuing of Imperial edicts posted all over the city for the people to protect, or at least cease their attacks on the Legations—were powerless to do more than intermittently check the attacks.

Finally the Allies reached and entered the city! The Empress Dowager, discouraged and finding herself powerless, finally succumbed to the fears of her entourage for her Person. She, herself, became almost panic-stricken at the thought of falling into the hands of the foreigners, whose depredations and cruelty to the Chinese on that memorable march from Tientsin had all been reported to her with the usual exaggerations. Her indomitable spirit was broken. She consented, in an agony of womanly fear, to fly. She was disguised as a common woman, her long finger nails, which would have revealed her exalted rank, were cut off, and, in a common cart, she made her escape from the city. As she had refused to go until the last moment, everything at the Palace was left in the wildest confusion. Neither her jewelry, nor hardly sufficient clothing, was taken. She did not leave the Palace until several hours after the foreign troops had passed the Water Gate and were already within the walls of the English Legation. She had held out as long as possible.

The memorable flight to Singan Fu began that night. The Court was accompanied by a regiment of Imperial troops, but such was their demoralized condition, so many Boxers were among the soldiers, that rank insubordination prevailed. Neither the officers, nor even the presence in their midst of the Sacred Persons, served as any check upon the soldiers. The greatest confusion prevailed. The maddest of the insurgents had begun to look forward to retribution and to realize that punishment would be inevitably visited upon them either by the foreigners or by the Chinese Government when things calmed down, and this thought seemed but to madden them further.

As the flight led the Imperial party through the section of country where the society of Boxers had the greatest number of adherents, the people, in many instances, refused food and shelter to the Imperial fugitives. They felt the Court had been against them and for the foreigners. Prince Su, in his account of the journey to Singan Fu, relates that neither Her Majesty nor the Emperor had enough to eat; that the soldiers stole the food that was prepared for Their Majesties. I heard at the Palace that it was only His Majesty who suffered the pangs of hunger. He, as well as all in the great company that formed the Court party, deprived himself rather than see the Empress Dowager suffer. I heard Her Majesty say that the Emperor's food was stolen, and she did not know for several days that he was depriving himself for her. She thought all the Imperial party had her own, meager enough allowance.

The Empress Dowager saw and heard many new and strange things on that memorable journey, but she bore it all bravely. After the first panic of fear, her indomitable spirit resumed its natural poise. Her capacity for seeing the humorous side of things also helped her to bear it, and furnished her with a fund

of witty anecdotes later, though she once remarked
that, at the time, she did not appreciate the humorous
side to its full extent. Their experiences at this time
were often the theme of conversation among the Ladies
at the Palace. While I was there they were constantly
referred to by the Princesses and even by the eunuchs
of the Court. These pampered individuals had then
their first experience with the hardships of the outer
world, though, to do them justice, they rarely referred
to their own hardships, which must have been severe,
only speaking of what Their Majesties and the Ladies
had to endure. This flight from Peking to Singan Fu
marks an epoch in the Palace. Everything is dated
as before or after that time. After Her Majesty had
accomplished this perilous journey and borne it so
bravely, she was given a new title, a dearer, higher one.
She was called Lao-Tzu-Tzung (the Great Ancestress)
by her enthusiastic admirers.

[1] Since the above was in type I find the following in F. Laur's
" Siège de Péking." In speaking of the cause of the Boxer rising, he
quotes Dr. Matignon as saying:

" C'est l'Europe tout entière qu'il faut mettre en cause. C'est parce
qu'elle n'a pas compris les Chinois, c'est parce qu'elle a cru que ce
peuple doux, somnolent, passif, pouvait, sans regimber, accepter toutes
les innovations, toutes les humiliations, que l'Europe s'est laissée en-
trainer, et par ses missionnaires, et par ses ingénieurs. . . .

" Voilà pourquoi le mouvement Boxeur s'est produit. Ce mouvement, c'est l'éveil du patriotisme chinois, avec toute l'intransigeance
d'un *nationalisme* aveugle, ignorant, mais légitime."

CHAPTER XXXI

THE EMPRESS DOWAGER'S CHARITIES, SENSE OF JUSTICE, EXTRAVAGANCE, AND PERSONAL CHARACTERISTICS.

THE Empress Dowager's charities are extensive; she feeds the poor and succors the unfortunate. When her sympathies are aroused, she gives freely and generously. Her edicts are constantly ordering sacks of rice and food to be distributed among the poor and sent to districts where famine reigns. There is a great refuge in Peking, which she supports, where ten thousand poor are succored and fed during the year. During the winter, edicts are constantly appearing similar to this—commanding "The distribution from the Imperial granaries of fifteen hundred piculs (133⅓ pounds to the picul) of rice for refuges and gruel stations for the poor in North Tung Chow." Edict of November 6, 1904.

She also sympathizes with misfortune, tries to right the wrongs she knows of, and correct the abuses that come to her ears. From the "North China Herald" of November 19, 1904, I copy the following, and this paper cannot be accused of viewing any of Her Majesty's acts with a partial spirit (much to the contrary):

"During the Boxer troubles a bad character, by the name of Wang, owed money to a certain Chinese Mohammedan. Wang

270

had been frequently dunned, and was finally condemned by the courts to pay the debt; he was, besides, ordered to be beaten, as he had been insolent to the Mandarin trying the case. This incensed Wang, and he swore vengeance. When the Boxer troubles were in full swing in Peking, he became the leader of a band of insurgents and led his band to the house of the Mohammedan whom he had been forced by the courts to pay. Wang and his band massacred not only his old enemy, but eleven members of his family; leaving only a young daughter-in-law who had hidden in a loft and saw the whole tragedy; she also saw them march off, carrying, on spears, the heads of the old man and four of his sons.

"The poor daughter-in-law escaped from Peking soon after, and was not able to return there until a few months since, in 1904. She discovered the dwelling of the murderer of her husband's family, and had a petition drawn up on the subject.

"One day when Her Majesty was proceeding from one Palace to another, the young widow threw herself before the Empress Dowager's cortège. Her Majesty saw the prostrate girl (only nineteen years of age), and commanded her guards to ask what she wanted. The girl, dressed in deep mourning, held above her head her petition, calling for justice against her husband's murderers. Her Majesty read the petition, and her brow became black as night. She called to a eunuch in her train and commanded him to take the young petitioner and her petition to the 'Board of Punishments,' and deliver the Imperial Commands that no time be lost in arresting the murderers; that they should be tried, and the result reported to Her Majesty. This was done, and on the first of November, 1904, the chief murderer Wang, his two sons and a nephew were decapitated to expiate their cruel crimes."

The Empress Dowager is said to be recklessly extravagant in her own habits as well as in the management of Palace affairs. As for extravagance in the Palace, bad management doubtless exists, and extravagance does prevail. Abuses always creep in where the management of great establishments is intrusted to money-seeking officials, and to eunuchs, as is the case in·the Palace at Peking.

Extravagance in the Palace has been the theme of Chinese economists for many generations, for hundreds of years before the Manchu Dynasty came to the Throne. Several of the Emperors have themselves attempted to stem this extravagance by personal efforts and private economy, but to no avail. It is related of one Emperor that the sleeve of his State robe being a little worn, he called up his Master of the Household to ask what a new robe would cost. He found that it would cost three thousand taels, and as only the right sleeve of this gown was worn (as he used his arm a great deal in writing), he decided, in order that he might himself show a good example, and inaugurate economy, to have a new sleeve made, instead of ordering an entire gown. He gave his commands, in consequence, and the gown was taken out of the Palace and remained several months. When it was returned, what was His Majesty's astonishment and chagrin to find that the cost of the new sleeve had exceeded that of a new gown!

In his walks outside of the Palace, another Emperor bought an article of food for a few pence. The next time he had it in the Palace he asked what the dish cost and was told it was "four taels." When he remonstrated, saying what he had paid for it outside of the Palace, his Master of the Household told him it was impossible to have it "inside" the Palace or on His Majesty's table at any less than the sum of four taels. If His Majesty wished it for a few pence, His Majesty might buy it outside the Palace and bring

Her Extravagance

it in himself for that sum, but no one else could bring it inside for the price it could be bought outside, as it had to go through so many official hands before it reached His Majesty's table, that it actually cost the sum of four taels.

After several efforts of this kind at reducing the Palace expenses, even these wise and economical Emperors were obliged to give it up. If these Emperors of ancient times, when the Palace was conducted on more simple lines than it is to-day, were powerless to check extravagance in the Imperial household, how much more difficult must it be to do so now that the system has become petrified with age—especially for the Empress Dowager, who can never go outside and see things for herself! It is said that each egg at Their Majesties' table costs three taels, but Palace reform, necessary as it is, must come from without, from the officials, and no private effort of Their Majesties can change things.

As for the Empress Dowager's personal extravagance, aside from present-giving, I saw no evidence of it. Her wardrobe, in point of actual cost, aside from her jewels, would not be superior in price to that of the wives of some of our American millionaires; for the styles do not change in China, and furs and embroideries are handed down from generation to generation. Her jewels, even, are not more gorgeous or more numerous, though they are more unique, than those of any of the European sovereigns. She has an immense number of pearls—for the pearl is her favorite precious stone, besides being the jewel of the Dynasty—but she has no diamonds, no emeralds, and very few European

273

precious stones. She has a quantity of fine jade jewels, but these, as well as pearls, are cheaper in China than elsewhere.

I saw several incidents which seemed to point rather to personal economy on Her Majesty's part than to extravagance. While I was painting one of the portraits, she decided that the trimming on the gown must be changed. She had bolts of different kinds of ribbon brought in to select from and finally decided upon a certain piece. She called a maid to sew some around the neck. When I wanted to have this piece cut off, so that some might be sewed around the hem where it was also visible, she said the ribbon had better not be cut, for it was a " handsome piece," and, if cut, it might spoil it for use in " trimming another gown." These pieces of ribbon and embroidery come in lengths for one dress only. One day when she was drinking some fruit juice, her hand slipped on the polished jade bowl and some of it fell upon the front of her jacket. She was most annoyed, and after several ineffectual attempts of her own and the attendants to remove the spot, she said she had heard that the foreigners had some wonderful processes of cleaning and she must have them investigated, for it was too bad to have a thing spoiled by an accident of that kind when a good garment was rendered useless for any one !

She had the good of China at heart and was really a patriot; in fact, I observed more patriotism, more National pride among the people I saw at Court, than I ever noticed elsewhere in China. I feel convinced the Empress Dowager has strong National feeling and really loves her country, and is as patriotic a Chinese as there is in China. When there were internal troubles, or exterior complications, she seemed to be really worried and to grieve, as if it were a personal thing. She made mistakes, of course, and grave ones, but when it is remembered that her knowledge of what takes place " outside," comes entirely from the reports made to her, that she has no opportunity of seeing things for herself, it seems wonderful she does not make more.

Last winter a new scheme of taxation, by which the revenue would be largely increased and which taxation would be scarcely felt by the people, was presented to Their Majesties for consideration. Her Majesty soon grasped the entire scope of the scheme and thought it good and feasible; but though the payment of the foreign indemnity made it imperative to increase the revenue by every means possible, she hesitated over the inauguration of this new scheme, fearing it might give the officials a new opportunity to oppress the common people, for it is not the laws that oppress the people in China. This is done by the officials who enforce them. She evidently realized this power that the officials have of " squeezing " the people, and she wished to be assured of the manner in which this taxation would be enforced before she gave her consent to the scheme. At the first presentation to her of this plan of taxation, she repeated several times, " I fear it may harass the people; we cannot harass the people; they have enough burdens to bear." She was not so particular about not harassing the Officials, for they were called upon all over China to make great contributions to the Imperial Treasury for the purpose of assisting in paying the foreign indemnity.

Notwithstanding her penetration of character, her naturally good judgment, she made mistakes in her appreciation of those who surrounded her; but this was not strange, for she had almost no opportunity of seeing them in their true light. She was a good physiognomist, but one cannot always trust to physiognomy. She was in the habit of giving all who surrounded her a certain amount of latitude, until they came to rely on her favor and revealed themselves in their true light to her. Then she would quickly suppress them or cast them aside. This often seemed cruel and heartless. She sometimes would take another's estimate of a character which she had favorably judged, for, of course, there is a great deal of jealousy and intrigue among her entourage, and she was influenced by reports that she heard; for she was obliged, in order to form an opinion, to listen to the gossip of the Palace. Her own penetration, however, would generally come to her aid and, in the end, her judgment would right itself.

She had strong prejudices, and often allowed herself to be deceived by the favorites to whom she had given her confidence. After several preliminary trials of their character, and when she thought she had arrived at a proper estimate of it, she was an easy victim. These favorites could then act with impunity, and she was sometimes made the dupe of their schemes. Thus Ministers, courtiers, friends, and attendants, who had once thoroughly established their positions with her, could often get the advantage of her and impose upon her natural acumen.

She could be most sarcastic, sometimes cruelly so, but I generally found there was some reason for her sarcasm. She was very impulsive and had her share of temper, but there was never any unladylike display of it. When she was angry her voice was never raised; it simply lost its silvery sweetness and took the quality of some ordinary metal, and she was always quiet and well-bred.

From what I saw of the Empress Dowager, it seemed to me she would not brook interference in the accomplishment of a design she had set her heart upon— that she would not hesitate even at crushing an individual who stood in the way of the realization of some plan she had fixed upon. But her judgment was so good, she did not decide upon a thing unless she felt it was absolutely imperative to carry it out.

As for tact and social savoir, she is remarkable. I never knew any one to possess these qualities to a greater degree. At her first Audience to foreigners, Sir Claude MacDonald, in reporting it, spoke of the Empress Dowager as "a kind and courteous hostess, who displayed both the tact and softness of a womanly disposition." Lady Susan Townley says of her: "Where has she learned the ease and dignity with which she receives her European guests?" These opinions of her social tact, so far as I could learn, are held by all the members of the Foreign Legations in Peking.

When the young Prince Adalbert of Prussia was received in special Audience by Their Majesties, on his visit to Peking, he was accompanied not only by the

With the Empress Dowager

German Minister and his staff, but by a number of officers as his personal escort. This made an unusually large number of presentations necessary. I have been told that at the Audiences of the Diplomatic Corps, where only gentlemen were present, the Empress Dowager had a sort of shyness and did not show the same ease of manner as when she received the ladies. But at this Audience of the young Prince she became interested in talking with him, and I heard one of the gentlemen who was present say it was the first time he had seen Her Majesty thoroughly at ease at one of the Audiences to the Diplomatic Corps, and that on that day she was perfectly charming, seeming to take the liveliest interest in questioning the young Prince and conversing with him in a motherly way, and that he then realized to its full extent her wonderful charm and her great social instinct.

I have heard it said that the Empress Dowager puts all this charm on for these occasions; that she is a consummate actress, but during the whole time I was in the Palace I never saw her other than the charming hostess, considerate of the comfort of those who surround her and readily sympathizing with sorrow, and I have seen her under all circumstances, at Audiences and in private, in anxiety and sorrow and in joy. She was too great a lover of Nature in all its phases to be cruel and heartless, and I am convinced she is really genuinely kind. She apparently greatly admired intelligence, and goodness always seemed to appeal to her. She was ever a fascinating study, and her magnetic personality full of charm. I found her thoroughly human and perfectly womanly.

CHAPTER XXXII

THE CHINESE NEW YEAR—OFFICIAL AUDIENCE

THE Chinese New Year, the greatest of the popular festivals, is, of course, celebrated with much pomp and enthusiasm at the Palace. Splendid decorations, hundreds of beautiful horn lanterns, with their long, red silk tassels, the great red "Sho" emblazoned on their sides, made the courts and verandahs gay with color. Painted figures of red-clothed gods regarded one at every turn. Hideous monsters with vermilion faces, painted on the outside doors, brandished spears to frighten away the bad spirits. There were the usual gala representations at the Theater ; and the Palace, as at all festivals, was filled with visitors.

The Chinese pay all their debts at the New Year. If they have not the ready money to do so, they will dispose of anything valuable they have, in order to begin the New Year free from debt. It is considered tempting Heaven to begin it otherwise. A great deal of silver imitation money is exchanged at this season. This is an old custom and supposed to bring abundance during the year. At the New Year, present-giving reaches its culminating point in China. Every one, rich and poor, high and low, gives presents then.

Their Majesties not only gave to all the Ladies and

279

With the Empress Dowager

Princesses, but to every inmate of the Palace, and even the beggar at the gate was not forgotten; but the presents exchanged at the New Year are never so handsome as those given for a birthday. The presents the Empress Dowager received on this occasion were principally flowers (her Throne-room was full of them, as well as her private apartments)—dwarf fruit-trees twisted into fantastic shapes, laden with fragrant blossoms and splendid plants of peonies in full flower, and countless vases of the Chinese Lily, as they call the Narcissus in China. The Empress Dowager tried to be cheerful and not dampen the gaiety of the Festival by her alarm, but the long-looked-for and much-dreaded war between Russia and Japan had then actually begun, and she was mortally anxious! The Japanese were already in Manchuria, and no one knew how it might affect China!

Though I did not work on the portrait during the New-Year's festivities, it was now really advancing. When Her Majesty saw how the hands looked when they were drawn in, with the palms of the hands hidden by the long fur undersleeves, in the position I had dared to find fault with at the first sitting, she at once suggested having the fur undersleeves taken off, but she still said nothing about changing the position of the hands, though I saw she had her doubts about them, and I felt confident her good taste would finally prevail and she would want them changed. I painted them in with a thin wash of color, knowing they would be changed later. A few days after this, she remarked that my "idea about the position of the hands was not bad," and suggested that the left hand "would look well on a

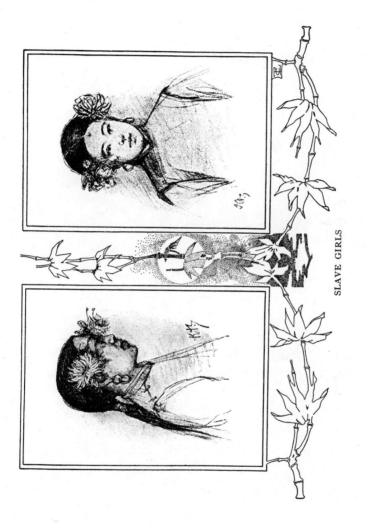

SLAVE GIRLS

cushion." I made this change in the small study, much to her satisfaction, and then did the hands likewise in the large portrait.

The New-Year festivities were hardly over before the Empress Dowager decided to move the Court to the Sea Palace. This Palace, though not so much a favorite with her as the Summer Palace, she liked better than the Winter Palace; the latter's small, shut-in courts, walled-in walks, and rigid traditions seemed to depress her. At the Sea Palace she had gardens for her promenades and there was a lake. It was not so beautiful as the Summer Palace, but was an improvement over the Winter Palace.

This move to the Sea Palace necessitated another change of studio for me, just as I was comfortably installed in my quarters in the Winter Palace, and had begun to progress with my work. I knew I should be obliged to have the new place arranged with upper glass windows and that I would again lose time, and the date of the opening of the St. Louis Exposition was approaching! But there was no help for it; I must go with the Court to the Sea Palace. I was told that there I was to have a magnificent pavilion on the lake, with a perfect light for painting. As to the pavilion's being magnificent, I had no doubt, but I did doubt, from past experiences, whether the light would be all that could be desired.

One morning our chairs carried us to the Sea Palace instead of to the Winter Palace. All my painting-things, materials, canvases, as well as Her Majesty's Throne, on which she was seated for the portrait, had been moved. Not the smallest piece of paper, nor even a bit of charcoal was missing. I had painted until the last moment at the Winter Palace, the day before; and early the next morning my things were in perfect order—the portrait on the easel, and the Throne in the proper position in my quarters at the Sea Palace. It was an "Aladdin's-Lamp" move.

The group of buildings that had been set aside for my painting fronted on the lake, and were really charming, but the overhanging verandahs to each pavilion forced me again to have the upper windows put in. After this was accomplished, it was the best working-room I had ever had at any of the Palaces. The days were getting longer and the light better, and I hoped now to soon finish the portrait.

A few days after the Court moved to the Sea Palace, the members of the Corps Diplomatique were received in Audience to present their congratulations to the Emperor and Empress Dowager on the occasion of the Chinese New Year. They were received in the Great Audience Hall; but the ladies of the Legation, whose reception took place the following day, were received in Her Majesty's Throne-room opening on the Court of the large Theater at the Sea Palace. As it was cold, the Theater and its court were entirely inclosed and roofed over in glass, in panes of about a foot and a half square. On each pane was painted, in red, the ever-present character "Sho" (longevity), surrounded by five bats. The marble pavement of the court and the steps leading up to the Throne-room were carpeted in red; and when the great doors were thrown wide, there was a good effect of size given, although this Throne-room was one of the smallest in the Sea Palace.

As this was to be a formal reception, several members of the Wai-Wu-Pu were present as interpreters. The ladies of the Legation were presented by the Baron Czikan, the Austrian Minister, Doyen of the Corps. He made a graceful address in French, wishing Their Majesties a Happy New Year, and China much prosperity. This was translated into Chinese by one of the Secretaries of the Wai-Wu-Pu. The Empress Dowager replied for herself and the Emperor, in Chinese. Her Majesty's words were interpreted by His Excellency Liang Fang, a good French scholar. Then the Doyen presented the ladies individually, and the usual order of ceremonies followed. When the presentations were over, the Doyen, foreign attachés and interpreters, with the Chinese officials, repaired to the hall which had been set aside for their luncheon, while the ladies, accompanied by the Princesses, went to their repast in another part of the Palace!

Only a few days after this, came the lantern festival; but this was not an interruption to my work, for I painted all day, and only went to the Theater for the final piece and the spectacular tableau. We dined in the Imperial loge, and after dinner there were beautiful lantern and torch-light processions. In the court opposite the Throne-room where we dined, there was a beautiful pai-lou of transparent gauze, painted in charming designs, illuminated from within, and hung with luminous flowers and quaint lanterns. Tall eunuchs, in gala red, stood around the courts, holding great lanterns aloft, like huge caryatides with luminous burdens. Others with fanciful vermilion lanterns wound in and out through corridors and courts. When they reached the court of the softly glowing pai-lou, they manœuvered and made intricate designs and luminous tableaux, holding aloft their red-globed lanterns to form characters and phrases of "felicitous omen." These huge, luminous characters were wonderfully accurate.

After the torch- and lantern-lit processions, and the glowing tableaux, a pair of illuminated dragons writhed into the court and struggled for the "flaming pearl," which flitted around with elusive fantastic movements, ever beyond their grasp. I was not able to find out the origin of the Imperial legend of the Double Dragon and the Flaming Pearl, representations of which appear everywhere at the Palace on whatever is meant for Imperial use, or for any official function over which the Emperor is supposed to preside. It is on all the Thrones of the Dynasty; it adorns the Imperial pennant; it is cut into stone, carved into wood, and painted in pictures. It decorates the gowns of the higher officials, and is embroidered upon the Court dresses of the Ladies of the Palace. At the Birthdays of the Emperor and Empress, and at all Dynastic celebrations there are realistic representations of the immortal struggle where the Double Dragon strives to absorb the "flaming pearl." The significance of the legend seems to be: The Double Dragon represents the Powers of Earth or Evil which try ever to absorb the Flaming Pearl, Emblem of the Dynasty, symbol of Heaven or Perfection. The Flaming Pearl, the Unattainable, keeps ever beyond and above their grasp, seeming to serve always as an incentive for further effort.

For a fortnight after the lantern festival, there were fireworks every night on the banks of the lake. We would dine in the Throne-room, and then Her Majesty and the Emperor, accompanied by the Ladies, and attended by the usual number of eunuchs (each bearing transparent horn lanterns), would go through the courts and paths of the garden to the lake, on the banks of which the fireworks were sent up. Here, in full view of the set pieces, stood four large, roomy sleds. When the lake was frozen, these sleds were used to push Their Majesties and the ladies over its glassy surface. They had not been used as sleds this winter, for the ice had not been sufficiently firm, the winter having been comparatively mild. But when the lake was well frozen, as is usual at this season in Peking, Their Majesties viewed the fireworks from these sleds as they skimmed along over its smooth surface. There was a sled for each of them—one for the Empress and second wife, and one for the Princesses. They were cloth-covered, lined with fur, and had great fur rugs. There were seats around the three sides; the wadded curtain, with its large square of plate glass that hung down over the front, was taken off for the fireworks. Their Majesties occupied each of theirs alone, but the Empress had several of the Ladies in hers.

The fireworks were superb. There were beautiful set pieces, pagodas, with ladies on balconies, pavilions with grapevines, wistaria arbors, and beds of flowers so lifelike they seemed to grow at the side of the luminous cascades, and many other effects I had never seen before in fireworks. One day, during the time of the lantern festival, we had fireworks in the brilliant sunshine. When these day rockets exploded, all sorts of curious paper devices fell to the ground—fish dragons and animals, as well as flags and baskets. When anything interesting was revealed, Her Majesty would send the eunuchs to pick it up as it fell and bring it to her that she might examine it. Many fell outside the Palace walls, and she said these would give pleasure to the "poor people outside."

Formerly, at these fireworks in the Palace to celebrate the lantern festival, the public was admitted into the Inclosure, but this practice stopped when the two Empresses were Co-Regents for the first boy Emperor, Tung-Chih. As this was coincident with the establishment of the first Foreign Legations in Peking, the latter fact may have had some influence in changing the custom. The Chinese people were shut out because it was feared that the foreigners might also come into the Precincts. These beautiful fireworks I could enjoy without any qualms of conscience, for I could not paint at night, and they were consequently no interruption to my work.

CHAPTER XXXIII

CONTINUATION OF THE ST. LOUIS PORTRAIT—SPRING
DAYS AT THE SEA PALACE

THERE began now to be some discussion as to
what would be the most propitious date for finishing the portrait. I had thought I might finish
when I could, but this was not to be the case. The
almanacs were consulted, and it was decided that
the nineteenth day of April would be an auspicious time to finish and before four o'clock! The
Empress Dowager informed me of the "happy
augury" of this date and asked me if I thought it
possible to finish then. Not only had the date for
beginning the portrait been carefully chosen, but
there was much deliberation as to the proper time for
finishing! Her Majesty seemed very anxious until
she received my reply as to whether it would be possible to finish at this happy date, for I could not say
at first, as I had never thought of finishing at any
particular moment! When I finally told her I could
finish it before four o'clock, April 19th, she was delighted. She said "How good" and asked me to
please "not disappoint her." As the portrait neared
completion she came very often to the studio and
watched over the painting-in of all the accessories,
which she seemed to consider quite as important as

287

the likeness itself. As she was tired after the Audiences, she gave me two or three sittings at this time before she went to the Audience Hall, and I painted from half-past six to eight A.M. for two or three days. The jewels in the head-dress, all official, were the subject of much deliberation. After a jewel was painted in, she would decide she did n't like it and that something else would be better. She seemed to think it was as easy to take it from the picture as to remove it from her person. All these requests for changes were so graciously made, I never complained. She would sometimes say, "I am giving you a great deal of trouble, and you are very kind." I did n't mind the trouble, only these changes took away the freshness of the painting and did not add to the artistic effect of the picture.

Her Majesty ordered a magnificent frame for the portrait. She, herself, made the design. The Double Dragon at the top struggled for the "flaming pearl" with the character "Sho" on it. The sides were elaborately carved in designs representing the symbol of "ten thousand" years with the characters for longevity. The frame was to be set in a superbly carved stand, as the Chinese do their mirrors. The whole, of rare camphor-wood, was made by Her Majesty's own artisans at the Palace—the most expert workmen in China.

The days were lengthening now, the trees beginning to bud and the flowers in the courts to bloom. The icy fetters that had locked the lake were broken; the boats again glided over its bosom. In the mornings we no longer had to take the winter "chairs" and be carried the long distance from the gates to the Throne-room. The comfortable boats once more lay moored at the foot of the landing-steps, just within the gates, and we enjoyed again those ideal trips across the lake.

The Empress Dowager began to take long promenades now and was much out-of-doors. Sometimes in the mornings, on our arrival, she would already be in the gardens. One day we met her on the banks of the lake and made our morning salutations there. Another day, she and the Emperor were inspecting the new buildings which were being erected to replace those burned during the occupation of Peking by the Allies, when Count von Waldersee had his headquarters in the Sea Palace. Splendid buildings were being erected on the site of those burned. The Emperor and Empress Dowager, each with his own suite, carefully visited every part of these new constructions and seemed much interested in their progress. Of course, the workmen were banished during the visit of Their Majesties. One of these new halls was to be used for the entertainment of foreigners, when they are invited to the Palace, and many concessions had been made to foreign ideas in its construction. Let us hope it may not lose its Chinese character! I am sure the foreigners will regret this innovation and would prefer the typical Chinese interior, even though it be less suited to the exigencies of a modern reception.

Sometimes we would see the Empress Dowager in her Japanese "jinricksha." This was a beautiful, gold-lacquered affair in dragon form, the two dragons' heads in front. It had splendid gold-lacquered shafts and wheels—the latter with rubber tires. It was pulled by one eunuch and pushed by another, and Her Majesty seemed greatly to enjoy this novelty for a while, but she said she preferred to walk or to be carried in her open chair, as a usual thing.

Two other modern and novel methods of locomotion had been installed in the grounds of the Sea Palace. There was a small railway, which ran from the outer gates to the dwelling Palaces, which had its engine and complete running outfit. This had been constructed by some progressive Mandarins, who wished to get the Empress Dowager's support for some railway scheme, but though she often spoke of how much she had enjoyed her one trip on a real railway, her spirit was too utilitarian to care for toy pleasures. She could n't stand the puffing of the engine, the tiny cars, and all this trouble for so short and useless a jaunt.

There was also in the Sea Palace, as well as at the Summer Palace, a number of automobiles, which had been presented to Their Majesties by Chinese nobles and officials who had been abroad, as examples of the curiosities of European civilization. One of these was gorgeously fitted up in the Imperial yellow and gold lacquer, with the Double Dragon. The body was inclosed in glass and there was a throne-like seat within for the Empress Dowager. The question of how the chauffeur should run the machine standing, as he would be obliged to do if Her Majesty were inside, had not then been solved. She was, however, willing to throw tradition to the winds in this instance, and was most anxious to try one of these motor-cars. Her entourage was, however, bitterly opposed to it, even for

Spring Days at the Sea Palace

a short distance in the grounds. They were afraid of an accident. She never tried one while I was there, but I am confident that her venturesome spirit will not rest content until she has had a ride in one of these modern carriages.

In April, kite-flying time begins in China. High Officials and dignified literati indulge in the pastime as well as children and young people. The popular pastimes of the people, as well as their serious occupations, being always honored in the Palace, kites were, of course, sent off by the Empress Dowager and the Ladies. The first day the kites were to be flown Her Majesty sent for me to come into the garden, where the kite-flying was to take place. The kites were of paper, wonderfully fashioned, representing birds, fish, bats, and even personages. The strings were wound on curiously shaped reels and the cleverness with which Her Majesty let out the string and manipulated the kites was wonderful. After she had let one go, she graciously handed me her own reel and told me she would teach me to fly a kite. I was hard at work at my painting when I was called out into the garden and I wished to return to it as soon as possible; and as I knew I would not be very clever at kite-flying, I begged her to allow me to watch her instead. The young Empress and Princesses were also very proficient in flying them, and Her Majesty flew hers as she did everything else, with unusual grace.

One of these beautiful spring mornings as we were softly gliding across the lake, propelled by the graceful Palace boatmen, I lay back on my cushions reveling in the scene of quiet loveliness before me and drinking in the ineffable perfume of the spring, when my glance, roaming lazily around in perfect content, caught sight of a group of gentlemen on the bank of the lake beyond. The rays of the morning sun, glinting upon the gold of their embroidered costumes and touching, with iridescent rays, the peacock's feathers upon their hats, revealed their rank and official standing.

As it was a most unusual thing to see gentlemen in the Palace Inclosure, I was at once all attention, knowing there must be some important event on hand, especially as, on looking closer, I saw one small figure in their midst more plainly dressed than the others, whom I at once recognized as His Majesty the Emperor. As we slowly approached I saw the Emperor go over to a plow to which was hitched an ox, and which stood at a little distance off in the field. Fortune favored me! I was to see the Emperor plow the first furrow of the year! For it was only on the morrow that the official public ceremony was to take place at the Temple of Agriculture, near the great triple altar of Heaven. I was to see the private plowing, done in the Palace grounds and viewed only by the Princes of the Imperial Family and the highest Manchu nobles.

When all was ready the Emperor took the handles of the plow and guided it down a furrow marked off the ground, and when the furrow was upturned, the seed was dropped in. The ox for this ceremony, which I had heard was white, was (at the Palace function) of a soft doe color. He seemed to have been trained for the purpose and performed his part with a dignity in

Spring Days at the Sea Palace

harmony with the attitude of all the assistants and in keeping with the solemnity of the occasion.

I was rejoiced to have an opportunity of seeing this interesting ceremony and to learn that even this great rite, which I had thought, like the sacrifice to the Invisible Deity on the triple altar, was only performed in the grounds of the Temple to Heaven; and to learn that every custom dear to the people, or incorporated in the National life, is observed in the Palace by the Emperor and Empress—that His Majesty really plants the first furrow of the year and gathers the first sheaves of ripened wheat, and that the Ladies of the Palace really spin the first silk and pull the first fruits.

The slow movement of the Palace boats was never so appreciated by me as on this morning, for I was thus enabled to see well this curious National ceremony, which I would never have seen but for the accident of the hour of my crossing the lake and the time it took to do so; for, as at all ceremonies where men are present, there were, of course, no members of Her Majesty's entourage, and none of the Ladies or Princesses had ever seen this ceremony!

CHAPTER XXXIV

FINISHING AND SENDING OFF THE PORTRAIT

THE nineteenth day of April was approaching, and the portrait steadily advancing. As it neared completion Her Majesty's interest in it seemed to grow. She spent a great deal of time in my pavilion watching its progress, and expressed herself as much delighted with it. A few days before the nineteenth, I asked Her Majesty to allow Mrs. Conger to come and see it on that day. She immediately consented, and invitations were sent through the Foreign Office, not only to Mrs. Conger, but to the wives of the Ministers and First Secretaries of Legations to come to the Palace on the nineteenth day of April, for the purpose of "seeing the portrait of Her Imperial Majesty, the Empress Dowager, painted by the American artist."

The ladies of the Legation, of course, responded to the invitation, and on the morning of the nineteenth the portrait was placed in the splendid frame. Her Majesty decided she would receive the ladies first in her Throne-room, after which they were to come to my studio to see the portrait. As I was still working until the "fateful hour," I did not go up to the Throne-room but awaited the ladies in my own place. Her

Finishing and Sending the Portrait

Majesty did not accompany the ladies when they came
to see the portrait, but she sent the young Empress
and Princesses to my pavilion to assist me in receiving and to lend a proper dignity to the occasion. The
portrait, in a Chinese milieu, and seen in the light in
which it was painted, made a better effect than it
could in any other surroundings. The ladies were, of
course, much interested in seeing this long-talked-of
picture—the first ever painted of Her Majesty—and
the novelty of the precedent, as well as the interest of a
visit to the Palace, favorably predisposed them, and
they expressed themselves as most interested in the
work, finding it a good likeness. The admiration it
received from the young Empress and the Ladies of
the Court was almost embarrassing, and the eunuchs
said it was so lifelike when they passed the windows
that it inspired the same awe Her Majesty's own
presence did.

After the ladies had duly looked at and commented
upon the portrait, they repaired to one of the halls in
connection with my studio, where a repast had been
prepared by the orders of Her Majesty. Here, for the
first and only time, while I was in the Palace, the
young Empress sat down at the table with the foreign
ladies, and acted as hostess, and very gracefully she
filled her rôle.

After the visit of the ladies of the Legation, Her
Majesty informed me that the Princes and nobles,
whose rank entitled them to enter the Palace Inclosure, were to come to see it the following day. As
it would not have been " according to the Proprieties "
for gentlemen to enter the quarters reserved for ladies,

or the buildings where even a foreign lady worked, the portrait was, for their visit, carried out into the open court of my pavilion.

To place the portrait in its carved pedestal, it was necessary to erect a scaffolding by which the framed picture was raised into the air, and then lowered into its stand. When all was finally arranged, the scaffolding was removed, the debris cleared away, and the Princes and nobles, in full dress, came into the court to see the portrait. Each one approached the picture and closely examined it, even touching the canvas. Unfortunately, I could not hear their comments, as I only saw the ceremony discreetly ensconced behind a curtain, but I could watch their faces and study their expressions, though I must confess that they revealed very little.

A young Manchu, who had been attached to a Legation abroad and had learned photography in an amateur way, had been ordered by Her Majesty to make a photograph of the portrait. This was done while the Princes and nobles were still in the court. When it was photographed, and the Princes had retired, the scaffolding was again put up, the picture was raised out of its carved wood pedestal and was replaced in my studio. All this took the greater part of the day.

Her Majesty was so pleased with the comments she heard upon the portrait (of course no unfavorable ones were made to her), that she decided to accede to the prayers of several of the high officials, and allow the Sacred Picture to be viewed by a number of other high functionaries. For this purpose, the portrait was removed to the Wai-Wu-Pu (Foreign Office); for many of the highest Officials are not permitted to enter the Palace Inclosure.

At the Foreign Office, not only the high Chinese Officials, but the foreign Ministers and their staffs were invited to see it. Many of the foreigners went in full-dress uniform for this visit, in deference to Chinese prejudices. After it had been duly viewed by all in Peking of sufficient rank to have that honor, it was inclosed in a satin-lined camphor-wood box, covered with satin of Imperial yellow, and the box was closed with great solemnity. The pedestal was placed in a similar box. Each had splendid bronze handles and huge circular locks. These boxes were inclosed in others, also lined with the Imperial color, and were finally ready for shipment. The packing-cases, containing the framed picture and its carved pedestal, were placed upon a flat freight car, which had been elaborately decorated with red and yellow festoons of silk. The boxes were covered with yellow cloth, painted with the Double Dragon. A special railway had been laid from the Wai-Wu-Pu to the station outside the Chien-Men, for it was not considered fitting that ordinary bearers transport the picture of Her Majesty.

The Officials of the Wai-Wu-Pu, as well as many other of the high Officials in Peking, dressed in full dress, accompanied it to the station, and stood to watch the Sacred Picture start off on its long journey to St. Louis. The special train carrying it was met at Tientsin by the Viceroy of the Province, surrounded by all his official staff. It was there placed with great ceremony upon the steamer on which it was to make the journey to Shanghai, and was accompanied from Peking to Shanghai by an official specially appointed for the purpose.

At Shanghai it was received in the same formal state and with the same official pomp as at Tientsin. It was met at the steamer by the Governor of the Province and all his staff and transhipped with great ceremony to one of the Pacific Mail Steamers for San Francisco. The Sacred Picture was accompanied on its journey from Shanghai to St. Louis by a high Official and his suite. A special car conveyed it from San Francisco to St. Louis.

His Imperial Highness Prince Pu L'un, Imperial Commissioner and personal representative of Their Majesties at the Exposition of St. Louis, awaited the arrival of the portrait there, delaying his departure for several days in order to be able himself to assist at the reception and placing of the portrait. At four o'clock on the afternoon of the 19th of June, His Imperial Highness and the Imperial Chinese Commission repaired to the Art Gallery, where the cases containing the portrait and pedestal were awaiting their presence to be opened. The Director of the Art Gallery, the Assistant Director, and several other members of the Board of Fine Arts, were also present.

The cases containing the portrait, one within the other, were opened, and finally within the last, lined with yellow silk, lay the "Sacred Picture," covered with a screen of brocaded satin of Imperial hue. This satin cover was ceremoniously removed, and the picture was "unveiled." The Prince proposed the health of Her Majesty and the Prosperity of China, which the assistants drank in sparkling champagne. This opening of the cases and unveiling of the picture lasted from four o'clock to nine P. M. A few days later, when the Gallery where it was placed was opened to the public, it lost, for the first time since its inception, its semi-sacred qualities. Only then did it stand upon its own merits and become as other portraits. Then, for the first time, it could be seen by the ordinary individual—then only it became the subject of comment as any other picture at the Fair. Then it was open to the gaze of the vulgar and the comment of the scoffer.

At the close of the Exposition, a delegate was sent from the Chinese Legation in Washington to arrange for the transportation of the picture to the latter place. The portrait and its carved support were again placed in their satin-lined cases, and it began the journey to Washington. Her Majesty had decided when the portrait was completed to her satisfaction that it would be a suitable present for her to make to the United States. She thought this would be particularly appropriate, as the painting of the portrait for the St. Louis Exposition had been thought of by the wife of the American Minister to Peking, and as it had been executed by an American artist. Thus the United States received the gift of the first portrait ever painted of a Chinese Ruler.

When the portrait arrived in Washington, His Excellency Sir Chentung Liang Cheng, the Chinese Minister to Washington, attended by his Secretaries, made a formal presentation of the portrait to the President, which Mr. Roosevelt received on behalf of the United States Government.

CHAPTER XXXV

RETURN TO THE SUMMER PALACE

SENDING off the picture to St. Louis did not sever my connection with the Palace, for I had still other work to finish! At the end of April, a month later than usual, the Court moved out to the Summer Palace for the rest of the year. The country was beautiful, the trees were almost in full leaf, and lilacs, blue and white, bloomed everywhere. My garden in the Park of the Palace of the Emperor's Father was full of them, and over my entrance gate clambered a beautiful yellow rose-bush laden with masses of blooms. Wild flowers were springing up at every turn, and my dog "Melah" in his wild races through the park, when we were out for our walks, would often start up coveys of birds; or rabbits would scurry away at his approach. I went back to my favorite haunts in the park, to the summer-house, where upon the threshold, cut in stone, lay the plaint of the Seventh Prince! It was a delightful change to be in this beautiful spot after the four months in Peking, and to see Nature everywhere budding into perfection. The grounds of the Summer Palace were one maze of delight. The peonies in all their royal splendor, the fragrant lilac, the stately magnolia, and the budding

Return to the Summer Palace

elms, each added their charm to this beautiful spot, where everything was lovely. I could not wonder at the Empress Dowager's desire to come back again to all this beauty.

A charming studio was fitted up for me at the Summer Palace on our return. Her Majesty saw how much more satisfactory it was for me to have a proper place to work in, where I would be undisturbed, and even had she not seen the utility of a studio, I think she would have granted my request for one, for she was always kind and considerate. Upper windows of plate glass were put into the north side of one of His Majesty's Throne-rooms, behind the Imperial loge. It looked over a charming terrace of the garden. The days were long, and it was a delight to live and breathe, and the quiet of the studio, where I could work at leisure, made me resume my work with renewed vigor.

I began at once to finish up the small sketch of the St. Louis portrait, which Her Majesty wished to keep, and then to put the final touches on the two portraits begun at the Summer Palace. The Throne-room that was now my studio had only one disadvantage. It was so near the Theater that on theater days I could hear the music and the voices of the actors. And on those days, the court outside my windows was filled all day with eunuchs and Their Majesties' attendants, moving to and fro. I decided if it was necessary for me to go into Peking at any time, to take a "Theater day" to do so.

One Theater day I did go into Peking, and on my return to the Summer Palace the next day I found that His Majesty the Emperor had taken advantage of my absence to occupy his Throne-room the day before, for I found his Theater program, distinguishable by being written on Imperial yellow paper, and he had also left a few papers scattered around with characters and phrases written with the "Vermilion Pencil," which may only be used by His Majesty. On one paper he had evidently been trying to draw a plan of the part of Manchuria where the war operations were then being carried on. He had also drawn a part of the Great Wall of China, and the dividing line between China and Manchuria.

So the Emperor, notwithstanding his stoical smile, his apparent unconcern, was not indifferent to affairs in Manchuria. He was watching the course of events there, and he probably worried and grieved as much as even the Empress Dowager, about what might be the result for China. He had probably schooled himself to appear indifferent. The ceremonies and festivals at the Palace had been going on as usual, but the two central figures of all these functions had their own secret anxieties and cares. The Emperor was following the campaign in Manchuria, and the Empress Dowager was probably planning and thinking of the best course for China to follow.

In May, the Empress Dowager had another Garden Party for the ladies of the Legation, at which she, as usual, asked me to assist. When I went into the Audience Hall for this reception, a few moments before the ladies were to arrive, Her Majesty, after greeting me and scanning my toilet, which was all in gray without any color, took a pink peony from a vase at hand, and pinned it on my dress, saying I needed a little color. I had just finished the largest of the other three portraits I had painted at the Summer Palace, and Her Majesty told me she liked it so much that she had decided to show it to the foreign ladies at this Garden Party. As I had heard nothing of this plan before leaving my studio that morning, I had made no preparations for it. The picture was on my easel, unframed, and I told her I would prefer it to be placed in its frame, before it was shown. This frame, designed also by the Empress Dowager, and made by the Palace workmen, was a magnificent piece of work, elaborately carved and beautiful in form. It was in the natural color of teak-wood, and this quiet tone admirably set off the vivid color of the gown and accessories, and was a great improvement to the picture. When she heard what were my wishes on the subject, Her Majesty said she would see that the picture was placed in the frame, and it was arranged that as soon as I had finished my luncheon, I would return to the studio and overlook things myself, and arrange the portrait as I wished.

The Audience passed off as usual. Immediately after luncheon the ladies were invited to go to the studio to see the portrait. The Empress Dowager had evidently forgotten about my wish to go there first, and as she herself, contrary to all precedent, led the way, followed by the ladies, I could not, of course, precede her. I had not thought that she would make such an innovation as to, herself, accompany the ladies to the studio. I felt greatly honored, but I feared the eunuchs had not arranged things as they should be, and knew I could do nothing with Her Majesty present, and what was my chagrin on reaching the hall in the wake of the Empress Dowager and the ladies, to find that the portrait, though placed in the frame as I had desired, was in the center of the narrow hall, and every window on both sides had been opened to its widest extent, and the light came in from all sides! I had shut off all the lights of this hall, except the double windows to the north, where I had the upper glasses put in, and this is where the picture should have been placed, but as Her Majesty's Throne always occupies the center of the Throne-rooms, the eunuchs evidently thought that was the proper place for her portrait when on exhibition. As the halls are narrow in proportion to their length, no one could get further off than four feet from this life-size portrait. This, added to the cross-lights, was heartrending. I was in despair. Her Majesty's presence prevented my ordering the eunuchs to change the position of the portrait, and, besides, every one had already seen it! The ladies, who could not do otherwise than express their admiration in the presence of both the August Subject and the artist, duly praised the portrait. Her Majesty, who knew how it looked in its proper light, and who only glanced at it here, did not realize at what a disadvantage it appeared, and was perfectly satisfied with the effect.

An amusing little incident took place while the ladies were looking at it. The Empress Dowager, in her cursory examination in this light, noticed a part of the trimming of the gown where the design was not

THE PORTRAIT OF THE EMPRESS DOWAGER IN ITS FRAME

This Frame is Made of Camphor-wood Carved in the Palace after the Empress's own Designs and under Her Direction

well worked out. She came up to me, as I stood in a group of ladies, and pointed out the defect. She took my hand in hers, and said in an almost pleading way, "There is a bit of trimming that is not well finished. You will arrange it for me, will you not, Ker-Gunia?" She did not believe in leaving anything to the imagination, and wished every detail fully worked out!

This portrait was very successfully photographed, and Her Majesty concluded she liked it much better than the one which had been sent to St. Louis. She said it would make me "famous." But when I thought of how I might have painted this wonderfully interesting woman in the unique setting in which she was placed, I realized that "it might have been" are really the "saddest words of tongue or pen."

The precedent having been established, the idea of a representation of the Sacred Person of a Chinese Majesty being seen by the world having been accepted, the painting of Her Majesty's first portrait not having been followed by the dire results that the Chinese had prophesied, the traditional prejudice was overcome, and when she saw how quickly the photograph was made of the portrait, and how satisfactory it was, she decided she would have the photographer try one of herself, and she was not one to stop at a single trial. After waiting sixty-eight years to see a counterfeit presentment of herself, I know she will now indulge this new fantasy of hers to its fullest extent, and perhaps some other artist may at some time paint her according to western ideas, and represent her attractive personality in its best setting.

But there must always be a pioneer, and he it is who suffers the hardships and makes the way clear for others, which must be my solace and consolation for not being able to paint ¹ r as I should have liked. The Empress Dowager "consented" to have a portrait of herself painted. Before I finished the first one she told me she wanted "many," and suggested my passing the rest of my life out in Peking. I painted four. Who will do the others?

I felt I could not go on forever painting portraits, according to Chinese traditions, of the Empress Dowager. I could not spend my life in this dalliance with Oriental splendor. The world beyond the Palace gates called me. I hurried to finish my task. The last portrait was nearing completion. My sojourn at the Palace was drawing to a close. Though I longed to be where I might paint in a freer way, I looked forward with real regret to leaving the Palace, and especially to leaving the Empress Dowager and the young Empress, for I had come to really love them. I found Her Majesty by far the most fascinating personality it had ever been my good fortune to study at such close range. The young Empress was a sweet, kind nature, full of dignity and pathos, for whom I prayed there might be greater happiness in store than had yet fallen to her lot. My sojourn at the Palaces of Her Imperial Majesty the Empress Dowager of China, my association with herself and the Ladies of her Court, I shall always remember as one of the most charming experiences of my life.